STAR WARS

ABSOLUTELY EVERYTHING YOU NEED TO KNOW

UPDATED AND EXPANDED

Written by
**ADAM BRAY,
KERRIE DOUGHERTY,
COLE HORTON,
AND MICHAEL KOGGE**

CONTENTS

PROTECTORS OF THE GALAXY   4
Jedi of the Republic   6
Head Honchos   8
The Maverick   10
The Mentor   12
Free Agent   14
The Jedi Legend   16
Clone Troopers and Commanders   18
Super Troopers   20
Seasoned Veteran   22
Armed and Dangerous   24
The First Rebels   26
True Believer   28
The Blind Jedi   30
Last of the Padawans   32
Bombs Away!   34
The Big Bruiser   36
Cranky Mech!   38
Dangerous Firebrand   40
The Rebel Alliance   42
Rebellious Rogue   44
Caring Cutthroat   46
Brutal Honesty   48
Reluctant Rebel   50
Warrior Monk   52
Fallen Guardian   54
The Last Jedi   56
Fly Boy   58
Warrior Princess   60
Furry Fighters   62
Double Trouble!   64
Defiant Ones   66
The Resistance   68
Rey of Hope   70
Courageous Defector   72
One Hell of a Pilot   74
Rock and Roll   76

BAD GUYS, BOUNTY HUNTERS, AND THE UNDERWORLD   78
The Sith   80
Pure Evil   82
Blood Brothers   84
The Great Betrayer   86
The Fallen One   88
The Separatists   90
Greedy Grubs   92
Cyborg Fiend   94
Deadly Witch   96
The Empire   98
Command and Control   100
Calculating Commander   102
Secret Service   104
Opposing Visions   106
Jedi Hunters   108
Bucket Heads   110
Troopers Through Time   112
The First Order   114
Ruthless Leaders   116
Raging Storm   118
Bounty Hunters   120
Family Business   122
Hired Gun   124
The Underworld   126
Slime Lords   128
Shadow Army   130
Pirate Menace   132
Crimewave!   134

WEIRD AND WONDERFUL BEINGS   136
Intelligent Beings   138
Warrior Tribe   140
Buzzing Swarm   142
Jabba's Cronies   144
Clumsy Gungan   146
Scrap Dealers   148
Aquatic Allies   150
Rogues' Bar   152
Maz's Menagerie   154
Madcap Musicians   156
Cheats and Champions   158
Desert Warriors and their Banthas   160
A Galaxy of Droids   162
Monsters   164
Tooth and Claw   166
Pets   168
Arena Beasts   170
Charge!   172
Monsters from the Deep   174
Hitching a Ride   176
Ice Beasts!   178
Space Invaders   180
Winged Wonders   182
Creepy-Crawlies   184
Crazy Critters   186
Terror Below!   188

IN A GALAXY FAR, FAR AWAY....   190
Planetary Systems Across the Galaxy   192
Lawless Land   194
Serene Realm   196
Mega City   198
Clone World   200
Hives of Death   202
Sunken Cities   204
Hell Planet   206
Frozen Wasteland   208
Swamp Hideout   210
Up, Up, and Away   212
Forest Moon   214
Captive Territory   216
Paradise of Doom   218
Sacred War Zone   220
Ship Graveyard   222
World Wrecker   224
Space Travel and Weapons   226
Full Throttle!   228
Aerial Combat!   230
Hide and Seek   232
A Piece of Junk?   234
Fast Flyers   236
Mighty Fleet   238
Deadly Blades   240
Doomsday Weapons   242

THE BATTLE CONTINUES...   244
Hermit's Hideout   246
Playground of the Rich   248
Relentless Evil   250

Index   252

Acknowledgments   256

Which weapon does **Han Solo** give to **Rey** on Takodana?

PROTECTORS OF THE GALAXY

Whose starship does **R2-D2** save from certain **destruction**?

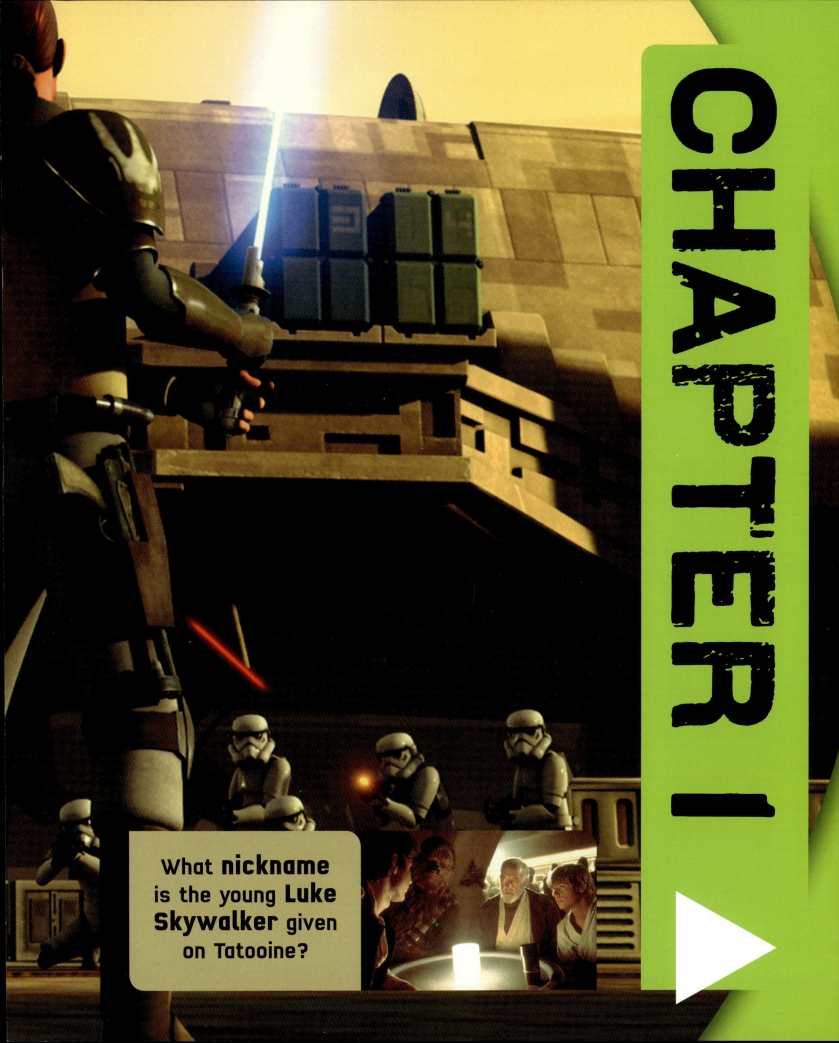

CHAPTER 1

What **nickname** is the young **Luke Skywalker** given on Tatooine?

JEDI OF THE REPUBLIC

"KOH-TO-YAH!"
"GREETINGS!"
In Kel Dor, the language of Plo Koon's people.

Q: So what *is* a Jedi?
A: A **protector** and **peacekeeper**—the good guy who upholds **justice** and **keeps harmony** in the galaxy (or tries to... it's not easy!). The Jedi do this by using the **Force**, a **powerful energy** coursing through every living thing in the galaxy. Jedi also use the Force to **defend** themselves, but it has a **dark side**, too...

PLO KOON
Kel Dor from Dorin • Jedi Master and General • Frequently undertakes dangerous missions

YARAEL POOF
Quermian from Quermia • Jedi Master • Expert at Jedi mind tricks and illusions

In numbers
1,000 generations
The length of time the Jedi have been the guardians of peace throughout the galaxy.

Q: Why does Plo Koon wear a breath mask and goggles?
A: Oxygen is **poisonous** to Plo Koon's species, the Kel Dor. Koon's breath mask **filters** the air on Coruscant, while his goggles **protect his eye fluids** from evaporating!

ADI GALLIA
Tholothian from Coruscant • Uses Form V lightsaber combat • Great starfighter pilot

Yarael Poof has **TWO BRAINS**—one in his **HEAD** and the second in his **CHEST**.

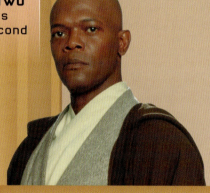

Adi Gallia joins Obi-Wan Kenobi on his **VITAL** mission in the Outer Rim to **FIND AND STOP** the evil Darth Maul and Savage Opress.

How did Even Piell receive the **SCAR** on his face? The scar is an old **BATTLE WOUND** that he carries as a badge of honor.

MACE WINDU
Human from Haruun Kal • Jedi Master, Master of the Order • The Council's greatest battlefield General and warrior

YADDLE
Jedi Master • Same mysterious species as Yoda • Skilled in little-known Jedi powers • Highly sought after for her great wisdom

COOL!!
As a senior Council member, Mace Windu makes sure his **VOICE IS HEARD**—both in noisy negotiations *and* with his **UNIQUE AMETHYST-BLADED** lightsaber!

EVEN PIELL
Lannik from planet Lannik • Jedi Master • Revered for courage and telekinesis powers • Enhanced hearing thanks to large ears

...BUT TRUE
Yaddle is only **half the age** of Yoda, but still **more than 400** years old.

JEDI OF THE REPUBLIC

Fast Facts

LEADER: Master of the Order, elected by a unanimous vote of the Council's members

HOMEWORLD: Coruscant

AFFILIATION: Galactic Republic

AIM: To serve the will of the Force, to train new Jedi

WOW!...
10,000
The number of Jedi Knights in the Order

KI-ADI-MUNDI
Cerean from Cerea • Jedi Master and General • Lightsaber expert • Leader of the Galactic Marine clone troopers

COUNCIL CHAMBER
Located in Jedi Temple • 12 customized chairs ring a fern-patterned floor • Stunning bird's-eye views over the city of Coruscant

SAESEE TIIN
Iktotchi from Iktotch • Jedi Master and General • Ace starfighter pilot • Natural superior telepathic powers

Saesee Tiin's **HORNS** will **GROW BACK** if damaged!

REALLY?!
The **COMPLEX BRAIN** inside Ki-Adi-Mundi's long, **CONE-SHAPED HEAD** relies on **BLOOD PUMPED** from his **TWO HEARTS**!

"We're keepers of peace, not soldiers."
— MACE WINDU

Peek behind the scenes
Episode I originally featured a **puppet version** of Yoda. In later releases, George Lucas substituted a more polished **digital version**, to give Yoda a consistent appearance throughout the prequel trilogy.

YODA
Jedi Master, Grand Master, Master of the Order • Famous teacher • Perhaps the greatest Master of the Force ever

HEAD HONCHOS

Who **rules** the Jedi **roost**? Only twelve of the wisest and finest Jedi Masters get to sit on the **High Council**. These noble leaders keep the Jedi Order **out of trouble**, maintain **balance in the Force**, and **handpick future Jedi stars**.

Fast Facts

HOMEWORLD: Tatooine
AFFILIATION: Jedi Order and the Republic
ABILITIES: Expert pilot, superior Force abilities, talented mechanic, speaks Huttese
OCCUPATION: Slave, podracer pilot, Jedi Padawan, later Knight
SPECIES: Human

Q: What are midi-chlorians?
A: Midi-chlorians are **tiny, intelligent life-forms** that live inside the cells of **all living things** in the galaxy. They do no harm, and help their host **use the Force**. The **more** midi-chlorians someone has, the **more powerful** a Jedi they may become.

MECHANICAL MASTER
Anakin has always had a talent for engineering. He enjoys **tinkering** with **podracers** and **droids** as a boy, and graduates to **starfighters** and his new **prosthetic arm** as an adult!

REALLY?!
Young Anakin has a **TRANSMITTER CHIP** hidden inside his body. If he tries to sneak away from Watto, he could be **BLOWN UP!**

UNHAPPY ENDINGS
All of Anakin's relationships seem to **end in sadness**—especially with the women closest to him.

- **Shmi Skywalker**
Anakin's kind, loving mother, Shmi, is **taken captive** by Tusken Raiders. When she **dies** in their camp, Anakin is **devastated**.

- **Padmé Amidala**
After falling **in love**, Anakin and Senator Amidala **secretly marry** on Naboo. In a tragic turn of events, Padmé **perishes during childbirth**.

- **Ahsoka Tano**
Ahsoka is Anakin's **Padawan** during the Clone Wars. He is distressed when she **leaves** the Jedi Order.

- **Princess Leia Organa**
Anakin does not meet his **daughter**, Leia, until he becomes Darth Vader. He doesn't even **realize** that she *is* his daughter until it is far **too late!**

THE MAVERICK

Rescued from **slavery** and squalor by the **Jedi**, Anakin Skywalker quickly rises to the rank of **Knight**. His Force potential is **so strong** that some Jedi believe he will **save the galaxy** from darkness. But things don't go quite as expected…!

Timeline

- **23 years old**—joins the Jedi Council, but is caught between loyalty to the Jedi and his friend Chancellor Palpatine; becomes Darth Vader.
- **20 years old**—marries Padmé Amidala; fights for Republic as a general during the Clone Wars.
- **14 years old**—builds first lightsaber on Ilum; trains with Obi-Wan Kenobi on Coruscant.
- **10 years old**—is accepted into the Jedi Order as a gifted youngling.
- **9 years old**—is discovered on Tatooine by Jedi Master Qui-Gon Jinn; wins Boonta Eve podrace.
- **3 years old**—slave owner Watto wins Anakin from Gardulla the Hutt.

You know you're strong with the Force if you can…
1. Perform astonishing, circus-worthy acrobatics.
2. Move objects without touching them.
3. Speak with some people using only your mind.
4. See visions of the future (although this is a troubling ability that may lead to the dark side!).

JEDI OF THE REPUBLIC

"**Not again! Obi-Wan's gonna kill me.**"

Anakin is very unlucky with **lightsabers**! He **drops** his Padawan blade during a mission, which Obi-Wan returns (with a telling off), only for Anakin to accidentally **destroy** it in a droid factory! Anakin's **replacement** lightsaber is then taken and kept by Obi-Wan after he wins their epic duel on Mustafar. Decades later the Jedi finally hands it to Anakin's **son, Luke.**

"Next time, try not to lose it… This weapon is your life."
OBI-WAN TO ANAKIN

Anakin is trained by a line of **unusually independent** Jedi. **Count Dooku's stubborn** ways are a strong influence on his apprentice **Qui-Gon**, who pushes for Anakin to be trained as a Jedi. Could Dooku's teachings be an influence on Anakin's **dark future**?

In numbers

700kph (435mph)
The maximum speed of Anakin's ship, the *Twilight*

105m (344ft 6in)
The maximum altitude Anakin's podracer can fly

15 min 42 sec
Anakin's winning time in the Boonta Eve Classic podrace

2 witnesses
Attend the wedding of Anakin and Padmé—R2-D2 and C-3PO

1.85m (6ft)
Anakin's adult height

Tell me more!

LIFE AS A SLAVE
Anakin's mother, Shmi Skywalker, is **captured by pirates** and sold into **slavery** when she is just a girl. She and Anakin end up as the property of **Gardulla the Hutt** on Tatooine. Later, a Toydarian **junk-dealer** named **Watto** wins them both in a **bet** with Gardulla.

"Someday I will be the most powerful Jedi ever!"
ANAKIN SKYWALKER

Peek behind the scenes
Colin Hanks, Paul Walker, and Ryan Phillippe all auditioned for the part of Anakin Skywalker, but the role was given to Hayden Christensen.

WOW!...

20,000+

Anakin's midi-chlorian count per cell (the highest ever recorded)

DESERT SHOWDOWN
After decades of **vowing revenge** on Obi-Wan, Maul tracks down the aging master on Tatooine. **Years** of quiet **meditation** help Kenobi defeat Maul in mere **seconds**!

BEST KNOWN FOR
CUTTING OFF ANAKIN'S LEGS AND ARM IN ONE SLICE!
Obi-Wan Kenobi

> "Look what has become of you, a rat in the desert."
> **MAUL TO OBI-WAN ON HIDING ON TATOOINE**

NO WAY!! Obi-Wan once **FELL** into a **NEST** of nasty **GUNDARKS** and was saved by Anakin!

Q: Why is Obi-Wan called "Ben" on Tatooine?
A: Obi-Wan uses his **old nickname** so that he won't be found by the Empire, which is **hunting down** Jedi survivors after the Clone Wars.

THE MENTOR

Obi-Wan Kenobi is a **noble knight, skilled swordsman**, and **nifty negotiator**, who serves as **Jedi Master** for **Anakin Skywalker**. As one of the few remaining Jedi during the dark times of the Empire's rule, he also **mentors Luke Skywalker** in the ways of the Force.

Peek behind the scenes
Creator George Lucas named Obi-Wan's homeworld "Stewjon" after talk show host John Stewart.

Love interest...
Obi-Wan falls in love with Satine Kryze, Duchess of Mandalore, but the Jedi code forbids attachment!

In numbers
212th
The Attack Battalion led by Obi-Wan

57 years old
When struck down by Darth Vader

19 years
Spent living on Tatooine

3 saber strikes
To defeat Maul in their final duel

Fast Facts

OCCUPATION: Jedi Master

AFFILIATION: The Jedi Order

ABILITIES: Jedi mind tricks, lightsaber combat, negotiation

LEAST FAVORITE JOB: Flying

MODES OF TRANSPORTATION: Jedi starfighter (during the Clone Wars), dewback (while hiding on Tatooine)

JEDI OF THE REPUBLIC

Clone Commander Cody **betrays** Obi-Wan and tries to destroy him when Palpatine issues **Order 66**, the execution of Jedi. Obi-Wan is caught in the trap, but he manages to **escape**!

"Help me Obi-Wan Kenobi, you're my only hope."
PRINCESS LEIA

Obi-Wan **lectures** Anakin about **never losing** his lightsaber, but Obi-Wan has lost his own lightsaber **many times**!

STRANGE ...BUT TRUE
Jedi General Obi-Wan once wore **Mandalorian armor and a jet pack**! It was a **disguise** to infiltrate the Mandalorian capital and **save** Duchess Satine from Darth Maul!

OBI-WAN'S HERMIT HUT
Small home on Tatooine • Hermit hideout for a wanted Jedi • 136km (85 miles) from the Lars homestead, to keep watch on Luke Skywalker

Q: How does Obi-Wan reappear after Darth Vader defeats him?
A: After being **struck down** by Darth Vader on the Death Star, Obi-Wan becomes **one with the Force**. He appears as a **Force spirit** and is able to communicate with Luke and Yoda.

"Well, I don't know anyone named Obi-Wan, but old Ben lives out beyond the Dune Sea."
LUKE SKYWALKER

REALLY?! To keep Obi-Wan's location a **COMPLETE SECRET**, Bail Organa tells everyone Obi-Wan is **DEAD**. Even his old friend Captain Rex believes the lie.

FREE AGENT

The Clone Wars make headstrong Ahsoka Tano a **Jedi legend**—until she realizes her destiny doesn't lie with the Jedi at all. It may intertwine with Anakin's, but ultimately it rests in her own hands and heart.

Fast Facts

OCCUPATION: Former Jedi Padawan and Knight, rebel leader

AFFILIATION: Jedi Order during Clone Wars, later joining the first rebels

HOMEWORLD: Shili

SPECIES: Togruta

ABILITIES: Strong leader, quick reflexes

BEST KNOWN FOR
WISECRACKS AND SNARKY WIT
Ahsoka Tano

> "My master could never be as vile as you."
> — AHSOKA TO VADER

Peek behind the scenes
The Clone Wars producers hired a martial artist to model Ahsoka's acrobatic moves so that they could be realistically animated using computer graphics.

Ahsoka wields her lightsaber in a **REVERSE GRIP**, to accord with the ancient **SHIEN** style of Jedi combat.

REALLY?!
Ahsoka's lightsabers use an **INQUISITOR'S KYBER CRYSTALS**. They change from red to white via the Force.

WOW!...
25
The echolocation distance Ahsoka can detect with her hollow montral horns in meters (82 feet)

Q: If Ahsoka uses lightsabers, isn't she still a Jedi?

A: Ahsoka **uses the light side** of the Force, but she **isn't a Jedi**. The **white color** of her lightsabers shows she is no longer aligned with the Jedi Order. This is why Ahsoka does not help Kanan and Ezra open the Lothal temple, though she does catch a **glimpse of Yoda**.

JEDI OF THE REPUBLIC

WHO TRAINED WHOM?

Ahsoka shares Anakin's **rebellious streak**, just as Anakin does of his **Jedi Master Obi-Wan Kenobi**. In this way, the teachings and legacy of **Qui-Gon Jinn** live on.

QUI-GON JINN → Master of... → OBI-WAN KENOBI → Master of... → ANAKIN SKYWALKER → Master of... → AHSOKA TANO

Q: Who are the Fulcrums?

A: A fulcrum is a **balancing point**—a meaningful idea to a Force-user like Ahsoka. Acting as a **secret rebel agent and go-between**, she goes by the **codename** Fulcrum. Other informants like **Agent Kallus** and **Cassian Andor** also use her codename and **symbol** later.

TOP 4
AHSOKA'S BRUSHES WITH VADER

1. When Vader attacks Phoenix Squadron, he **senses Ahsoka's presence**, though **his identity is a mystery** to her.
2. Ezra tells Ahsoka that the **Inquisitors** are under orders from the Sith Lord to **hunt for her**.
3. Ahsoka visits the Jedi temple on Lothal and has a **vision of Anakin with terrifying implications**.
4. Ahsoka confronts Vader and **confirms the truth** she didn't want to believe: **Anakin is Darth Vader**.

Tell me more!
THE LIFE-CHANGING MEETING

Jedi Master Plo Koon discovers the toddler Ahsoka's **sensitivities to the Force** while on a mission. He brings her to the Jedi Temple on Coruscant to be trained, and **maintains a strong bond** with her throughout her Padawan years.

In numbers

32 years old
Ahsoka's age when she faces Vader

14 years old
Age when Ahsoka is apprenticed to Anakin Skywalker

3 years old
Ahsoka's age when she is found by Plo Koon and taken to join the Jedi Order

2 years
Time spent as Anakin's Padawan trainee

2 lightsaber colors
Ahsoka uses green, then white

1.88m (6ft 1in)
Ahsoka's adult height

TOP 7 SUCCESSFUL CLONE WARS MISSIONS

1. Helps save Jabba the Hutt's son.
2. Liberates her fellow Togruta who were enslaved.
3. Breaks the Separatist blockade of Ryloth.
4. Halts the spread of the Blue Shadow Virus.
5. Rescues Baron Papanoida's daughters.
6. Stops bounty hunter Aurra Sing from slaying Senator Amidala.
7. Exposes the Mandalorian Prime Minister's corruption.

A REBEL HEART TAKES HER OWN PATH

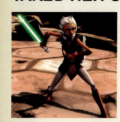

Fiery Ahsoka relies on her **instincts** as much as her **Jedi skills**. As Anakin's Padawan, she learns that **planning and patience** are as vital as courage.

A **wiser but no less gutsy** Ahsoka helps the rebels fight the Empire. Now a **mature warrior**, she takes on Imperial Inquisitors.

Falsely accused of **blowing up** the **Jedi Temple** and almost expelled, Ahsoka loses respect for the Order. She leaves the Jedi to **create her own destiny**.

Ahsoka's journey comes full circle and she **faces her former friend** and mentor. Ahsoka duels with Darth Vader and is **lost to shadow and rubble**.

REALLY?! Yoda learns how to **SURVIVE as a FORCE SPIRIT AFTER DEATH** from the late Qui-Gon Jinn. He then teaches this **SECRET** to both Obi-Wan Kenobi and Anakin Skywalker.

"Growing your abilities are, and with them, danger."
— YODA TO EZRA

How to talk like Yoda

Yoda speaks Basic in the phrasing of his native language, which can sound a little strange.

"HELP YOU, I CAN."

"POWERFUL, YOU HAVE BECOME."

"WHAT KNOW YOU OF READY?"

"HOW JEDI CHOOSE TO WIN, THE QUESTION IS."

Peek behind the scenes
Yoda's face takes inspiration, in part, from two real-life faces. Working from a design by Joe Johnston, sculptor Stuart Freeborn used his own face—and Einstein's!

In numbers

20,000 Jedi
The estimated number that Yoda has trained over his lifetime

900 years old
Yoda's age

800 years
How long Yoda has been training Jedi

23 years
Period of Yoda's exile on Dagobah

Fast Facts

HOMEWORLD: Unknown

SPECIES: Unknown

AFFILIATION: Jedi Order, Galactic Republic

JEDI RANK: Grand Master of the Jedi Order (leads Council)

REPUBLIC ARMY RANK: General

DISLIKES: Luke's rebel pilot food rations (he spits them out!)

Yoda's feet are like those of many **birds**, with **three toes** at the **front** and **one** at the **back**.

Q: Why is Yoda unsure about young Anakin Skywalker?

A: Yoda senses **strong anger in Anakin**. **Rage and fear** can make a Jedi turn to the **dark side of the Force**, and Yoda is worried that this may happen to Anakin. Much to his regret, he turns out to be right!

LONG-DISTANCE MEETINGS
In the Jedi temple, Yoda tells Kanan that, **"I am here, because you are here."** Qui-Gon says the same to Obi-Wan on Mortis. Jedi can **see each other from afar**, as Yoda and Ezra do, if they are **somewhere strong in the Force**, and are themselves strong in it too.

Mind the furniture! Yoda confronts evil enemy Darth Sidious in a **ferocious lightsaber duel** that includes **Force-throwing huge Senate pods at each other** inside the Senate chamber!

Peek behind the scenes
The *Star Wars Rebels* version of Yoda is voiced by the legendary puppeteer from the movies, Frank Oz. This version's design is based on the 1980's Kenner action figure.

Tell me more!

HOW TO MASTER THE FORCE
Don't let his small size or quirky manner fool you—Yoda is one of the **most powerful and respected** Jedi in history. As well as having **formidable fighting skills**, he is a **brave** and **wise** general. Yoda's deep connection to the Force makes him a **gifted teacher** and **philosopher**, who always seeks to understand the Force better.

THE JEDI LEGEND

Yoda's history may be **shrouded in mystery**, but there's nothing uncertain about the ancient Jedi Master's **legendary Force power** and **lightsaber combat expertise**—especially to his unlucky foes.

Yoda may be in **exile** on Dagobah, but he still uses the Force to **watch over and advise** surviving Jedi like Kanan Jarrus and his Padawan, Ezra.

Q: Why does Yoda give Anakin a Padawan?

A: Yoda knows Anakin still carries many fears and cannot let go of his **tragic past**. He hopes that by **teaching the Padawan Ahsoka Tano**, the young Jedi will learn that he does not need to be **so protective** of those he loves.

NOT JUST A STICK
Yoda's walking cane, made from a **gimer** stick, symbolizes a Jedi Master's **ancient wisdom**. But it's not just a status symbol—when Yoda **chews** on the gimer bark it releases natural plant substances that help him **meditate**. Plus, the nutritious juice inside **eases thirst** and acts as a **natural painkiller**.

YODA'S TOP 4 JEDI ABILITIES
1. Master of all lightsaber fighting styles.
2. Ability to sense the future.
3. Impressive levitation capabilities.
4. Can deflect Force lightning with his hands.

Yoda's Dagobah home is not just built of mud and stones. It also includes **pieces of the escape pod** that secretly brought him to the planet.

NO WAY!!
Rey hears Yoda in her **FORCE VISION** on Takodana, telling her "Its energy surrounds us, and binds us."

FAN FACT
Originally, photos were taken of a **monkey** in a robe with a **cane** and a **mask**, to see if that would work to play Yoda.

CLONE TROOPERS AND COMMANDERS

SUPER TROOPERS

Bred in their millions, these identical, loyal, and relentless clone soldiers of the Republic are the future of galactic warfare. But they also come with a lethal secret—a command code to make them destroy their Jedi officers!

WOW!... 192,000
Clone troopers present at the Battle of Geonosis

When plans backfire!
Commander Gree receives Order 66 during the Battle of Kashyyyk and **tries to eliminate Yoda**. But sensing betrayal, the Jedi draws his lightsaber just in time, and **Gree loses his own head instead!**

Tell me more!
SILENCING YOUR ENEMIES
When Chancellor Palpatine's **true identity** as Sith Lord Darth Sidious is discovered, he issues **Order 66**, telling all clone troopers that the **Jedi** have betrayed the Republic and **must be eliminated immediately!**

BEST KNOWN FOR
TRYING TO BUMP OFF OBI-WAN (UNDER ORDER 66)
Commander Cody

Q: Who asks for this huge army to be made?
A: **Sifo-Dyas**, a Jedi High Council member who **senses a looming galactic war** and tasks the Kaminoans to create a clone army for the Republic. When the Sith learn of this, they **murder Sifo-Dyas** so they can **control** the clones' creation.

Peek behind the scenes
In Episodes II and III, actor Temuera Morrison wore a blue bodysuit to play troopers Cody, Odd Ball, and Jag. The suit was later digitally replaced with computer-generated armor.

CLONE TROOPERS AND COMMANDERS

TOP 5
CLONE COMMANDERS

1. **CAPTAIN REX (CT-7567)**—Reports to Jedi Anakin Skywalker. Mentor and friend of Jedi Padawan Ahsoka Tano.
2. **COMMANDER CODY (CC-2224)**—Reports to Jedi Master Obi-Wan Kenobi. **Close friend** of Obi-Wan and Captain Rex.
3. **WOLFFE (CC-3636)**—Reports to Jedi Master Plo Koon. Commands the famous "Wolf Pack" Battalion.
4. **COMMANDER FOX (CC-1010)**—Reports to Chancellor Palpatine. **Rescues** Padmé Amidala and **arrests** Ziro the Hutt.
5. **COMMANDER GREE (CC-1004)**—Reports to Jedi Master Luminara Unduli. Named after a **tentacled alien species**.

Clone Lieutenant

> "No clone uses their number. I am Fives. Call me Fives."
> **FIVES TO AZI-3 ON KAMINO**

Commander Deviss

STRANGE ...BUT TRUE
Count Dooku secretly orders the Kaminoans to put **computer chips in the brains** of every clone trooper, which makes them **obey Palpatine** without question.

Just following orders
Clone Commander Fox arrests Padawan Ahsoka Tano when she is **wrongly blamed for bombing the Jedi Temple**. He also destroys clone trooper Fives, who has been **falsely accused of trying to harm Chancellor Palpatine**.

Clone Commander

Traitors in the ranks
Some clones don't follow orders. Jedi General Pong Krell **plans to execute Fives and Jesse** for disobedience, but when Captain Rex learns **Krell is a traitor**, he arrests the Jedi. Ultimately, clone trooper Dogma slays Krell himself.

REALLY?!
Echo fights alongside teammates **Heavy, Cutup, Fives,** and **Droidbait.** When Captain Rex slaps his hand, covered in **BLUE EEL BLOOD,** on Echo's armor, the mark becomes Echo's symbol!

In numbers

80kg (176lbs)
Average clone trooper weight

13 years
Clone service time from the first clone birth to the founding of the Empire

10 years old
Age when clones are combat-ready

2+ x
Growth rate of clones compared to normal people

Fast Facts
AFFILIATION: Galactic Republic

LEADER: Supreme Chancellor Palpatine

CLAIM TO FAME: The devastating galaxy-wide conflict known as **the Clone Wars is named after them**

Fast Facts

DESIGNATION: CT-7567

AFFILIATION: Republic, rebels

HOMEWORLD: Kamino

TOP CLONE COMRADES: Commanders Wolffe and Gregor

BEST KNOWN FOR LEADING THE 501ST LEGION
Captain Rex

The **blue symbols** on Rex's helmet are **Jaig Eyes**. This is short for jai'galaara'la sur'haii'se, which means "shriek-hawk eyes" in Mando'a. They are a combat honor.

A CLOSER LOOK

SEASONED VETERAN

Captain Rex is the ideal clone soldier: **brave, loyal,** and **honorable**. He serves as second-in-command to **Anakin Skywalker** through most of the Clone Wars. After a brief **retirement** from the Republic's army, Rex is back, and ready to **fight against the Empire!**

In numbers

5576-39
Gregor's birth number

245lbs (111.13kg)
Rex's retirement weight

56 years old
Rex's equivalent age when he meets the rebels

28 standard years old
Rex's actual age when he meets the rebels

1.83 (6ft)
Height of Rex and the other clones

2nd generation clone armor
Rex's rebel outfit

Tell me more!

THE AHSOKA CONNECTION
Ahsoka Tano is more than just Rex's **superior officer**. They are **close friends** who have known each other since the **Battle of Christophsis**. Ahsoka sends the rebels to look for Rex on **Seelos**, in hopes that Rex can find a base for the rebels to hide at.

Résumé
CAPTAIN REX CT-7567

YOUNG CAPTAIN
As a young clone captain, Rex begins working with Anakin, Obi-Wan, and Ahsoka Tano.

THE TRUTH OF WAR
Just prior to Order 66, Rex begins to see the ugly side of the Republic.

RETIREMENT'S OVER!
Rex joins the rebels of Phoenix Squadron and moves to Atollon.

REBEL COMMANDO
Rex takes an active role in the Rebellion, which leads to him meeting some old comrades like Saw Gerrera.

Ending an old war
Rex and the rebels visit **Agamar** in search of proton bombs. There, they are captured by Kalani, a **Separatist tactical droid**. The rebels convince Kalani that his **former enemy** (the Republic) is now their **mutual enemy** (the Empire) and finally "end" the Clone Wars.

CLONE TROOPERS AND COMMANDERS

"Oh! You want some more, you lousy clanker?! I'll show you more!"
REX

MOBILE HUNTING LODGE

Customized Republic AT-TE • Retirement home for Rex, Wolffe, and Gregor • Contains bunks and kitchen • Modified for hunting joopas on Seelos

"Now we spend our days just telling stories and slinging for joopas."
REX TO EZRA

Top 5

Clone Wars missions

1. **THE CITADEL** Rex must help save Tarkin and Jedi Even Piell from a Separatist prison.
2. **DARKNESS ON UMBARA** Rex and the 501st Legion attempt to capture the Umbaran capital.
3. **ESCAPE FROM KADAVO** Rex helps liberate a colony of Togruta slaves from Zygerrian captivity.
4. **THE WRONG JEDI** While under orders to capture Ahsoka, Rex and Anakin try to prove her innocence.
5. **THE SIEGE OF MANDALORE** Under Ahsoka's command, Rex and the 501st attempt to free Mandalore from Maul's stranglehold.

Talk like a clone trooper

"SHINIES" CLONE CADETS IN NEW ARMOR

"CLANKERS" BATTLE DROIDS

"DROID POPPERS" ELECTROMAGNETIC PULSE GRENADES

"AIWHA-BAIT" KAMINOANS

"BUZZERS" BATTLE DROID AERIAL PLATFORMS

"BUGS" GEONOSIANS

"ROLLERS" HAILFIRE DROIDS

"ROLLIES" DROIDEKAS

Q: Why is Gregor so nutty?
A: Clone commando Gregor is marooned on **Abafar** with **amnesia** during the Clone Wars. While aiding Meebur Gascon and D-Squad on their mission, he is **caught in an explosion**, which **alters his personality**. Gregor then joins Wolffe and Rex toward the end of the war.

REALLY?! After Fives reveals the truth about the clones' **BRAIN BIO-CHIPS**, Rex, Wolffe, and Gregor remove theirs before Order 66. They have the **SCARS** to prove it!

23

ARMED AND DANGEROUS

During the **Clone Wars**, the Republic builds a **formidable arsenal**. These **vehicles and weapons** trigger the transformation of the **peaceful Republic** into the **invincible military machine** that is the **Empire!**

BEST KNOWN FOR

WITHSTANDING SUB-ZERO TEMPERATURES

CK-6 swoop bikes

Q: How do clone soldiers enter a combat zone?
A: They ride to a planet's surface in either heavily armed *Acclamator*-class **assault ships** or smaller, but lethal, **assault gunships**.

DC-15 BLASTER RIFLE

EMP PULSE GRENADE

In numbers

700 crew members
Required to operate *Acclamator*-class assault ships

99.71m (327ft)
Length of the Republic's experimental stealth ship

66
Secret clone order number given to execute all Jedi

4.15kg (9lbs 2oz)
Weight of DC-15A blaster rifle

1.83m (6ft)
Height of a clone trooper

TOP 4
CLONE TROOPER WEAPONS
1. **DC-15 blaster rifle**—standard issue long-range weapon with 500 shot capacity.
2. **DC-15a blaster**—smaller weapon with 500 shots, but a shorter range.
3. **DC-17 blaster pistol**—ideal for close combat, 50 shot capacity.
4. **EMP pulse grenade**—electromagnetic emission disables battle droids' circuits.

DC-17 BLASTER PISTOL

STRANGE ...BUT TRUE
The **cloaking device** on the Republic's radical new **stealth ship** makes the vessel **invisible to scanners**—and even the **human eye!** Blink and you'll miss it!

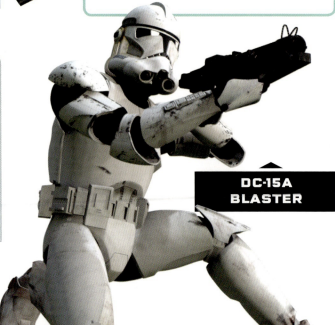
DC-15A BLASTER

CLONE TROOPERS AND COMMANDERS

TETH

Planet of jungles and flat-topped mountains • Site of revered B'omarr monastery, turned Separatist fortress • Testing ground for new clone vehicles and weaponry during Battle of Teth

"Teth? That's Wild Space. The droid army isn't even in that sector."
ANAKIN SKYWALKER

The Republic's stun tanks bring down not only Separatist WARSHIPS, but also the fearsome ZILLO BEAST!

Peek behind the scenes
The clone trooper DC-15 blaster rifle is based on the design of the German MG 34 machine gun from World War II.

REALLY?!
The turbo tank's TEN wheels and COCKPIT AT EACH END allow this war machine to make quick turns.

AT-TE   AT-AP   AT-RT

WOW!...

1.137

Length of a Republic *Venator*-class Star Destroyer in kilometers (3,730 feet)

TOP 3
REPUBLIC WALKERS
1. **AT-TE**—six-legged walker able to carry troops and climb steep slopes.
2. **AT-RT**—reconnaissance walker built for speed and maneuverability.
3. **AT-AP**—three-legged "pod walker" used for long-range artillery attacks.

25

THE FIRST REBELS

Fast Facts

OCCUPATION: Starship captain, rebellion starter
SPECIES: Twi'lek
HOMEWORLD: Ryloth
ABILITIES: Makes flying the *Ghost* look easy, charismatic leader

GHOST

> "Whatever it takes, this Rebellion is worth it."
> **HERA TO MON MOTHMA**

Tell me more!

REBEL ROLE MODEL

Hera is a **trailblazer**! She test-flies the **B-wing prototype** and her piloting skills get her **promoted** to Phoenix Leader. She delivers Mon Mothma to a rebel meeting at **Dantooine**, resulting in a historical alliance. She is even promoted to **General** and flies at the **Battle of Scarif**!

Top 5

Ways to be a great rebel leader

1 HONE YOUR FLYING SKILLS
Fly straight through Thrawn's blockade of Atollon and on to a new home on Yavin.

2 BE READY FOR ANYTHING
Fight off a flurry of fyrnocks on an abandoned clone trooper asteroid base.

3 LOOK AFTER YOUR TEAM
Rescue your crewmates from a well-guarded Imperial communications tower.

4 BREAK THE RULES!
Disobey your rebel contact's orders and lead a mission to save co-leader Kanan.

5 BE A TALENT-SPOTTER
Convince Kanan to train Ezra—the boy has talent!

> "Do I have to do *everything* myself?"
> **HERA**

Hera's **childhood home** on Ryloth is confiscated by the Empire and turned into their headquarters. Hera **infiltrates** it, pretending to be a servant, and ends up **blowing it all up**!

HOW TO GESTURE WITH LEKKU

Hera's species has developed a unique sign language using their lekku. They can communicate without saying a single word!

"HELLO."
RIGHT LEK TIP RAISED

"GOODBYE."
LEFT LEK TIP DIPPED

"LOVE YOU."
BOTH LEKKU TIPS CROSSED OVER, TWICE

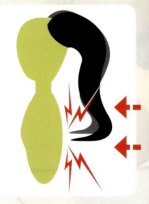
"MAY SPICE SALT YOUR WOUNDS!"
BOTH LEKKU TIPS JABBED INTO SPEAKER'S BACK

THE FIRST REBELS

FAMILY HISTORY AS LIVING ART

"WHAT'S A... 'KALIKORI?'"
EZRA

"A TOTEM PASSED DOWN THE LINE OF A TWI'LEK FAMILY. IT HONORS ALL WHO HAVE COME BEFORE."
NUMA

"EACH PARENT ADDS TO THE ARTWORK, TO INCLUDE THEMSELVES IN THE LEGACY."
GOBI

BEST KNOWN FOR

MAKING ENEMY PILOTS SPACESICK

Hera

STRANGE ...BUT TRUE
Hera's father and greatest inspiration, **Cham Syndulla**, is a reluctant Twi'lek hero. His leadership of the **resistance on Ryloth** against the Separatists is **celebrated in song**.

Peek behind the scenes
Hera (voiced by Vanessa Marshall) wasn't a tall Twi'lek in the early design stages of *Rebels*—she started out as a short, motherly woman.

TRUE BELIEVER

Don't just call Hera Syndulla an expert pilot—she is the **gutsy leader** of Phoenix Squadron, and her own motley rebel crew aboard the *Ghost*. Her belief in battling evil and her wise strategies help hold this family of misfits together!

In numbers

5,929 Twi'leks
Of the Syndulla clan taken as Hutt slaves

24 years old
When she accepts Ezra Bridger into her crew

2 head-tails
On each Twi'lek

1.76m (5ft 9in)
Hera's height

Spectre-2
Hera's rebel codename

Tell me more!

WHAT ARE TWI'LEK TENTACLES FOR?
The **two long tentacles** that grow from Hera's skull are known as **lekku**, or head-tails. Super-sensitive lekku can **grab and hold things** and react to the slightest touch. **Never mess with them**—a damaged lek can cause **serious harm** to a Twi'lek's health.

29

Fast Facts

OCCUPATION: Jedi, rebel

AFFILIATION: Lothal rebels, Phoenix Squadron, Rebel Alliance

HOMEWORLD: Coruscant

SPECIES: Human

Q: What is "Form Three"?

A: When the Inquisitor confronts Kanan on the planet Stygeon Prime, he notes that **Kanan favors Form Three** to a "ridiculous degree." Form Three, also known as **Soresu** or the **Way of the Mynock**, is one of **seven styles** of **lightsaber combat**.

In numbers

100 shots
Capacity of Kanan's DL-18 blaster

14 years old
Kanan's age when the Jedi Order is destroyed

3 fights
Kanan's bar fight record for one night

2 names
Kanan Jarrus's real name is "Caleb Dume"

1.9m (6ft 3in)
Kanan's height

Peek behind the scenes
Kanan is voiced by actor Freddie Prinze Jr., famous for his roles in 24, Freddie, Scooby-Doo, I Know What You Did Last Summer, and She's All That.

WORST 3

ENCOUNTERS WITH MAUL

"Well, if at first you don't succeed... Try, try again." **MAUL TO KANAN**

1. Maul **blinds Kanan** with his lightsaber at the Sith temple on Malachor.
2. Maul **pushes Kanan out an airlock** on the space station Vizsla Keep 09.
3. Maul abandons Kanan and Sabine to **evil Nightsister ghosts** on Dathomir.

> "Battles leave scars, some you can't see."
> **KANAN TO REX**

Tell me more!

SECRETS OF THE HOLOCRON

Holocrons are **storage devices** used by both **Jedi and Sith**. Only a Force-user can **open a holocron**, activate the crystal at its core, and then project the **information** within as a **hologram**. Kanan's holocron contains a message from **Obi-Wan Kenobi**, as well as large star maps and databases.

Q: Who is the Bendu?

A: This **ancient being** dwells on Atollon. He represents the **center of the Force**, between the light and dark side. Bendu helps Kanan regain his **connection to the Force**—something than the **Jedi lost along with his sight**.

THE BLIND JEDI

Kanan Jarrus is a quick-witted gunslinger who emerges from exile. Once a wayward Jedi on Lothal, he becomes a wise mentor to Ezra Bridger and helps lead the *Ghost*'s rebel crew in a growing war with the Empire!

WHO TRAINED WHOM?

Kanan's Jedi line boasts one of the **greatest Jedi Masters**, Mace Windu, while Kanan's own Master, Depa Billaba, **sacrifices herself** to save Kanan. The rebel with a cause only completes his training as a Jedi Knight after **taking Ezra as a Padawan** and **defeating the Inquisitor**.

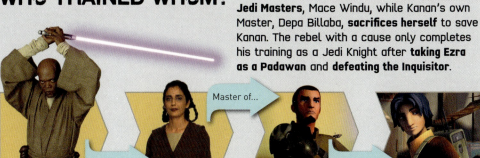

MACE WINDU — Master of... → DEPA BILLABA — Master of... → KANAN JARRUS — Master of... → EZRA BRIDGER

REALLY?!
The Inquisitor uses **THE CORPSE** of Jedi Master Luminara Unduli as **BAIT** to catch Kanan!

TOP 3
AN UNCONVENTIONAL JEDI
1. **Emotional attachments**—Kanan has feelings for Hera.
2. **Fists and blasters**—Kanan doesn't always seek peaceful solutions.
3. **Criminal contacts**—Kanan does deals with gangsters.

JEDI KNIGHTHOOD

"By the right of the Council, by the will of the Force, Kanan Jarrus. You may rise."
JEDI SENTINEL TO KANAN

Kanan is not knighted by **members of the Jedi Council** on Coruscant. They are **nearly all gone**. In a desperate time with few Jedi left, an **apparition of the Inquisitor** (when he was a Jedi) knights Kanan in the **Jedi Temple** on Lothal.

STRANGE ...BUT TRUE
Kanan lives **in hiding** for a decade, **rarely using the Force** or his lightsaber. He **doesn't complete his own Jedi training** before he begins mentoring Ezra. So after leaving Atollon, Kanan believes he may have **nothing left to teach** his apprentice.

> "The Force resides in all living things. But you have to be open to it."
> **KANAN TO HERA**

LESSONS FROM UNUSUAL TEACHERS

YODA
Kanan's childhood instructor appears in Lothal's temple to help Kanan gain confidence.

JEDI SENTINEL
A vision of the former Inquisitor helps Kanan let go of his fear of losing Ezra to the dark side.

BENDU
Teaches Kanan to gain new sight through the Force, and helps him restore balance with Ezra.

In numbers

328 rocks
Missed by Ezra when thrown at him during lightsaber practice

150m (492ft)
Range of Ezra's slingshot

24 passengers
Ezra's *Gauntlet* starfighter drop-seat bay capacity

8 credits
Fee Ezra charged passengers for speeder rides across Lothal's Capital City

GROWTH BRINGS DANGER
Yoda tries to aid Ezra. In their first encounter at the Jedi temple, Yoda appears as a cloud of lights, guiding Ezra to a kyber crystal. In their second meeting, Ezra is stronger in the Force and they see each other clearly. This time Yoda sends him to Malachor.

STRANGE …BUT TRUE
Ezra and Maul **join Sith and Jedi holocrons** to gain secret knowledge. Maul looks for "hope" in **revenge against Kenobi**, while Ezra seeks a solution to **defeating the Sith**. The experiment leaves their two minds **dangerously linked!**

REALLY?!
Ezra uses the dark side of the Force to open the **SITH HOLOCRON**, which alarms Kanan!

Tell me more!

A TALE OF TWO LIGHTSABERS
Ezra builds his **first lightsaber** with a kyber crystal from Lothal's Jedi temple and spare parts on the *Ghost*. This unconventional **blue lightsaber-blaster hybrid** is destroyed by Darth Vader. After his trip to Malachor, Ezra constructs a traditional **green-bladed replacement lightsaber**.

> "How we choose to fight is just as important as what we fight for."
> — **EZRA TO GOOTI**

Peek behind the scenes
Each costume change in *Star Wars Rebels* requires a new CG character model. By the end of season 3, Ezra has at least 10 versions, including a scout trooper uniform and pajamas!

SITH TEMPLE OF MALACHOR
Located below the surface of a crater • Site of ancient battle between Sith and Jedi (The Scourge of Malachor) • Maul deceives Ezra and blinds Kanan here • Contains a Sith holocron that operates a super-weapon

> "Maul tricked us! This temple's a weapon!"
> — **EZRA TO KANAN AND AHSOKA**

THE FIRST REBELS

Q: Who are Ezra's parents?

A: **Ephraim** and **Mira Bridger** are two of Lothal's first rebels, broadcasting messages of resistance. After hearing **Ezra's broadcast**, they plan a revolt within an Imperial prison. They perish while **helping Ryder Azadi and others escape**.

> "Come on, when have I asked you to trust me and it hasn't worked out?"
> **EZRA TO THE *GHOST* CREW**

STRANGE ...BUT TRUE

Ezra was **born** on "Empire Day," the same day that the **Emperor founded his Galactic Empire**. All citizens must attend the **parades** and **festivities**—whether they want to or not!

Peek behind the scenes

Ezra (voiced by Taylor Grey) was the **first character** producer Dave Filoni sketched. He drew inspiration from the **strong-willed, feisty** Ralph Macchio in *The Karate Kid*!

Tell me more!

EZRA'S MISINTERPRETATION

Kenobi isn't pleased to meet Ezra on **Tatooine**! The Jedi instructs Ezra that he has been deceived by Maul. Ezra only saw in the holocrons what he **wanted to be true**. As a result, Ezra **has lead Maul to Kenobi**, which forces Kenobi into a duel he **did not want**!

LAST OF THE PADAWANS

Orphan Ezra Bridger **grows up the hard way** on the streets of Lothal's Capital City. After meeting Kanan Jarrus and the *Ghost* crew, he discovers a bigger destiny as a **Jedi in the Rebellion**!

> "Not looking for trouble... but it sure has a way of finding me."
> **EZRA**

Fast Facts

OCCUPATION: Street urchin (formerly), Jedi Padawan, rebel

SPECIES: Human

HOMEWORLD: Lothal

UNIQUE ABILITY: Connecting with creatures and Force-sensitive beings through the Force

Starting the Jedi path: HOW OLD IS TOO OLD?

9 YEARS OLD?
Anakin Skywalker is said to be **too old** to be trained as a Jedi when he is just 9 years old... look how that turned out!

14 YEARS OLD?
When Ezra starts his training he is **even older** than Anakin at 14 years, but Kanan Jarrus can see his strong Force potential.

19 YEARS OLD?
19-year-old Luke Skywalker is **much older** than Anakin or Ezra were when his Master starts to teach him the ways of the Force.

33

Fast Facts

HOMEWORLD: Krownest

ABILITIES: Languages, computer hacking, art, explosives, customizing weapons and gear

AFFILIATION: Phoenix Squadron (*Ghost* crew), Clan Wren

SPECIES: Human

WATCH YOUR HEAD!
From Death Watch to Sabine, Mandalorians wear helmets with a **distinctive and menacing** design.

IMPERIAL SUPER COMMANDOS (Gar Saxon) — **CONCORD DAWN PROTECTOR** (Fenn Rau) — **CLAN WREN** (Countess Ursa Wren, Sabine's mother)

DEATH WATCH — **SHADOW COLLECTIVE** — **PRE VIZSLA** — **NITE OWLS** — **SABINE WREN**

Top 3
Sabine's Gear

1. **DARKSABER** — Retrieved from Maul's refuge on Dathomir. A weapon with influence on Mandalore.
2. **JET PACK** — Taken from an Imperial super commando. Features a powerful firing rocket.
3. **MANDALORIAN VAMBRACES** — A gift from Fenn Rau, complete with paralyzing darts and repulsor.

Q: What are the creatures on Sabine's armor?

A: The **starbird** on Sabine's chest becomes the **symbol** for her **rebel group**. She changes the animal on her shoulder: first an **anooba**, then a **fyrnock**, and later a **convor**.

STRANGE ...BUT TRUE
Between her time at the Imperial academy and years with the rebels, Sabine is a **bounty hunter**. Ketsu Onyo is Sabine's partner in crime—until she **leaves Sabine for dead** and works for **Black Sun**.

TOP 10
KANAN'S FAST-TRACK DARKSABER TRAINING
1. Kanan trains Sabine with **wooden training sabers**.
2. Ezra teaches Sabine **lightsaber forms** (a couple of days).
3. Sabine **practice fights** with Ezra.
4. Sabine incorporates **Mandalorian weapons**.
5. Kanan presents and explains her **Darksaber**.
6. Kanan teaches Sabine a **series of strikes**.
7. Kanan **free-form spars** with Sabine.
8. Kanan pushes Sabine **psychologically**.
9. Sabine faces her **painful past**.
10. Basic training is complete!

BOMBS AWAY!
Sabine is the **weapons expert** and **resident artist** aboard the *Ghost*. She's **smart**, speaks **many languages**, and is always ready to **blast** some stormtroopers!

COOL!
Some of Yavin's **REBEL PILOTS**, like Brace Marko (Gold Six) and Farns Monsbee (Blue Five), wear versions of Sabine's famous **STARBIRD** on their helmets!

Through the ages: HAIR COLOR COMBOS

BLUE AND ORANGE — BLUE AND GREEN — WHITE AND PURPLE

THE FIRST REBELS

> "Everything I did was for family, for Mandalore!"
> **SABINE**

In numbers

3272 LY (Lothal Year)
The year Sabine meets Ezra in the Lothal Calendar

250kph (155mph)
Top speed of Sabine's speeder

18 years old
Sabine's age when she returns home to her family on Krownest

3 colors
Sabine's blaster model can fire red, blue, and yellow plasma

1.84m (6ft)
Length of Sabine's speeder

1.70m (5ft 7in)
Sabine's height

1 sibling
Tristan Wren, formerly one of Saxon's Imperial super commandos

Peek behind the scenes
Sabine is voiced by actress **Tiya Sircar**. She is best known for her roles in the movies *17 Again* and *The Internship*, and the TV series, *The Vampire Diaries*.

STRANGE ...BUT TRUE
Sabine's artistic and political **inspiration** comes from some unusual quarters, including **Janyor**, a **rebel artist** on Bith and the **rebel senator Gall Trayvis**, who turns out to be a secret **Imperial agent**!

HOPE FOR PHOENIX SQUADRON
When Mon Mothma refuses **to send aid** for the Battle of Atollon, Ezra turns to Sabine and her family. Together they **destroy** Thrawn's *Interdictor*-class Star Destroyer, allowing the rebels to escape.

Tell me more!

STANDING ALONE
While Sabine is a cadet at the Imperial Academy on Mandalore, she builds **weapons** that the Empire then uses **against her own people**! Horrified when she learns the truth, Sabine escapes from the academy. However her family sees her as a **traitor**.

Sabine decorates **Zeb and Ezra's room** with a picture of Chopper playing a **prank** on them!

ART ATTACK
Sabine loves to give everything her **own personal touch**. She sprays her rebel graffiti on **walls and Imperial vehicles**, over **propaganda posters**, and even on **unconscious stormtroopers**!

Fast Facts

OCCUPATION: Former Honor Guard Captain of Lasan, now a rebel

SPECIES: Lasat

AGE: 43 dust seasons

HOMEWORLD: Lasan

ABILITIES: Bo-rifle expert, fighting stormtroopers (or in rebel-speak, "bucket heads")

TOP 2
ZEB'S KEEPSAKES
Zeb hides mementos of his life on Lasan in his cabin on the *Ghost*.
1. Honor Guard medallion
2. Tiny bag of Lasan dust

Peek behind the scenes
Star Wars concept artist Ralph McQuarrie first came up with what became Zeb's look during his early design work for Chewbacca.

How to let off steam like Zeb
"KARABAST!" THE MOST COMMONLY USED WORD THAT EXPRESSES EXTREME FRUSTRATION

THE BIG BRUISER

If there are **bucket heads to bash**, the rebels call on the brawniest of their bunch, Garazeb "Zeb" Orrelios. Zeb is as **strong as a Wookiee**— and **equally prickly**, especially around Chopper, AP-5, or that Loth-rat kid, Ezra.

Q: Who were the Honor Guards of Lasan?
A: They were Lasan's **elite warriors**, who defended Lasan when the Empire invaded. As a captain, Zeb **fought to the last**, until a bomb destroyed the palace. He was nearly dead when Kanan found him.

FIGHTING INSTINCT
Stronger, swifter, and **stealthier** than humans, Lasats are **built for fighting**. Stormtroopers really **don't stand a chance**.

Bo-rifles have a **third mode**, used by the "ancients" for **music** and ceremonies.

BO-RIFLE HONOR
In Lasat culture, only a true **Honor Guard of Lasan** has the privilege to wield an **AB-75 bo-rifle**. With a **click of a button**, the weapon can change from a **high-capacity blaster rifle** to an **electrostaff**.

REALLY?!
Zeb refuses to use the Empire's **LETHAL T-7 DISRUPTORS**. He still has **NIGHTMARES** about the Imperials **DISINTEGRATING** his people **ATOM BY ATOM** with T-7s.

THE FIRST REBELS

Peek behind the scenes
Steve Blum, Zeb's voice actor, also plays the smooth talking, snappily dressed, HoloNet News anchor Alton Kastle.

Tell me more!

NOT ALONE AFTER ALL
Zeb discovers two **Lasat survivors**, Chava and Gron. They tell him that a **prophecy** will lead them to a new land called **Lira San**, which turns out to be the **original Lasat homeworld**!

> "There's something about the feel of their helmets on my fists."
> **ZEB ON STORMTROOPERS**

SERIOUSLY?!
Confronted by stormtroopers, Hera and Kanan pose as bounty hunters and claim that Zeb is a **RARE HAIRLESS WOOKIEE** they've captured. No one is fooled, so Zeb sorts things out with a well-placed **PUNCH**.

> "I owe those hairy beasts. They saved some of my people."
> **ZEB ON WOOKIEES**

STRANGE ...BUT TRUE
Zeb is **so flexible** he can squeeze his hefty 2.1m (6ft 11in) frame into the cockpit of a TIE fighter with room to spare.

THE PROPHECY
Zeb assumes the warrior in a Lasat prophecy refers to him, and is surprised to learn the warrior, child, and fool could all be one person!

"THE PROMISE OF LIRA SAN WILL FOLLOW THE FATE OF THE THREE: THE FOOL; SIMPLE AND SELFISH, HE WOULD LEAD... THE WARRIOR; BOLD AND BLOODTHIRSTY, TO HUNT THE HOPE OF TOMORROW... THE CHILD... TO DESTROY HIM. WE WILL FIND OUR NEW HOME ONLY IF... THE CHILD SAVES THE WARRIOR AND THE FOOL."

Q: Why did Zeb think he was the last Lasat?
A: Zeb's native planet, Lasan, is **invaded** by the Empire, just like the Wookiees' homeworld, Kashyyyk. Yet **instead of taking slaves** as they did with the Wookiees, the Imperials **devastate** Lasan and **exterminate** most of the Lasat.

ARCH FRENEMIES

Agent Kallus orders the destruction of Zeb's **homeworld**. However, when they are trapped together on **Bahryn** these enemies become **comrades**.

37

Fast Facts

AFFILIATION: Ghost's crew

TYPE: C1-series astromech droid

MANUFACTURER: Irrelevant, seeing how often he's been patched up

PERSONALITY: Grouchy, mischievous

> **REALLY?!** AP-5 knows Chopper is **REPROGRAMMED** by the Empire when he **BEHAVES NICELY** for a change!

TOP 5 FAVORITE GADGETS

1. **Computer probe**—connects to computers to dig out information, open doors, and control ships.
2. **Electroshock prod**—Chopper's favorite gadget, which he uses to zap both enemies and friends!
3. **Arc welder**—for repairs or cutting into objects using a tiny blowtorch.
4. **Antenna**—receives and sends data wirelessly.
5. **Grasping arms**—to pull levers, push buttons, and grab things.

BEST KNOWN FOR SQUABBLING AND TEASING ZEB AND AP-5 — Chopper

CRANKY MECH!

Old and grumpy, Chopper is Hera Syndulla's **faithful droid... mostly**. He's a valued member of the Ghost's rebel crew, but **hates being bossed around**.

Q: What does Chopper actually do?

A: As a **C1-series astromech droid**, Chopper is the Ghost's mechanic and an assistant to Hera and the crew. He also goes **undercover** as an Imperial droid on spy missions, often working with **Ezra or AP-5**.

In numbers

32kg (71lbs) Chopper's weight

4 visual sensors Including a hidden telescope

3 retractable arms Two on his head, one on his body

2-6-4 Chopper's Imperial alias

2 mismatched legs Cover plates from different droids

1 booster rocket Hidden inside his body

C1-10P Chopper's model number

STRANGE ...BUT TRUE
Chopper *really doesn't* like other astromech droids! He squabbles with R2-D2 when they meet and has been known to **push Imperial astromechs** down **sewer pipes**—or out of **starship airlocks**!

Top 5 Chopper antics

1. **WISECRACKS** He always has a snarky answer or insult at the ready, but Zeb can't understand a thing he says!

2. **ELECTROSHOCK PRODS** He loves to zap Ezra and others with a jolt of electricity.

3. **DE-BUNKING** He removes the screws from Ezra's bunk and sends him crashing down on Zeb.

4. **PITCHING OVERBOARD** He helps Ezra with lightsaber training by hurling so many empty milk jugs at him that he knocks the kid off the ship!

5. **FUN FIRST** He teases Zeb and Ezra rather than repairing the Phantom, and the ship breaks down when Hera and Sabine use it later!

THE FIRST REBELS

> "Wabuh wa wa waboo."
> Mind your own business.
> **CHOPPER TO IMPERIAL DROID**

Peek behind the scenes
Chopper's look is inspired by the original designs for R2-D2, by legendary Star Wars concept illustrator Ralph McQuarrie.

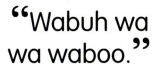

Tell me more!

FINDING CHOPPER BASE
Chopper makes friends with an **Imperial protocol droid** named AP-5. When Phoenix Squadron discover that the planet they plan to hide on has an **Imperial blockade**, AP-5 suggests **Atollon** instead. In recognition for the droids' help, the rebels name their new base after Chopper, and put AP-5 in charge of inventory.

> "Bha! Blap ba wah waah"
> Watch the paintjob, jerks!
> **CHOPPER TO RYDER, KANAN, AND EZRA**

COOL!!
Chopper is made almost entirely of many **REPLACEMENT PARTS** from **OTHER DROIDS**. Not much of him is original!

Peek behind the scenes
"If Artoo-Detoo is your favorite dog, Chopper is the cat," says Star Wars Rebels executive producer Dave Filoni, on his approach to Chopper's personality.

TOP 3 WAYS CHOPPER GETS AROUND... AND AROUND

3 wheels—but sometimes rides along on just one, like a unicycle.
2 legs—slowly shuffles or wiggles forward... with attitude.
1 rocket booster—lets him fly, usually off the handle, for short distances.

STRANGE ...BUT TRUE
Chopper is a former **Republic droid** who flies Y-wing missions during the Clone Wars. Hera finds Chopper and repairs him after **his ship crashes** in front of her family's home on Ryloth.

Tell me more!

HOW TO LOSE A DROID AT SABACC
Lando Calrissian **wins Chopper** from Zeb in **Sabacc**, a popular card game. Zeb's hand totals **23** (a "**Pure Sabacc**"), but Lando holds a **2**, a **3**, and an "**Idiot**" card (an "**Idiot's Array**"). Lando's cards are the only combination that can beat Zeb's—and **Chopper's not happy** about it!

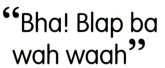

CHOPPER'S CRANK-O-METER
LOATHE ← → LOVE
Orders, R2-D2, Zeb, Missions, C-3PO, AP-5, Hera, Lando, Ezra, Holochess, Pranks

In numbers

143kg (315lbs)
Saw Gerrera's weight with gear

8 years
Length of time Saw raises Jyn Erso

2 cycles
Length of time that Saw is out of contact on Geonosis

1.87m (6ft 2in)
Saw Gerrera's height

1 mind-reading creature
An octopus-like telepath named Bor Gullet used for interrogations

Fast Facts

ROLE: Freedom fighter, rebel cell leader, smuggler
MEDICAL DEVICES: Artificial leg, pressure suit, respiratory aid
HOMEWORLD: Onderon
SPECIES: Human

TOP 5

SAW'S HIDEOUT HIGHLIGHTS

1. **G2-1B7 Medical droid**—treats the rebels from his diagnostic station.
2. **Cavern Angels X-wings**—starships that are kept flying with spare parts.
3. **Weapons cache**—traded and stolen blasters with custom upgrades.
4. **Hand-made dejarik game**—provides entertainment between raids.
5. **Ancient, religious stone carvings**—mysterious and crumbling, their stories have been lost in history.

Q: What's wrong with Saw's health?

A: Saw is in **rough shape** from so many battles. His lungs are **contaminated** with Geonosian pesticides. He develops severe **breathing problems**, and also **loses his leg** during the final two years of his life. He needs **constant** medical treatment to stay alive.

SACRIFICE FOR THE DREAM

Saw and Steela Gerrera are trained as rebels by the Jedi Ahsoka Tano. Later, Saw raises Jyn Erso, the daughter of his friends, Galen and Lyra. In the end, they all give up everything for the rebellion.

AHSOKA TANO
Trainer of Saw and Steela, missing on Malachor

STEELA GERRERA
Sister of Saw, perished on Onderon

SAW GERRERA
Perished on Jedha

JYN ERSO
Foster-daughter of Saw, perished on Scarif

Tell me more!

SAW'S SYMBOL

At times, Saw wears a **three-pronged symbol** on his cape or shoulder. It also appears on the **helmets** of his band of soldiers. The symbol originates with the rebels of Onderon. Combined with **Sabine Wren's rebel starbird graffiti tag**, it becomes the crest of the **Rebel Alliance**.

THE FIRST REBELS

Saw spends some **20 years** looking for the Empire's **secret**! He almost uncovers it when he helps capture the Geonosian **Klik-Klak**. Saw finally learns of the **Death Star** when he shows Jyn a **secret message** from Galen.

BEST KNOWN FOR

USING BOR'S TELEPATHIC TENTACLES TO QUESTION BODHI

Saw Gerrera

Through the ages: SAW GERRERA

DREAMER
Saw fights for freedom from the Separatists on his homeworld. In the process, he is tortured and loses his sister.

REALIST
Convinced the Empire is planning something big, but disappointed in his allies, Saw considers more violent tactics.

EXTREMIST
Saw leads his own band of insurgents in a rebellion independent from the Alliance council.

Tell me more!

A MOTLEY MIX
Not all of the fighters in Saw's rebel cell **actually believe** in the cause. Moroff is a Gigoran mercenary who fights the Empire for **profit**. Saw's rebels are not merely violent warriors either. Kullbee Sperado is **deeply religious**, and goes on long retreats to **pray**.

"Your methods are soft, Jedi! We lost the last war because of you!"
SAW TO KANAN JARRUS

Working with Dressellian smuggler Has Obitt, Saw helps the **Erso family escape** the Empire and their life on Coruscant. He remains **friends** with them and comes to **Jyn's rescue** when Orson Krennic discovers their whereabouts.

Q: What's in Saw's pocket?
A: Saw keeps a personal **holoprojector** marked with the symbol of the Onderon rebels. It contains an image of his **sister**—the only thing left to **remind** him of her.

Steela Gerrera

Peek behind the scenes
Saw Gerrera was first voiced by Andrew Kishino in *The Clone Wars*. He was played by Forest Whitaker in *Rogue One*, and then voiced by the latter in *Rebels*.

STRANGE
...BUT TRUE
Saw's eye color changes from **teal** to **green** to **brown** over time.

DANGEROUS FIREBRAND

From his **hideout** in the Catacombs of Cadera on Jedha, **daring** Saw Gerrera leads a **rebel cell** against the Imperial occupation. However, this renegade is **shunned** by the Rebel Alliance—they consider him a **troublemaker**!

THE REBEL ALLIANCE

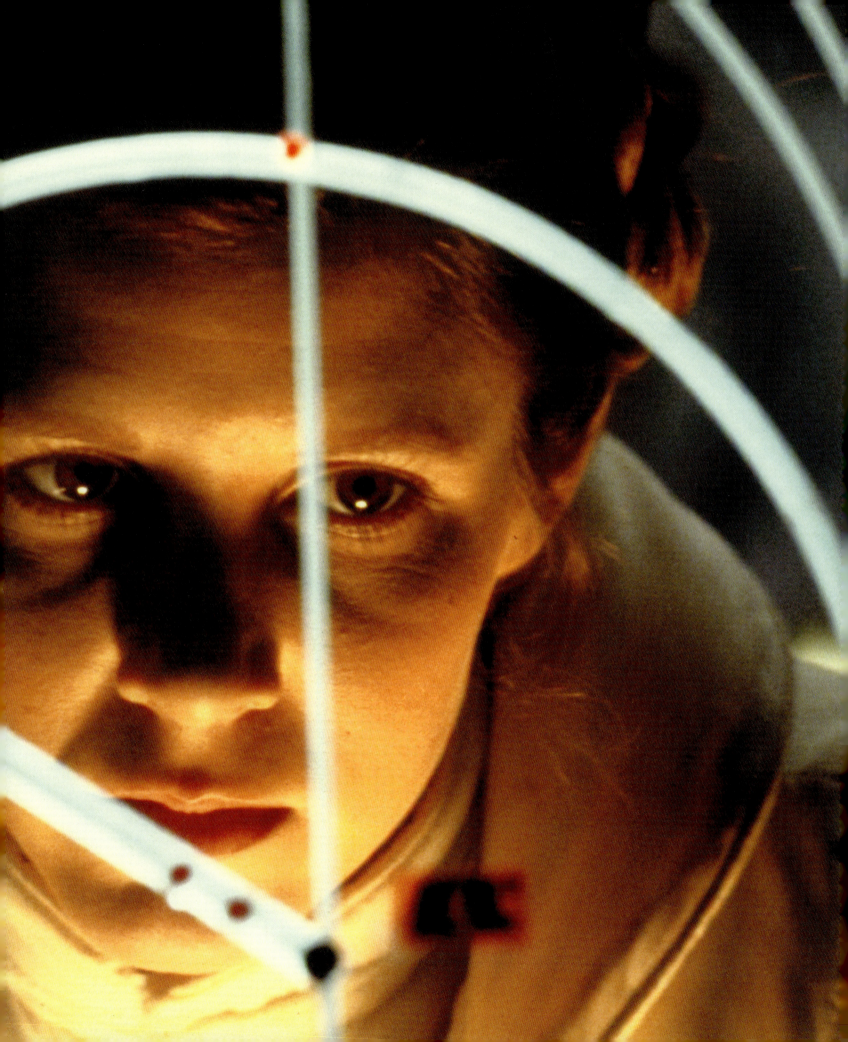

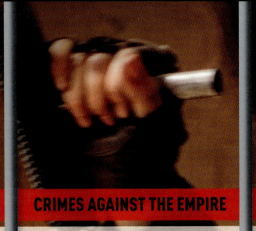

CRIMES AGAINST THE EMPIRE

- Aggravated assault
- Escape from custody
- Possession of unauthorized weapons
- Forgery of Imperial documents
- Theft of Imperial data tapes
- Breaking and entering
- Leading a revolt against the Empire
- Impersonating military personnel

In numbers

5,400+ days
Since Jyn has seen her father

20 years
Jyn's sentence of hard labor on the planet Wobani

16 years old
Jyn's age when Saw Gerrera abandoned her

1.60m (5ft 3in)
Jyn's height

BEST KNOWN FOR
STRONG SURVIVAL INSTINCT
Jyn Erso

Q: Where does Jyn get her kyber crystal necklace?

A: Jyn's mother gives her the crystal to remind her to trust in the Force.

Known Aliases
JYN RARELY USES HER REAL NAME...
1. Liana Hallik
2. Tanith Ponta
3. Kestrel Dawn
4. Stardust (by her father)
5. Prisoner 6295A
6. Little Sister (by Baze Malbus)

> "I'm not used to people sticking around when things go bad."
> — JYN ERSO

MOST WANTED
Throughout her life, Jyn Erso finds herself pursued by many.

BATTLE DROIDS
The Erso family is caught in the middle of a battle at the end of the Clone Wars.

ORSON KRENNIC
The Imperial tracks down the Ersos on Lah'mu. Young Jyn narrowly escapes.

SAW GERRERA
The rebel outlaw finds Jyn hiding under a hatch and rescues her from Lah'mu.

THE EMPIRE
Imprisoned for multiple crimes, Jyn is sent to a labor camp.

REBEL ALLIANCE
The rebels must find Jyn in order to learn more about the Death Star.

TOP 4
JYN'S WEAPONS
1. Truncheons
2. Fists
3. Blastech A180 (stolen)
4. Imperial E-11 (stolen)

REBELLIOUS ROGUE

Resilient and rebellious, Jyn Erso is just 21 years old. She has spent nearly her entire life **fighting and hiding** from authority. When she realizes how much destruction the **Death Star** will bring to the galaxy, she puts aside her independent nature and takes up the mantle of **rebel leader**.

JYN'S MISSION
When she **learns** about the Death Star flaw, Jyn decides to lead the mission to steal **plans** to the space station. Jyn makes an **impassioned plea** to the leaders of the Rebel Alliance to help her in her mission.

Tell me more!

A STUDENT OF DISORDER
Rescued by **Saw Gerrera** after her father is taken into Imperial custody, Jyn spends the next eight years **learning how to be a rebel**. She becomes Saw's best soldier, but he **abandons** her at the age of 16 when he fears others will find out her secret: that she is the child of an Imperial scientist. After this, she **trusts no one**.

Fast Facts

AFFILIATION: Saw Gerrera's group and the Rebel Alliance

SPECIES: Human

BORN ON: Vallt

PARENTS: Galen and Lyra Erso

SKILLS: Plotting against the Empire, giving inspiring speeches

IMPERIAL DETENTION CENTER AND LABOR CAMP LEG-817
Located on Wobani in Bryx Sector, Mid Rim • Jyn held prisoner here • Inmates carry out forced labor • 5-year life expectancy for inmates

CARING CUTTHROAT

Captain Cassian Jeron Andor is a **hardened rebel agent** who carries out **brutal orders** for the Rebel Alliance. But **new friendships** lead him to put his **trust** in his team members, **disobey** his commanders, and **save the galaxy**!

BEST KNOWN FOR
DEFYING THE ALLIANCE AND HELPING JYN
Cassian Andor

Top 4 Cassian's cryptic codenames

1. **WILLIX** — A government agent operating on Ord Mantell.
2. **AACH** — A Republic Senate contact on Darknell.
3. **JORETH SWARD** — An assistant to Imperial Admiral Grendreef.
4. **FULCRUM** — A rebel recruitment agent in the Albarrio sector.

RING OF KAFRENE
Trading post occupied by Empire in Kafrene asteroid belt • Overcrowded stopover point for human and nonhuman travelers alike • Here, Cassian learns of Saw, Galen, and Death Star from informer Tivik

In numbers
- **89 stormtroopers** — Stand between Cassian, Jyn, K-2SO, and the Vault in Scarif's Citadel
- **26 standard years** — Cassian's age
- **8 compressed eleton blaster gas ampules** — On Cassian's belt
- **2 blue pips** — On Cassian's Alliance Captain badge

Cassian entered the conflict when he was just a kid. He became a child soldier at the tender age of **six**!

WHAT IS CASSIAN WEARING? A **Corellian-cut** khaki field jacket, popular in shops in **Kor Vella**.

DANGEROUS DUTIES
Cassian works for the **Intelligence Operations division**, with spy duties putting him in **constant danger**. Later in his career he is transferred to the **Retrieval division**, where his orders are to **break Jyn Erso out of prison**, then locate Saw Gerrera and Galen Erso.

Q: Cassian hates the Empire, but does he love the Republic?
A: Not really. Cassian isn't officially a Separatist, but he disagrees with the Republic's military control of areas during the Clone Wars.

REALLY?!
SABOTAGE, ASSASSINATION, and **BETRAYING FRIENDS**—being an intelligence agent means Cassian must carry out tasks that he isn't always proud of!

Fast Facts

AFFILIATION: Rebel Alliance

DUTIES: Spying, prisoner rescues, undercover missions, recruitment

HOMEWORLD: Fest

FAVORITE SHIP: A speedy Corellian starfighter

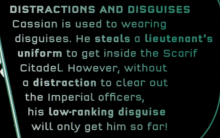

DISTRACTIONS AND DISGUISES
Cassian is used to wearing disguises. He **steals** a **lieutenant's uniform** to get inside the Scarif Citadel. However, without a **distraction** to clear out the Imperial officers, his **low-ranking disguise** will only get him so far!

Tell me more!

A SHOT IN THE DARK
Cassian's BlasTech A280-CFE can be extended with add-on modules to become a **sniper rifle** or **assault rifle**. The sniper mode features a long-distance **night-vision** scope—perfect for hunting Cassian's unsuspecting targets in the dark.

STRANGE ...BUT TRUE
Though Mon Mothma tells Cassian to **help Jyn** find her father, General Draven orders Cassian to **eliminate Galen** instead. Cassian has carried out **difficult orders** in the past, but he can not bring himself to **betray Jyn**!

> "We're not here to make friends."
> **CASSIAN ANDOR**

NOT SO FESTIVE BEGINNINGS
Cassian's homeworld of Fest is not a place that you want to rush to visit. It's **cold** and **mountainous** and, if you're a human, you will probably end up **laboring** in one of the planet's many industrial zones, occupied by the Empire.

CASSIAN'S SECURITY KIT
Cassian has to get past lots of **locked doors** and **sensors** as a rebel spy. He carries a security kit in a **sensor-baffling wallet** that is full of tools for hacking—or **destroying**—control panels and electronics.

Fast Facts

NAME: K-2SO

CLASS: KX-series Imperial security droid

PLACE OF CONSTRUCTION: Vulpter

MANUFACTURER: Arakyd Industries

AFFILIATION: Rebel Alliance Intelligence

MASTER: Cassian Andor

K-2SO's data spike is hidden in his knuckles. The spike allows him to access doors and computer systems.

BEST KNOWN FOR WITTY COMEBACKS! K-2SO

Lucky K-2SO doesn't need to steal an Imperial officer or ground crew uniform to **disguise** himself on Scarif, like Jyn and Cassian do. He **blends in** just as he is!

How to lighten the mood, by K-2SO

"THAT IS A BAD IDEA. I THINK SO, AND SO DOES CASSIAN."
—On Jyn coming with Cassian and K-2SO on their mission to Jedha

"I FIND THAT ANSWER VAGUE AND UNCONVINCING!"
—On the reason Jyn has a blaster

"THERE ARE A LOT OF EXPLOSIONS FOR TWO PEOPLE BLENDING IN."
—On Cassian and Jyn fighting while undercover in Jedha City

"THERE'S A PROBLEM ON THE HORIZON... THERE'S NO HORIZON."
—After the Death Star blasts Jedha

"JYN. I'LL BE THERE FOR YOU. CASSIAN SAID I HAD TO."
—On looking out for Jyn when the rebels head to Scarif

SNEAKY! After the Clone Wars, the Senate **BANS** battle droids. The Empire gets around this by classifying the KX-series as "security droids."

Q: Why does K-2SO tell Jyn and Cassian to climb?

A: K-2SO knows he can **no longer hold off the stormtroopers** from the Citadel's vault. He must **seal** the doors and **sacrifice** himself to **save** Jyn and Cassian. The only way for them to exit the vault now is **up**—so K-2SO tells them to climb the tower and transmit the Death Star plans from the roof.

THE REBEL ALLIANCE

BRUTAL HONESTY

Peek behind the scenes
For some scenes, K-2SO actor Alan Tudyk wore robotic hand extensions. The robot fingers moved in sync with his own, allowing him to manipulate objects!

K-2SO is both **intimidating** and **endearing**. This Imperial droid has been **reprogrammed** to serve the Rebel Alliance. A side effect of his personality shift leaves him offering **uninvited opinions**, that are not only **blunt**, but at times **unsettling**!

Cassian had a **lot** to change when he reprogrammed K-2SO, such as adding **restrictions** on **harming** non-Imperials, and **removing** K-2SO's **respect** for Imperial officers.

Tell me more!

DON'T JUDGE A BOOK BY ITS COVER
KX droids are not just made for security duty! Their **dexterous hands** can operate lots of complicated equipment and they are an **excellent shot**, too—much **better** than stormtroopers! These highly intelligent droids are also **experts** in **strategic analysis**, and good at making **complex calculations** quickly.

In numbers

111kg (245lbs)
K-2SO's weight

40+ Imperial vehicles
Number of ships K-2SO is pre-programmed to fly

35% chance of failure
K-2SO's calculation for the rebels making a safe landing on Eadu

12 standard years old
K-2SO's age

6 buttons
At K-2SO's primary programming port access door

2.16m (7ft 1in)
K-2SO's height

REALLY?!
When the rebels need a map on Scarif, K-2SO uses his data spike to **PROBE** another security droid's **BRAIN** for one!

Q: What does Arakyd Industries make?
A: Apart from K-2SO, the long-standing company also manufactures various **sinister military and spy droids**, including the ID9 seeker droid, DRK-1 Dark Eye probe droid, Viper recon and probe droids, and the RA-7 insect droid.

STRANGE

...BUT TRUE
Cassian won't let K-2SO have a blaster—a **precaution** against any **faulty** reprogramming! Even with no weapon, he makes some **rebels** on Yavin **nervous**. This **tall, powerful** droid alarms people who once fought battle droids.

Q: Why does Bodhi flee the Empire?

A: Bodhi feels **guilty** for things he's done in the Empire's service. When he meets scientist **Galen Erso** on Eadu, Galen convinces Bodhi that he can **make things right** by taking a **secret message** to the rebels. Bodhi may be timid, but his **bravery** and **sacrifice** make him a hero.

NEED A LIFT?

Bodhi is **trained to fly** all kinds of Imperial cargo vessels, including *Lambda* and *Zeta*-class **shuttles**. The rebels need him to fly the shuttle from Eadu to Yavin, and on to Scarif. Without his **Imperial clearance codes**, they would **never** have made it to Scarif!

> "He didn't capture me, I came here myself! I defected, I defected!"
> **BODHI TO SAW GERRERA**

Tell me more!

ALL IN A DAY'S WORK!

Bodhi must get a **signal** to General Raddus, telling him to open Scarif's shield gate. To do this, Bodhi must go out into the **fighting** and use his **cable reel** to connect the ship to the **communications tower**. To activate the line, Chirrut and Baze must **flip** the **master switch**, even **farther** away!

Fast Facts

AFFILIATION: Rebels, former Imperial cargo pilot

HOMEWORLD: Jedha

SPECIES: Human

PERSONALITY: Nervous, courageous, resourceful

Peek behind the scenes

British actor, **Riz Ahmed**—who plays Bodhi—sent fourteen auditions to director **Gareth Edwards**. In each one, he gave Bodhi a different costume or accent.

BODHI'S SCARIF MISDIRECTION GUIDE

1. Wait inside cargo shuttle SW-0608 on landing pad **nine**.
2. When the shooting starts, confuse the Imperials by telling them you spot 40 rebels heading west on pad **two**.
3. Tell Corporal Tonc to get on the radio and say the rebels are now on pad **five**!

Q: What's in Bodhi's pocket?

A: Bodhi loves **candy**. He steals Weeteef's **stash** at Saw Gerrera's hideout!

RELUCTANT REBEL

Bodhi Rook becomes an Imperial pilot in order to **survive** under the Empire's brutal occupation. But Bodhi can't keep ignoring the **suffering** of his people, so he decides to **do something about it**!

WOW!...

75,000

The Imperial reward in credits for Bodhi's capture

YUCK!!
Poor Bodhi is nearly driven insane by the slimy, fat **TENTACLES** of Bor Gullet. The creature reads Bodhi's thoughts and can tell if he **LIES**!

BEST KNOWN FOR
DELIVERING GALEN'S SECRET MESSAGE TO JYN
Bodhi Rook

STRANGE ...BUT TRUE
Bodhi has a **gambling** problem. He bets on **races** between **odupiendo**—large, flightless **avians** from Naboo. Bodhi has won **thousands** of credits, but he's also **lost** as many!

Top 8
Side-switching heroes

1 BODHI ROOK
From Imperial pilot to Rebel Alliance soldier

2 FN-2187 (FINN)
From First Order stormtrooper to Resistance soldier

3 LANDO CALRISSIAN
From making deals with Darth Vader to rebel general

4 ASAJJ VENTRESS
From Sith assassin to Jedi ally

5 KETSU ONYO
From bounty hunter to rebel ally

6 SABINE WREN
From Imperial cadet to rebel

7 FENN RAU
From the Empire's Journeyman Protectors warrior to rebel ally

8 AGENT KALLUS
From Imperial ISB agent to rebel spy

In numbers

25 years old
Bodhi's age

15.24m (50ft)
Length of the communications cable line on Bodhi's backpack

10 pouches
On Bodhi's vest

8 buttons
On Bodhi's data-relay wrist link

3 code cylinders
In the pockets on Bodhi's left arm

1.72m (5ft 8in)
Bodhi's height

BEST KNOWN FOR

TAKING OUT STORMTROOPERS WITH JUST HIS STAFF

Chirrut Îmwe

> "I don't need luck. I have you."
> **CHIRRUT TO BAZE**

When he is captured by Saw Gerrera and put in a cage, Chirrut senses that there is someone in the next cell before he hears them.

CHIRRUT'S LIGHTBOW

Powerful enough to take down a TIE fighter in one blast • Handcrafted by Chirrut • Powered by a diatrium power cell • 50 round capacity

> "The Force moves darkly near a creature that's about to kill."
> **CHIRRUT ÎMWE**

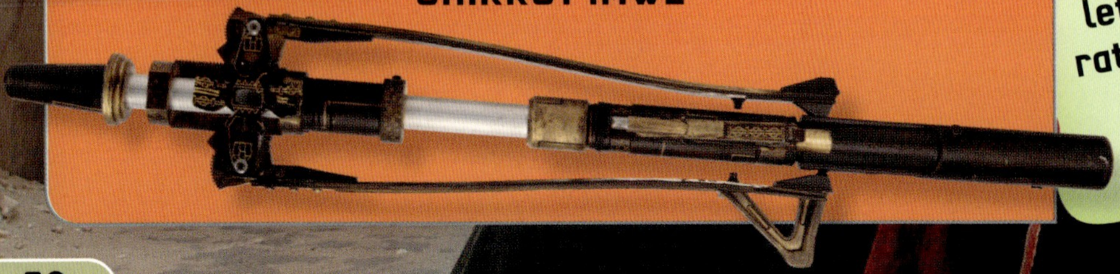

REALLY?! Chirrut's **ZAMA-SHIWO** martial arts skills are rumored to let him alter his heart rate and oxygen intake—giving him almost **SUPERNATURAL** powers!

Fast Facts

HOME PLANET: Jedha (moon)

SPECIES: Human

AFFILIATION: Guardians of the Whills (former), the Rebel Alliance

SPECIAL SKILLS: Breaking out of cages

OFTEN FOUND IN: The Holy Quarter of Jedha

Tell me more!

SPIRITUAL SOLDIER

Chirrut is a **skilled warrior**, and a faithful follower of the Force—even though he **doesn't** seem to have Force abilities like a Jedi. His **focus** and highly tuned **senses** make him a capable hand-to-hand **fighter** and an accurate shot.

Q: Just who are the Guardians of the Whills?

A: They are a devout religious order from Jedha. The monks protected the Temple of the Kyber and the pilgrims who visited it.

SPOOOOKY!

When the Temple of the Kyber is ransacked, Chirrut is left **jobless**. He earns money by using his **Force-sensing** abilities to tell people's fortunes.

HUH?! Saw Gerrera's rebels **TRUST NO ONE**. They put a blindfold on Chirrut even though he is already blind!

Peek behind the scenes
Chirrut is played by Donnie Yen, star of many martial arts movies such as *IP Man*.

Top 3

Pieces of kit

1 GUARDIAN ROBES
Chirrut still wears the traditional clothes of the Guardians of the Whills.

2 UNETI-WOOD STAFF
Tipped with a kyber crystal sliver, it serves as both a walking staff and a weapon.

3 ECHO-BOX TRANSMITTER
Emits a near-silent echo that helps Chirrut sense his surroundings.

WARRIOR MONK

A **true believer**, Chirrut Îmwe has not let the dark times **sway his faith** in the Force or his mission. He may be **blind**, but this hopeful hero is always hunting for a way to **strike back** against the Empire that has taken everything from him.

In numbers

∞ (infinite)
Chirrut's faith in the Force

52 years old
Chirrut's age

10 credits
Price charged by Chirrut to read someone's fortune on Jedha

8kg (4lbs)
Mass of Chirrut's lightbow

Fast Facts

SPECIES: Human
FAVORITE FOOD: Deep fried nuna legs
HOME PLANET: Jedha (moon)
AFFILIATION: Guardian of the Whills (former), the Rebel Alliance
NOTABLE BATTLES: Jedha, Scarif

CHALK AND CHEESE
Although they share a powerful bond, Baze and Chirrut have very different outlooks on life. But no matter how they might disagree, the duo always sticks together.

Baze Malbus	VS.	Chirrut Îmwe
Luck	HE BELIEVES IN	The Force
Modern	HIS PREFERRED WEAPONS ARE	Traditional
Blasting them	HE OPENS DOORS BY	Praying
Practical	HIS PERSONALITY IS	Optimistic

Tell me more!

LOST LEADER
Baze was one the most faithful members of the Guardians' religious order. But after the Empire destroyed the Temple of the Kyber, Baze lost his job… and his faith. He now puts his efforts into battling the Empire and protecting his friend, Chirrut Îmwe.

BEST KNOWN FOR
EAVESDROPPING ON IMPERIAL SOLDIERS
Baze Malbus

In numbers

53 years old
Baze's age

30kg (10lbs)
The mass of his blaster cannon

6 power cells
Carried on his chest plate armor

1.8m (5ft 11in)
Baze's height

COOL!!
Baze can let his **HAIR GROW OUT** now that he's no longer a Guardian of the Whills!

FALLEN GUARDIAN

Once a devoted believer in the Force, ex-Guardian of the Whills member Baze Malbus is now an armor-wearing, blaster-wielding **assassin**. But behind his **gruff** exterior is a loyal friend—willing to **sacrifice everything** for those he cares about.

Peek behind the scenes
Early drafts of *A New Hope* mention the "**Whills**," an idea that became the **Force** in the final film.

BIG BROTHER
Although Baze and Jyn haven't known each other for **long**, Baze puts all his **trust** in her. He fondly calls her "**little sister**."

THE REBEL ALLIANCE

"**You're welcome.**"
BAZE TO CHIRRUT AFTER *ALMOST* SHOOTING HIM

BAZE'S ARMORY
Baze adopts modern equipment for his battle against the Empire.

1. **MWC-35c repeating cannon** — More commonly known as "Staccato Lightning." For fast but accurate fire.
2. **High-density power cells** — To reload his fast-firing cannon.
3. **Weather shroud** — To keep warm on the frozen moon of Jedha.
4. **Cooling and power cell for cannon** — Worn on his back to distribute the weight.
5. **Quad-folded plastoid armor** — Protects against physical attacks and light blaster bolts.
6. **Handguards** — Hand armor stolen from an Imperial stormtrooper.

CLOSE CALL!
Baze takes down a **squad** of stormtroopers who have **surrounded** Chirrut. He **barely misses** his friend in the process!

Q: Why is Baze's cannon highly illegal?
A: This scarlet-and-silver weapon packs more power—and causes more damage—than any law-abiding citizen would ever need!

STRANGE ...BUT TRUE
Baze has a **long, curved scar** on his face. It's a **permanent reminder** of his **toughness** in battle.

NO WAY!! Baze's repeating cannon packs the **FIREPOWER** of **FIVE** laser rifles in **ONE!**

WOW!...
35,000
The number of blaster shots in Baze's cannon

55

Fast Facts

OCCUPATION: Moisture farmer, rebel, Jedi Knight, Jedi Master

AFFILIATION: Rebel Alliance

HOMEWORLD: Tatooine

ABILITIES: Piloting, lightsaber combat, the Force

VESSEL: T-16 skyhopper, T-65 X-wing fighter

How to become a Jedi Master—the Luke Skywalker way

1. FARM BOY
Dream big, aim high! Who says a farmer can't get into the Imperial Academy?

2. JEDI PADAWAN
Learn from the very best—Obi-Wan Kenobi and Master Yoda—and pay close attention!

3. JEDI KNIGHT
Resist the dark side, defeat your dad, Darth Vader, and bring balance to the Force. Easy!

4. JEDI MASTER
Save the galaxy and be the last Jedi standing after the fall of the Empire.

BEST KNOWN FOR DESTROYING THE FIRST DEATH STAR
Luke Skywalker

THE LAST JEDI

Wide-eyed and **restless**, Luke Skywalker **yearns to be a star pilot**, and dump his dull life as a moisture farmer. When he meets Obi-Wan, he learns that **his destiny lies** with something far greater—**the Force**.

STRANGE ...BUT TRUE
In their first duel, Darth Vader easily bests the **hot-headed, untested** Luke, slicing off his right hand. After barely escaping with his life, the young rebel has a **new, robotic hand** fitted.

LARS HOMESTEAD
Luke's home on Tatooine • Owen and Beru Lars's moisture farm • Underground living quarters

"Luke's just not a farmer, Owen. He has too much of his father in him."
AUNT BERU

Blade runner
The lightsaber is an **elegant weapon** for a more civilized age. The one Obi-Wan Kenobi hands to Luke connects the farm boy with his **infamous Jedi ancestry**.

TOP 3
JEDI LESSONS FOR LUKE
1. Dueling a flying remote droid while his vision is obscured.
2. Seeing his enemy's face as his own in the Dagobah cave.
3. Dropping his lightsaber and refusing to fight his father, Darth Vader.

THE REBEL ALLIANCE

In numbers

2,000 credits
Sale price for Luke's speeder

1,050kph (652mph)
Speed of Luke's X-wing in atmosphere

28cm (11in)
Hilt length of Luke's second, homemade green lightsaber

19 years old
Luke's age when he leaves Tatooine

1 more season
Length Uncle Owen asks Luke to work on the farm before he leaves

5. OLD MASTER
Go into **seclusion** on Ahch-To, a water-covered planet said to be home to the first Jedi temple.

BATTLE ON DEVARON
The **first time** Luke ever uses his lightsaber in a duel is in a **ruined Jedi temple** on the planet Devaron. He defeats a vicious alien known as **Sarco Plank**.

TOP 3
FORCE-FREE FEATS
1. Swinging across the immense Death Star chasm with Princess Leia.
2. Bringing down an Imperial walker single-handedly.
3. Defeating the ravenous rancor beast in Jabba's palace.

REALLY?!
After being savaged by a wampa, Luke is put in a bacta tank to recover. Bacta is a **CLEAR, SLIMY LIQUID** that helps the body regrow tissue, including **MUSCLES, NERVES, AND SKIN.**

JEDI JOURNAL
Obi-Wan leaves a **journal** in his Tatooine home for Luke Skywalker to find. It is full of stories about the **Jedi Order** and helps teach Luke about **the Force**.

Tell me more!

1 IN A MILLION! These are the odds of Luke hitting the Death Star's exhaust port with his proton torpedoes, according to Han Solo.

Q: Why does Luke leave the farm?

A: While hunting for C-3PO and R2-D2, stormtroopers **murder** Owen and Beru Lars when they discover the droids were sold to the couple. With no family left, Luke accompanies Obi-Wan on his **dangerous mission to Alderaan**.

STUDENT TURNED TEACHER
Without other Jedi to train him, Luke must **travel the galaxy** to learn more about the Force. His travels and adventures lead to many legends being told about him. With his new knowledge, he takes on the burden of training a **new generation** of Jedi. But his plan falls apart when one of the students turns to the **dark side**.

When he's not farming, young Luke relaxes by **shooting womp rats** for target practice or **racing through the treacherous Beggar's Canyon** in his T-16 skyhopper. He also hangs out with friends at Tatooine's Tosche Station, where he gets the **nickname "Wormie"**!

Fast Facts

OCCUPATION: Smuggler, gambler, starship captain, general
AFFILIATION: Rebel Alliance, Resistance
HOMEWORLD: Corellia
VESSEL: *Millennium Falcon, Eravana*

Peek behind the scenes
Han Solo was a big green alien in the original rough draft of Star Wars!

> "Hokey religions and ancient weapons are no match for a good blaster at your side!"
> **HAN SOLO ON THE FORCE**

SHOOT FIRST, THINK LATER
Han **almost blasts his friends** by shooting at a magnetically sealed door on the Death Star. It sends the **blaster bolt bouncing around the room!**

In numbers

- **224,190 credits** — The bounty that Jabba the Hutt puts on Han's head
- **17,000 credits** — Fee for transport from Tatooine to Alderaan in the *Millennium Falcon*
- **3 rathtars** — Captured by Han Solo for King Prana
- **1.8m (5ft 11in)** — Han's height
- **1 DL-44 heavy blaster pistol** — Han's favorite sidearm

Millennium Falcon

FLY BOY

The **dashing captain** of the *Millennium Falcon*, Han Solo, has flown from one side of the galaxy to the other, usually by the seat of his pants. Solo by name, solo by nature, this **mercenary, often cocky pilot** becomes **a selfless leader of the Rebellion**.

REALLY?!
Han loses his prized ship, the **MILLENNIUM FALCON**, to gunrunner Gannis Ducain. It trades hands multiple times before ending up on Jakku.

6 ways to INSULT Han!
He can **dish out the jibes**, but can he take them? Especially when they're **so close to the mark**.

- SCOUNDREL!
- HALF-WITTED!
- SCRUFFY-LOOKING!
- NERF HERDER!
- SLIMY!
- NO-GOOD SWINDLER!

THE REBEL ALLIANCE

REALLY?!
Ewoks try to **COOK HAN AS THE MAIN COURSE** at a big banquet in honor of C-3PO!

Q: How does a smuggler fall for a princess?
A: Han helps rescue Princess Leia in the hope of getting **a big reward**. Though he won't admit it at first, he **starts to fall in love** with her, and even becomes **jealous** that Leia is fond of Luke, not realizing until later that they are brother and sister.

TO THE RESCUE!
Just after **the Battle of Yavin**, Han and Chewie fly to the planet Cyrkon to **rescue** a member of **the Shrikes**—an elite rebel recon squadron. If the pilot, **Lt. Ematt**, falls into Imperial hands, the entire Rebellion would **be in danger**!

BEST KNOWN FOR
LEADING THE ATTACK ON STARKILLER BASE
Han Solo

Always the gambler, Han hangs **A PAIR OF DICE** in the viewport of the Millennium Falcon.

STRANGE

...BUT TRUE
Han, stumbling around **half blind from hibernation sickness** after being **frozen in carbonite**, accidentally hits Boba Fett's jet pack, sending the bounty hunter **crashing into the Sarlacc**.

RATHTAR ATTACK!
Han hires a crew of **grizzled mercenaries** to help him capture dangerous rathtars on Twon Ketee. Unfortunately, most of the crew are **eaten** in the process!

Résumé
HAN SOLO ZERO TO HERO

COCKSURE OUTLAW
On the run from Jabba the Hutt, Han Solo—smuggler, rogue, and all-around bad boy—is **only out for himself**.

REBEL HERO
Han surprises everyone, including himself, when he returns to **help the rebels blow up the Death Star**.

PETRIFIED PRISONER
To test the freezing process, Darth Vader **encases Han in carbonite**, and gives him to Jabba as a trophy.

REBEL GENERAL
Han's skills and boldness make him a **natural rebel leader**, as he heads the successful attack on Endor.

SENIOR SMUGGLER
Han returns to his dangerous life of crime after **his son, Ben**, turns to the **Dark Side**.

Tell me more!

WANTED, HAN SOLO... DEAD OR ALIVE!
Han Solo is a smuggler in the pay of **crime kingpin Jabba the Hutt**. When the Empire boards Han's ship, he has to **dump Jabba's illegal cargo**. The Hutt demands that Han repay him for the loss, but when he can't, Jabba puts **a big bounty on his head!**

Q: What is a nerf herder?
A: A shepherd who tends flocks of nerfs—**smelly, scruffy, surly beasts** bred for their **thick hides**. Their qualities are **shared by their herders**, in many people's opinion.

WARRIOR PRINCESS

Leia Organa's **quick wits** and **bold spirit** save the day as often as they land her (and her friends) in trouble. On the rare occasions that Leia's blaster doesn't hit her targets, her **wicked one-liners** will.

Q: How does Leia know that Luke needs rescuing from Cloud City?
A: She hears Luke's call in her mind, which is an early indication that she shares Luke's sensitivity to the Force.

Fast Facts

ROLE: Princess, senator, rebel leader, Resistance General

AFFILIATION: Rebel Alliance, Resistance

HOMEWORLD: Alderaan

ABILITIES: Strong will, sharp tongue, great shot, Force intuition

BEST KNOWN FOR SAVING THE REBEL ALLIANCE
Leia Organa

STRANGE... BUT TRUE
Leia braves the court of Jabba the Hutt disguised as the **bounty hunter Boushh**, with Chewie in tow as her "captive."

Peek behind the scenes
For Leia's hair, George Lucas was inspired by the hairstyles of rebel Mexican women fighting in the Mexican War of Independence in the early 1900s.

ON DEATH STAR

ON LOTHAL

"From now on, you do as I tell you. OK?"
— LEIA, TAKING OVER HER BUNGLED RESCUE

REALLY?!
Jabba takes Leia as his new favorite slave, drooling **UNWANTED ATTENTION** all over her. But she soon **TURNS THE TABLES** on the sickening slug.

THE REBEL ALLIANCE

Tell me more!

LIFE AFTER THE EMPIRE
Things aren't easy for Leia after the Battle of Endor. The public revelation that Darth Vader was her father **destroys her political career** as a senator. This prompts her to **found the Resistance**. Her son, Ben, brings heartache when he falls to the **dark side** and betrays her husband, Han Solo.

GROSS!! Leia's no **PRISSY** princess—she'll dive into stinking GARBAGE **CHUTES** that make grown Wookiees whimper!

ON D'QAR

ON ENDOR

ON HOME ONE

> "Not all the senators think I'm insane. Or maybe they do. I don't care."
>
> **GENERAL LEIA TO KORR SELLA**

TOP 6
HEROIC MOMENTS
1. **Mission to Lothal**—delivers 3 Hammerhead corvettes to Phoenix Squadron at age 16.
2. **Battle of Scarif**—accompanies Admiral Raddus for the rebels' first victory.
3. **Captured by Vader**—defies the Empire by not revealing the rebel base.
4. **Battle of Hoth**—helps lead the evacuation of Echo Base.
5. **Jabba's demise**—chokes disgusting Jabba the Hutt with her slave chains.
6. **Clash on Takodana**—leads the Resistance to rescue Han Solo and recover BB-8.

You know you're a great rebel when you…
- Hide the Death Star plans in R2-D2 so they safely **reach the rebel forces**.
- Assist Generals Dodonna and Rieekan at the **Battles of Yavin and Hoth**.
- Help **destroy Death Star II's shield generator** to seal the fate of the Empire.

ON CLOUD CITY

Love interest…

Han Solo may have won Leia's heart… but that doesn't mean he can let down his guard!

In numbers

50,000 credits
Leia's asking price for Chewie, from Jabba the Hutt

2187
Leia's Death Star detention cell number

100 shots
In Leia's small sporting blaster pistol

19 years old
Leia's age when she's captured by Darth Vader

1.5m (4ft 11in)
Leia's height

Tell me more!

FORCE-FUL FAMILY
When Luke abandons his Jedi training to **rescue his friends**, Obi-Wan's spirit sighs, "that boy is our last hope." But Yoda replies, "there is another," referring to Luke's twin sister, Leia. She is also **strong with the Force**, though she doesn't realize it at first.

61

Fast Facts

HOMEWORLD: Kashyyyk

DIET: Wild plants, berries, meat, spices—the hotter, the better!

AFFILIATION: Allies of the Republic and the Rebel Alliance

DISTINGUISHING FEATURE: Shaggy, water-shedding coat of hair

WOOKIEE GADGETS

Wookiees are expert craftsmen who blend modern technology like **blasters** and **lightsabers** with traditional materials such as **wood, precious stones, and metals**.

FURRY FIGHTERS

TEMPER TANTRUMS

Peace-loving Wookiees are aggressive **only when provoked**. But watch out—they have **ferocious tempers**.

"ALWAYS THINKING WITH YOUR STOMACH"

Chewie's big appetite lands the rebels in trouble on Endor. When he finds a **tasty dead critter** hanging in the forest, he tugs on it and **triggers** an Ewok **trap**!

Wookiees are big, strong, hairy creatures, but **don't** call them dumb—they're highly **intelligent** and easily take offense. Wookiee hero Chewbacca (aka Chewie) is Han Solo's **copilot**, a **loyal rebel**, and a **fine example** of his species.

Peek behind the scenes

Chewbacca is played by two actors: **Peter Mayhew** (the original 7ft 2in English-American actor) and **Joonas Suotamo** (6ft 10in) from Finland, who helps play Chewie in new films.

REALLY?!

When **MAZ** asks Han about her "boyfriend" **CHEWBACCA**, Rey and Finn don't know whether she is **SERIOUS OR JOKING!**

LIFE AFTER ENDOR

After the Battle of Endor, Chewbacca **returns to Kashyyyk** to free his people from Imperial occupation.

Chewbacca reunites with his **wife, Malla,** and **his young son, Lumpawaroo**, who both escaped from an Imperial slave camp.

When Han returns to smuggling, Chewie re-joins him, and later **meets Rey and Finn**.

Q: Why does Chewie get mad when Luke tries to handcuff him?

A: It **reminds** him of his time as a **captive** of the Empire, which **imprisons and enslaves many Wookiees**. Chewie escapes with the help of **Han Solo**, and the two form a **strong bond**.

STRANGE ...BUT TRUE

Wookiees can't speak Basic because of their **strange vocal chords**—but they can understand it. **Barking, growling, moaning,** and **roaring** are typical features of the Wookiees' many different dialects.

THE REBEL ALLIANCE

WOW!...
400
The average lifespan of a Wookiee in years

HOW TO INSULT CHEWIE
The kind-hearted Chewbacca puts up with a lot of name calling—even from his friends.

"Flea-bitten furball!"
C-3PO, as Chewie repairs him

"Big furry oaf!"
Han Solo, as the two of them climb into the Death Star's trash compactor

"Walking carpet!"
Leia, minutes after they first meet

"Hairy beast!"
C-3PO strikes again!

"THING!"
An unpleasant Imperial officer, who soon regrets his outburst

Spice Mine slaves
Wookiee Wullffwarro and his son Kitwarr are sent to **work as slaves** in the Kessel Spice Mines. Spice is **valuable** not only for its medicinal uses, but also as **an illegal drug**.

In numbers

234 years old
Chewbacca's young age at the battle of Starkiller Base

150kg (331lb)
Average weight of a male Wookiee

100kg (220lb)
Average weight of a female Wookiee

19 ammo cases
In Chewbacca's bandolier

7 dreadlocks
Hang from chieftain Tarfful's head when he fights in the Clone Wars

3 Wookiee languages
Shyriiwook, Thykarann, Xaczik

Peek behind the scenes
Chewbacca's voice was created by sound designer Ben Burtt. He used animal noises from walruses, dogs, and lions, but mostly from a bear named Pooh!

OUCH!! Chewie is a **SORE LOSER**—he's been known to **RIP** opponents' arms out of their **SOCKETS** if he doesn't win a game!

How to speak Shyriiwook

"WYAAAAAA!"
"HELLO!"

"ROOOARRGH UR ROO."
"I HAVE A BAD FEELING ABOUT THIS."

"RRRRUGH ARAH-AH-WOOF?"
"HOW DO YOU TAKE YOUR COFFEE?"

"WWWAH RRROOOAAAH WHA?"
"WANT TO PLAY HOLOCHESS?"

"AARRR WGH GGWAAAH!"
"JUMP TO HYPERSPACE!"

AWESOME!!
C-3PO was once **MISTAKEN FOR A GOD** by the primitive Ewoks on the moon of Endor!

In numbers

75kg (165lbs)
C-3PO's fully assembled weight

21+ bits and bobs
On R2-D2 including arms, scanners, and accessories

15 opening panels
On R2-D2's head

10 known masters
Of C-3PO

1.09m (3ft 6in)
R2-D2's height

DOUBLE TROUBLE!

Protocol droid C-3PO and his astromech ally R2-D2 are **an unlikely pair**. Although C-3PO dislikes excitement, he often follows R2-D2 on **thrilling exploits across the galaxy**.

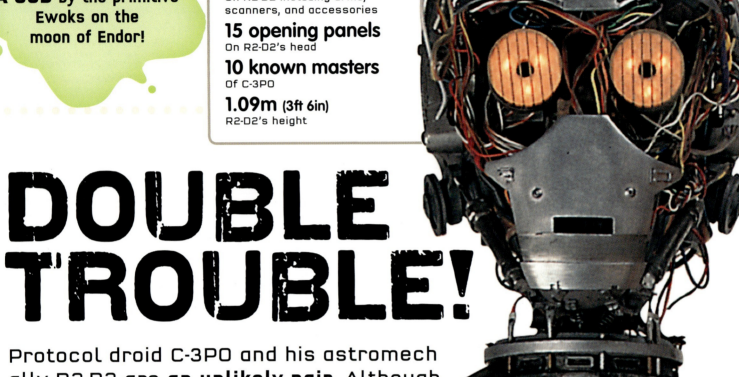

"We're doomed!"
C-3PO TO R2-D2

Peek behind the scenes
Sound designer Ben Burtt created R2-D2's voice, in part, by recording himself making baby noises on a synthesizer!

Q: What is R2's secret mission to Tatooine?
A: Princess Leia gives R2 the **stolen plans** for the Empire's **Death Star** battle station. He must deliver them safely to Obi-Wan Kenobi to **save the galaxy**.

STRANGE
...BUT TRUE
C-3PO is **blasted to bits** by Imperials on Cloud City. When Chewbacca reassembles him, the Wookiee **places C-3PO's head on backward**!

WOW!...

7,000,000+

Forms of communication known to C-3PO by the time he works for the Resistance.

Fast Facts

MANUFACTURER:
R2-D2: Industrial Automaton
C-3PO: Cybot Galactica

MAKE:
R2-D2: R-series astromech droid
C-3PO: Protocol droid

PRIMARY FUNCTIONS:
R2-D2: Navigation, repair
C-3PO: Etiquette, protocol, translation

DROID-IN-CHARGE:
R2-D2 (although C-3PO thinks it is him!)

Q: Why is R2-D2 so hard to understand?
A: R2 talks in **binary**, a language of **beeps** and **whistles**. C-3PO often has to **translate** to help everyone else understand what he's saying.

THE REBEL ALLIANCE

Peek behind the scenes
Actor Anthony Daniels **couldn't sit down** while wearing the C-3PO costume for the first film, and had to **lean against a board** between his scenes.

BEST KNOWN FOR
SAVING QUEEN AMIDALA'S ROYAL STARSHIP
R2-D2

TOP 5
ASTROMECH ACCESSORIES
1. **Lightsaber launcher**—for top secret missions.
2. **Electromagnetic power charge arm**—also handy for zapping Ewoks.
3. **Rocket boosters**—for flying through the air.
4. **Buzz saw**—to cut through almost anything.
5. **Drink dispenser**—to serve guests at parties.

R2-D2 is so **saddened** by Luke Skywalker's disappearance that he goes into **low-power mode**. He collects dust in the Resistance base on D'Qar.

What *is* R2-D2 saying?

"SPRRPFT!"
"PHOOEY!"

"WRRK-WRRK. WEEEEEOOP!"
"I SAID *COUNTER*CLOCKWISE!"

"WAH-WAH. WRRY-WRRY-NAHWIKOO!"
"LET'S GET OUTTA HERE!"

"PRRP-PAREE-PAREE PAIRREEOOP?"
"WHAT COULD POSSIBLY GO WRONG?"

Tell me more!

REPLACEMENT LIMB
After C-3PO crash lands on the hostile planet **Taul**, his left arm is torn off by a **six-eyed thidaxx monster**. Another protocol droid named **O-MR1** bravely sacrifices himself, allowing C-3PO to escape with both his life and with O-MR1's **red-painted arm**.

Fast Facts

AFFILIATION: The Alliance to Restore the Republic (the Rebel Alliance)

LEADER: Mon Mothma

ADMIRALS: Raddus, Gial Ackbar

GENERALS: Include Crix Madine, Jan Dodonna, Carlist Rieekan, Airen Cracken, Davits Draven, Antoc Merrick, Pitt Onoran, Baccam Grafis, Dustil Forell, Pharl McQuarrie, Hera Syndulla

SENATORS: Include Nower Jebel, Vasp Vaspar, Tynnra Pamlo

"Many Bothans died to bring us this information."
— MON MOTHMA

BEST KNOWN FOR LEADING THE BRIEFING TO DESTROY DEATH STAR II
Mon Mothma

ALLIANCE AT DANTOOINE
The *Ghost* crew eludes the Empire's new TIE defender to get **Mon Mothma to Dantooine**. There, she makes a broad call to **rebel cells** around the galaxy. An **alliance** is formed when several groups arrive above the planet.

MON MOTHMA
Uses title "Senator" • Human from Chandrila • Civilian head of state • Leads cabinet of six rebel senators

Mon Mothma, her cabinet, and the military leadership form a council known as the **HIGH COMMAND**.

Despite great trials and sacrifice, Bail is loyal to the Jedi, protecting **YODA** and **OBI-WAN**. Bail and his wife Breha even **ADOPT** the daughter of his friend Padmé.

There are **30 fighters** under Dodonna's command at the Battle of Yavin.

REALLY?! Dodonna orders the mission leading to **HOTH'S DISCOVERY**.

ACKBAR
Rebel Alliance Admiral • Mon Calamari from Mon Cala • Highly experienced soldier and revolutionary

BAIL ORGANA
Founding member of the Rebel Alliance • Human from Alderaan • Viceroy of the House of Organa

JAN DODONNA
Rebel Alliance General • Human from Commenor • Master tactician

During the **BATTLE OF ATOLLON**, Sato rams his ship into Admiral Konstantine's Star Destroyer. This obliterates the enemy's **GRAVITY WELLS**, and allows Ezra Bridger to escape.

Q: Who were the first rebel leaders?

A: After **unsuccessfully petitioning Palpatine**, Mon Mothma, Bail Organa, and a group of **trusted senators** form a **secret group** to oppose him. **Padmé Amidala** suggests they do not discuss the matter openly, but she might have joined the rebels, if she **survived the war**.

Jyn Erso sends the **DEATH STAR PLANS** to the rebels, but it is up to General Dodonna to locate the actual **FLAW** in the Death Star. He manages the attack on the battle station from the rebel command center on **YAVIN 4**.

JUN SATO
Commander of Phoenix Squadron • Human from Mykapo • Trailblazer and strategist

THE REBEL ALLIANCE

THROUGH THE AGES: REBEL BASES

CHOPPER BASE
Located on coral mesa on planet Atollon • Home to Phoenix Squadron • Suggested by former Imperial droid, AP-5 • Inhabited by kryknas and dokmas

YAVIN 4 BASE
Located on jungle moon • Base is in Great Temple, amidst ruins of ancient Massassi civilization • No other known intelligent life on moon

ECHO BASE
Located in Clabburn Range of planet Hoth • Seven secret levels • Overseen by General Carlist Rieekan • Home to tauntauns and occasional wampas

HOME ONE
Modified MC80A star cruiser • Most advanced ship in the rebel fleet • Rebel Alliance mobile command center (after Hoth)

RADDUS
Rebel Alliance Admiral • Mon Calamari from Mon Cala • Fleet commander and tactician

Admiral Raddus is the first military leader to back **JYN ERSO'S** plan to fight.

STRANGE ...BUT TRUE
General Crix Madine is a former **Imperial commander**. After **defecting** to the Rebel Alliance, Madine leads the Rebellion's **Special Forces**. He plans the mission to destroy the Empire's **shield generator** on Endor.

CRIX MADINE
Rebel Alliance General • Human from Corellia • Exceptional soldier and military planner

 General   Commander   Captain
 Colonel   Major   Lieutenant

REBEL INSIGNIA
The Rebel Alliance uses Alderaan's insignia system of **red pips** to indicate each member's **rank**.

Q: Why is Leia at the Battle of Scarif?
A: Admiral Raddus intends to escort Princess Leia to **Tatooine**, where they will meet with **Obi-Wan**. But when the battle begins, Raddus's ship is needed, and they are **diverted** into the **middle of the action** over Scarif.

LEIA ORGANA
Princess and rebel leader • Human from Alderaan • Incredibly brave when carrying out rebel missions

DEFIANT ONES

Senator **Mon Mothma** organizes individual rebel cells into a formidable **Rebel Alliance**. Once it is formed, the Empire pursues brave rebel leaders from base to base, until the Rebellion's **final victory at Jakku!**

THE RESISTANCE

REY OF HOPE

Rey grows up as a **lonely scavenger** on a desert world, waiting for a **family who abandoned her**. Her life gets a lot more exciting when she meets **BB-8 and Finn**, and discovers her own **connection to the Force**!

WHICH WEAPON?

QUARTERSTAFF VS. UNKAR'S THUGS
Rey's salvaged staff helps her to deal with the brutes on Jakku at close range.

BLASTER VS. STORMTROOPERS
Han Solo gives Rey an LPA NN-14 blaster, which is suitable for medium-range targets.

LIGHTSABER VS. KYLO REN
Luke Skywalker's lightsaber is the only weapon to use when facing a dark side user of the Force.

Q: Why doesn't Rey want to leave Jakku?
A: Though life on **Jakku is unpleasant** for Rey, she doesn't want to leave it. Rey intends to return to Jakku once she **helps BB-8**, so she can wait there for her **family**. **Maz Kanata** tells her that her family are **never coming**—and urges her to **seek Luke Skywalker!**

Peek behind the scenes
The voices heard in Rey's Force vision belong to a range of actors including Simon Pegg (Unkar Plutt), Ewan McGregor (young Obi-Wan), Alec Guinness (older Obi-Wan), and Frank Oz (Yoda).

Tell me more!

PERPLEXING VISION

Luke Skywalker's lightsaber calls to Rey through the Force from the basement of **Maz's castle**. Although her vision is confusing, it shows her sensitivity to the Force and suggests her **mysterious connection** to Luke Skywalker and Kylo Ren. Rey also glimpses her **sad childhood** and the menacing **Knights of Ren**.

Rey **marks off each day** of survival on Jakku on the inner walls of her home. She must deal with **thieving bandits**, a **lack of food and water**, toiling under the **oppressive sun**, and, occasionally, **dangerous desert pests**!

REY'S SALVAGE GEAR

- Salvage cleaning kit
- Survival satchel
- Salvage sack
- Salvage tray
- Stormtrooper goggles
- Quarterstaff
- Govath-wool boots
- Flashlight
- Knife
- Leather gloves

Top 5
SIGNS YOU ARE FORCE-SENSITIVE

1. You have natural fighting skills with lightsabers.
2. You can move objects with your mind.
3. You see visions of the past, present, or future.
4. You have acrobatic skills and fast reflexes.
5. You can resist or defeat dark side Force users.

THE RESISTANCE

BEST KNOWN FOR

DEFEATING KYLO REN IN A LIGHTSABER DUEL

Rey

Fast Facts

AFFILIATION: Resistance

SPECIES: Human

HOMEWORLD: Jakku

LIKES LISTENING TO: Stories about Jedi like Luke Skywalker and smugglers like Han Solo

> "I can do this, I can do this."
> **REY**

TOP 5

REY'S LANGUAGES

1. **Basic**—Standard galactic language. Its written form is called Aurebesh.
2. **Teedospeak**—Language of the pesky little Jakku natives.
3. **Shyriiwook**—Trade language of Wookiees. Very difficult to speak.
4. **Astromech binary**—Rey communicates with BB-8 in droidspeak.
5. **Ewokese**—Learned from a salvaged ship computer—but will she ever use it?

REY'S HOME

Ruined Imperial AT-AT, designated Hellhound 2, in Goazon Badlands • Protected by sensors and traps • Rey studies at home on Y-wing computer • Woven hammock serves as her bed

STRANGE ...BUT TRUE

Rey **builds her own speeder** for swiftness rather than hauling big loads. She carries **salvaged scrap in nets** slung over the sides. This means that she must take more trips—but smaller loads attract **less attention from thieves**.

71

Fast Facts

AFFILIATION: First Order (formerly), Resistance

OCCUPATIONS: Stormtrooper, being a big deal in the Resistance

PARENTS: Unknown

SKILLS: Explosives, starship gunnery, survival, melee combat

Healing on the go
Finn is badly wounded by Kylo's lightsaber on Starkiller Base, but his **injuries** are treated in a **mobile bacta recovery suit**. When Finn **wakes up** inside the suit, he's pretty **disorientated**!

COURAGEOUS DEFECTOR

Raised as stormtrooper FN-2187 of the First Order, Finn is **one of the finest soldiers** to ever come out of the trooper training programs. He **lacks just one trait** that every First Order soldier needs: **utter ruthlessness**. This single fault **forever changes his destiny**.

FINN'S JOURNEY

According to First Order records, FN-2187's training begins as an infant, and he grows into a promising cadet.

His first battle makes him question his orders and his loyalty.

Finn finds a new home in the Resistance, fighting against his former comrades.

WHO WORKS FOR WHO?

SUPREME LEADER SNOKE
↑
GENERAL ARMITAGE HUX
↑
CAPTAIN PHASMA

▲ **FN-2187** A high performer, but he cares too much about his fellow cadets.

◀ **FN-2003** Nicknamed "Slip," he is a proud but clumsy cadet.

▲ **FN-2000** Called "Zeroes," he does not question orders.

◀ **FN-2199** Known as "Nines," he feels betrayed when Finn defects.

YUCK!
After traveling through the Jakku desert, Finn is so **THIRSTY** he drinks out of an **ANIMAL TROUGH**!

THE RESISTANCE

BEST KNOWN FOR NOT KNOWING HOW THE FORCE WORKS!
Finn

"This is a rescue. I'm helping you escape."
— FINN TO POE DAMERON

STRANGE ...BUT TRUE
Stormtrooper cadets are **only allowed** to read **First Order-approved books** and watch **First Order-approved videos**.

Finn's Lie
Finn pretends that he is a big deal in the Resistance—but BB-8 and Han Solo know better.

REALLY?!
Finn is **SO AFRAID** of being recaptured by the First Order that he tries to join a **PIRATE CREW**.

FINN SNACK
Finn is **almost eaten** by a rathtar. Luckily, **Rey saves him** just in time!

TOP 5 WORST STORMTROOPER CADET JOBS
1. Taking out trash
2. Moving cargo
3. Mopping floors
4. Cooking meals
5. Cleaning dishes

STRANGE ...BUT TRUE
Finn spends his life being called by his **operating number, FN-2187**. This changes when **Poe** decides that his new **buddy** needs a **real name**!

Tell me more!

FAST FRIENDS
After Finn decides he must **leave** the First Order, he **escapes** with the help of **Resistance pilot Poe Dameron**. Even though they crash during their escape attempt, Finn and Poe form a **tight bond** for the future.

As a cadet, Finn worked on **Starkiller Base** as a **sanitation worker**.

In numbers

23 years
Of military training (his entire life)

6 times
Chewbacca almost kills Finn while he is trying to bandage the Wookiee's wounds

4 cadets
In a First Order fire team

1 chance
To flee the First Order before Captain Phasma finds out he disobeyed her

ONE HELL OF A PILOT

Fast reflexes, loyalty, and **charisma** make Poe Dameron **the most valuable** X-wing pilot in the Resistance. General Leia **personally** entrusts **crucial** tasks to brave Poe—ultimately leading to the **ruin** of Starkiller Base and the **discovery** of Luke Skywalker.

BEST KNOWN FOR

RAZING STARKILLER BASE

Poe Dameron

In numbers

32 years old
Poe's age

12.48m (40.96ft)
Length of Poe's X-wing

9 TIE fighters
Shot down by Poe all in a row, as witnessed by Finn on Takodana

1.75m (5ft 9in)
Poe's height

1 astromech droid
Faithful BB-8 belongs to Poe

THE IRRESISTIBLE KYLO REN
Poe doesn't have much fun as Kylo Ren's **prisoner**! Poe **resists** the interrogations of other First Order officers, but **brutal** Kylo uses the Force to **probe** Poe's mind. Kylo finds out that **BB-8** has the map to Luke.

HOW TO CLIMB THE CAREER LADDER BY POE

6. Beat the First Order to find Luke
Leia asks Poe to find the explorer Lor San Tekka so that he might lead the Resistance to Luke Skywalker—before the First Order reaches him.

5. Carry out Operation: Sabre Strike
Poe and his team hijack the ship of a senator collaborating with the First Order.

4. Get headhunted by your idol
General Leia Organa recruits Poe and his squad to the Resistance.

3. Become a squadron leader
Poe flies a T-85 X-wing in Rapier Squadron for the New Republic.

2. Grow up near work
Poe is raised in a colony near the original rebel base on Yavin 4.

1. Come from a family of rebels
Poe's father, Kes Dameron, is a Pathfinder soldier. His mother, Shara Bey, flies an A-wing in the Battle of Endor.

Top 5

Items in Poe's piloting gear

1 GLIE-44 BLASTER PISTOL
Handy Eirris Ryloth Defense Tech firearm.

2 EL-16HFE BLASTER RIFLE
Outdated Blastech surplus, but it still works!

3 TE4.4 FIELD QUADNOCULARS
Neuro-Saav device lets Poe see long-distance.

4 PILOT JUMPSUIT WITH INFLATABLE FLIGHT VEST
Includes "lucky" FreiTek life-support unit.

5 X-WING PILOT HELMET
Decorated with the Rebel Alliance crest.

While FN-2187 (Finn) is a **good guy**, his reasons for helping Poe escape are self-serving. The **only way** FN-2187 can escape the First Order's **Star Destroyer** is aboard a TIE fighter. There's just one problem. He **doesn't know how** to fly one—but Poe does!

THE RESISTANCE

STRANGE

...BUT TRUE
Poe's friend, Suralinda Javos, is a Squamatan **journalist** who can **spit acidic venom**. She **tricks** Poe into taking her to D'Qar so she can **write a story** about the Resistance. But instead of betraying them, she decides to **join** their cause instead!

Poe and Finn steal a two-person **Special Forces TIE fighter**—boasting a hyperdrive, deflector shields, and advanced weaponry—from the First Order. While Poe pilots, Finn has **fun** blasting their pursuers with the rear-facing laser turret.

REALLY?!
While searching for Lor San Tekka, Poe finds the Crèche—a **CULT** who worship a **GIANT EGG** that they believe contains their **SAVIOR**.

Fast Facts

ROLE: Squadron leader, pilot, commander
CALL SIGN: Black Leader
SHIP: Modified T-70 X-wing (*Black One*)
DROID SIDEKICK: BB-8
HOMEWORLD: Yavin 4
SPECIES: Human

> "The Resistance will not be intimidated by you."
> **POE TO KYLO REN**

Peek behind the scenes
Actor Oscar Isaac, who plays Poe, is from Guatemala. The scenery for Poe's homeworld on Yavin 4 was filmed in Tikal, Guatemala.

The orange and black ferrosphere paint scatters First Order scanners!

HOW IS POE'S CUSTOM X-WING DESIGNED FOR STEALTH MISSIONS?

Tell me more!

BLACK, RED, AND BLUE
Poe commands the **two** Resistance X-wing **squadrons** (known as Blue and Red) that attack Starkiller Base. He also leads a **stealth team** named Black Squadron, whose members he **handpicks**.

Q: Whatever happens to Poe on Jakku?
A: Poe and Finn **crash** in separate spots on Jakku. Finn finds Poe's tan-and-red **jacket**, and assumes his new friend has **drowned** in the Sinking Fields sands. However, Poe wanders off **alone** and gets a ride off-world with a Blarina scavenger named **Naka 1it**.

75

ROCK AND ROLL

Plucky astromech droid BB-8 accompanies pilot Poe Dameron on **dangerous missions** for the Resistance. Even if you don't understand his **beeps** and **whirs**, it's plain to see this **loyal, lovable** droid is unlike any other in the galaxy!

BEST KNOWN FOR

KEEPING LUKE'S SECRET LOCATION SAFE FROM ENEMIES

BB-8

REALLY?! A Teedo on Jakku **CAPTURES** BB-8 in a **NET**. He wants to **SCRAP** him for parts!

THE RESISTANCE INTELLIGENCE NETWORK

BB-8 plays a crucial role in the Resistance as part of a chain of intelligence droids working throughout the galaxy. No one suspects these droids of being secret Resistance spies!

C-3PO — Monitors the field reports from galaxy-wide droid agents.

PZ-4CO — PZ-4CO collates information and reports to C-3PO.

GA-97

CLASSIFIED GNK DROID

CLASSIFIED MSE-6 (MOUSE) DROID

Various droids report what they see and hear to PZ-4CO.

BB-8

Q: What does BB-8 have in common with a mouse droid?
A: Both roll around on the **floor** and are **scared** by a Wookiee's **roar**!

BB-8'S TOP TOOLS

1. Arc welder
2. Welding torch
3. Hydraulic suspension cables
4. Holoprojector
5. Magnetic-tipped bolt spinner
6. Manipulator arm
7. Computer interface arm

"He's a BB unit. Orange and white. One of a kind."
POE DAMERON ON BB-8

THE RESISTANCE

Fast Facts

ALLEGIANCE: Resistance

PRIMARY OWNER: Poe Dameron

PERSONALITY: Loyal to his owner but can be easily frightened

LIKES: Using his welding torch to give a thumbs-up

TOP 4 IMPORTANT MISSIONS

1. Flying with Poe in the attack on Starkiller Base.
2. Secret mission to Jakku where he meets scavenger, Rey.
3. Fighting the criminal Ranc Gang on the planet Kaddak.
4. Leading a droid mission to save Poe from the angry prisoners of Megalox Beta prison.

STRANGE ...BUT TRUE

BB-8 becomes **sad** when R2-D2 is found in **low-power** mode. This shows that BB-8 has an **exceptional** sense of emotion and devotion for a droid.

OH COOL!

BB-8's antenna is a remote communications module. It can even **OPEN THE DOORS** to Poe's starships.

Q: How does BB-8's head stay attached to his body?

A: The little droid has **powerful magnetic casters** that keep the head attached, even in **high-stress** scenarios.

In numbers

27th generation Droidspeak code
The language that BB-8 uses

6 swappable tool-bay disks
Panels on his body that can be easily replaced and updated

2 antennas
Stick up from his head

0.67m (2ft 2in)
BB-8's height

How to speak like BB-8

"BWA-WOO BOOP."
"LOOK AT THAT."

"BWA-WOOP?"
"FOR WHO?"

"WOOOOO."
"OH"

"BLOOPY BOO!"
"THAT'S RIGHT!"

"BLIP! BLIP! BLIP!"
"OK!"

"BLEEP BRRRO BEEP!"
"OH NO YOU DON'T!"

"BEE-BOORP!"
"THAT'S CLASSIFIED!"

"BEEP BOOP!"
"THANK YOU!"

BAD GUYS, BOUNTY HUNTERS, AND THE UNDERWORLD

Which **First Order** leader wears **armor** made from **chronium**?

What makes **Darth Sidious's** face melt during his **battle** with Mace Windu?

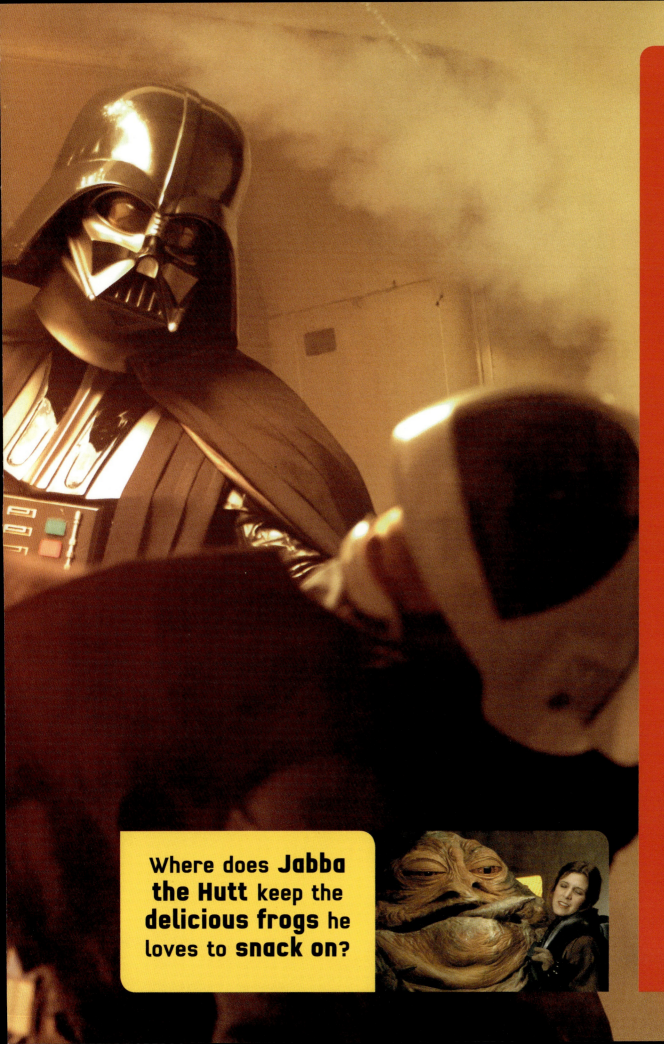

CHAPTER 2

Where does **Jabba the Hutt** keep the **delicious frogs** he loves to **snack on**?

THE SITH

Fast Facts

OCCUPATION: Politician and Sith Lord in hiding

HOMEWORLD: Naboo

ABILITIES: Force lightning, lightsaber dueling, keeping big secrets

> "You cannot stop what is to come."
> — **EMPEROR PALPATINE**

THAT FIGURES!!
Darth Sidious **ELIMINATES** his **OWN SITH MASTER**, Darth Plagueis, after learning everything he knows.

END OF AN ERA
The Emperor's reign comes **crashing down** when Darth Vader **hurls him down an energy shaft** on the second Death Star! Vader's dying efforts save his son, Luke, whom the evil Emperor was about to slay.

Q: What is a Sith?
A: The Sith are the **ancient enemies** of the Jedi. Long ago, a group of **Jedi fell to the dark side**, becoming the **first Sith**. Ever since, they have tried to **destroy the Jedi** and **rule the galaxy**.

Top 5 Reasons to rule the galaxy

1. **ABSOLUTE POWER!** No one will question your authority.
2. **APPLAUSE** The Senate will cheer your every move.
3. **EFFICIENCY** People work harder when they know you are visiting.
4. **THE BEST HEADQUARTERS** Your office on the Death Star comes with a great view!
5. **THE THRONE** Every Emperor deserves a big chair.

In numbers

23 years As Galactic Emperor

3 Sith apprentices Trained by Darth Sidious

2 red-bladed lightsabers Wielded with devastating skill and power

1.73m (5ft 8in) Palpatine's height

Q: Does Darth Sidious share his power with other Sith?
A: Never! Sidious **shares power with no one**. When **Darth Maul** and his brother **Savage Opress** become **rivals** to his power, Sidious **defeats them both**.

THE SITH

PURE EVIL

BEST KNOWN FOR

RULING THE GALAXY WITH AN IRON FIST!

Emperor Palpatine

Obsessed, devious, and absolutely ruthless, this scheming Sith Lord has been known by many titles—Senator from Naboo, Supreme Chancellor, and finally Emperor. His true identity is Darth Sidious, and ultimate power is his only goal.

STRANGE...BUT TRUE

Emperor Palpatine rarely leaves his palace and often appears via hologram. He prefers to let his minions do the dirty work!

Peek behind the scenes

It took four hours to apply the makeup and prosthetics to transform actor Ian McDiarmid into the Emperor!

Tell me more!

MASTER MANIPULATOR

Palpatine works for years to bring down the Jedi and the Republic. He secretly creates the crisis on Naboo to become Chancellor and then becomes both leader of the Republic and secret leader of the Separatists during the Clone Wars. With the galaxy in chaos, he uses the clones to wipe out the Jedi and takes full control of, well, everything.

DON'T MESS WITH THE DARK SIDE!

During a fight with Mace Windu, Palpatine fires Force lightning at his opponent, who reflects the dark energy back at the Sith, revealing his true, evil nature. Palpatine's face melts and his eyes, nails, and teeth turn a sickly yellow. After he becomes Emperor, he hides his disfigured appearance in Imperial propaganda broadcasts.

PALPATINE'S RISE TO POWER

EMPEROR...
With the Jedi destroyed and in full control of the Senate, Palpatine becomes Emperor.

CHANCELLOR...
During the Naboo crisis, Palpatine is elected Chancellor of the Republic.

SENATOR...
Sheev Palpatine represents the planet Naboo in the Galactic Senate.

BLOOD BROTHERS

Darth Maul and Savage Opress are brothers, but they are bound together by more than just family ties. Born into the Nightbrothers—a terrifying warrior clan—they inherit the same fierce desire to wreak revenge on their enemies, no matter the cost.

BEST KNOWN FOR
SLAYING FAMOUS JEDI MASTER QUI-GON JINN
Darth Maul

MAUL'S SUPER COMMANDOS
During his takeover of Mandalore, some Mandalorians paint their armor red or add horns to their helmets to reflect their new leader!

Top 3
Items in Maul's hunting kit

1. **PROBE DROID** Tiny "dark eye" can infiltrate small places Maul could never go.
2. **ELECTROBINOCULARS** Night vision and magnified zoom locate distant targets.
3. **SITH INFILTRATOR** Maul's personal starfighter is equipped with high-tech stealth systems.

Opress **DESTROYS** his other **BROTHER**, Feral, to prove his **LOYALTY** to the Nightsisters!

> "At last we will have revenge."
> **DARTH MAUL**

DARTH MAUL'S GUIDE TO LOOKING EVIL

- A **thick, hooded cloak** is a great way to carry out your Master's evil work in secret and frighten your foes into the bargain.
- Looking for **new legs**? Try scouring Lotho Minor's **junkyards**! An injured Maul finds himself **six arachnid-like legs** after his own are chopped off by Obi-Wan.
- Ask your **cronies** for help. Maul acquires a new set of **cybernetic legs** from the Nightsisters, to renew his vendetta against Obi-Wan.
- Walk with a **lightsaber cane**. Maul may be getting older, but he never goes far without his lightsaber, which he **hides** in a twisted walking stick.

THE SITH

DATHOMIR
Homeworld of Nightbrothers and Nightsisters • Planet bathed in blood-red sunlight • Place where Nightsisters use dark magic to enlarge and transform Opress into a vicious monster

REALLY?!
After opening a Sith holocron together, Maul and Ezra Bridger **MERGE THEIR MINDS** in a dark ritual. They can see each other's thoughts!

OLD MASTER
An aging Maul, long since betrayed by Darth Sidious and still thirsting for **revenge** against Obi-Wan Kenobi, attempts to make Ezra Bridger his apprentice.

TOP 8
LIGHTSABER DUELS
1. Maul vs. Qui-Gon Jinn. Victory
2. Maul vs. Obi-Wan Kenobi (Naboo). Defeat.
3. Opress vs. Adi Gallia. Victory.
4. Maul vs. Pre Vizla. Victory.
5. Maul and Opress vs. Darth Sidious. Defeat.
6. Maul vs. General Grievous. Draw.
7. Maul vs. Kanan Jarrus. Defeat.
8. Maul vs. Obi-Wan Kenobi (Tatooine). Defeat.

STRANGE ...BUT TRUE
Nightsister Asajj Ventress tests **six Nightbrothers** in brutal combat. The last warrior standing, Savage Opress, impresses Asajj enough to be chosen as her apprentice.

Fast Facts

AFFILIATION: Sith Lords, Nightbrothers

SPECIES: Dathomirian Zabrak

ABILITIES: Strong with the dark side of the Force. Both are skilled with double-bladed lightsabers, while Opress also wields an enchanted pike

Young Opress is raised in an **ISOLATED** Nightbrother village on Dathomir, where women and outsiders **RARELY** visit.

Q: How does Maul survive being cut in half?
A: The power of **anger!** Maul draws on his Master's dark side lessons to harness his **rage** and **stay alive** after Obi-Wan **maims** him in a duel on Naboo! **Rumor** has it that his top half fell down a reactor shaft into a **trash container**, which was then shipped to Lotho Minor.

Tell me more!

MANDALORIAN UPRISING
Maul's plot to **take over the galaxy** fails when Darth Sidious intervenes. Even with the Black Sun, the Pyke Syndicate, and Mandalorians on his side, **Maul is no match** for him. Sidious kills Savage Opress, and uses **Force lightning** to torture Maul. He is saving his former apprentice for a future scheme.

In numbers

26.5m (86ft 11in)
Length of Maul's Sith Infiltrator

12 years
Period of time Maul is believed to be dead after his battle with Obi-Wan

9 horns
Crown Opress's head

2.18m (7ft 2in)
Opress's height after Mother Talzin's shaman spell increases his size from 1.89m (6ft 2in)!

DOOKU'S PALACE
Headquarters of the wealthy House of Dooku • Located above a cliff on Serenno • Main tower is 119m (390ft) tall

BEST KNOWN FOR
LEADING THE SEPARATIST ALLIANCE
Count Dooku

TURNING TRAITOR
Dooku completes his fall from the light side when he **eliminates his friend, Jedi Sifo-Dyas**, under orders from Darth Sidious. With Sifo-Dyas gone, the **Sith take control of the Jedi's clone army**.

> "Welcome to Serenno. You have been invited here because you are the best bounty hunters in the galaxy."
> — COUNT DOOKU, AT "THE BOX" TOURNAMENT

THE GREAT BETRAYER

The **despicable Count Dooku** battles the Republic with his **massive droid armies**. The Jedi are in a desperate race to stop him before he **conquers the galaxy!**

Tell me more!

TAUGHT BY THE BEST
As a Jedi, Dooku is **trained by Master Yoda**, who considers him the Order's **greatest student**— and its **greatest failure**. In turn, Dooku takes Qui-Gon Jinn as his first and most famous Padawan.

In numbers

80 years old
Dooku's age when he duels Yoda on Geonosis

40 seconds
Length of lightsaber duel with Yoda

13 bounty hunters
Assembled for "The Box" tournament

7 radiator grooves
In Dooku's Sith lightsaber

2 lightsabers
1 as a Padawan, 1 as both Jedi Knight and Sith

1.93m (6ft 4in)
Dooku's height

Peek behind the scenes
George Lucas had a very different villain in mind for *Attack of the Clones*. But when Christopher Lee joined the cast, Count Dooku was specifically created for the legendary actor to play!

JOURNEY INTO DARKNESS

One of the **most brilliant Jedi Knights**, Dooku yearns for greater power and **leaves the Order** to lead the **Separatist army** as Count Dooku. He later **embraces the dark side as Darth Tyranus**, disciple to evil Sith Lord Darth Sidious.

Fast Facts

ROLE: Sith apprentice to Darth Sidious

ALIASES: Count Dooku, Darth Tyranus

HOMEWORLD: Serenno

SPECIES: Human

FASHION TO DIE FOR
Count Dooku **loves wearing fine clothes**! His **elegant cloak** is woven by famous tailors on the distant planet Vjun, and is a symbol of the Counts of Serenno. His boots are made of **rare rancor leather**, as is his belt, which holds his **stylish yet deadly red crystal lightsaber**.

> "I've become more powerful than any Jedi. Even you."
> **DOOKU TO YODA**

Q: Who are the "Lost Twenty"?

A: Count Dooku is the **20th Jedi Master to quit the Order** over differences with his fellow knights. There are **memorial statue busts** of each of these former Jedi displayed at the **temple on Coruscant**.

TOP 5
DOOKU'S COMBAT STYLE
1. Slashes his victims with a lightsaber.
2. Chokes the life from his opponents.
3. Zaps his rivals with Force lightning.
4. Force-smashes his enemies against a wall.
5. Runs away when all else fails.

REALLY?!
Dooku **CUTS OFF ANAKIN'S HAND** in the Battle of Geonosis. The young Jedi later gets his revenge in a duel with Dooku on General Grievous's flagship: **DOOKU LOSES BOTH HANDS— AND HIS HEAD!**

WOW!...
1,000,000
Hondo Ohnaka's asking price in credits for selling Dooku to the Republic

Darth Vader has developed his own style of **lightsaber fighting**, designed to overcome the restrictions of his life-support armor.

Embracing the **dark side** makes your eyes change color! Anakin has blue eyes, but they **turn yellow** when he becomes Vader.

NO HOPE
Vader comes face to face with his **former Padawan**, Ahsoka Tano, in a ferocious duel on the planet **Malachor**. She tries—and **fails**—to turn Vader from the dark side.

THE FALLEN ONE

REALLY?!
Darth Vader often wins arguments by **FORCE CHOKING** people who disagree with him.

Darth Vader is **feared greatly** as the **Emperor's Sith apprentice**. He was once the noble Jedi Knight **Anakin Skywalker**, but the **dark side** and **horrific injuries** have transformed him into a **terrifying cyborg**.

TOP 5
WAYS DARTH VADER DEFEATS HIS ENEMIES
1. Outfights them with his lightsaber.
2. Outflies them in his personal TIE fighter.
3. Hurls objects at them using the Force.
4. Picks them up and throws them around using the Force.
5. Force chokes them.

Peek behind the scenes
Darth Vader's face mask and helmet were inspired in part by the headdress worn by Japanese Samurai.

Fast Facts

HOMEWORLD: Tatooine (as Anakin Skywalker)

AFFILIATION: Galactic Empire

SITH MASTER: Darth Sidious

SPECIES: Cyborg (previously human)

CHILDREN: Luke Skywalker, Princess Leia Organa

SUBORDINATES: The Inquisitors, 501st Legion

Tell me more!

DWELLING ON THE PAST
Vader's limbless body hangs **suspended** as he **meditates** within a **bacta rejuvenation chamber** in his **menacing castle** on Mustafar. Meditation forces him to dwell on **painful memories**. It's all part of Darth Sidious's plan to drive Vader **closer** to the dark side!

> "Anakin Skywalker was weak. I destroyed him."
> **— DARTH VADER ON HIS TRANSFORMATION**

Q: Who turns Anakin to the dark side?

A: **Darth Sidious** takes advantage of Anakin when he is at his most **vulnerable**. Devastated by a **vision of his wife Padmé dying**, the young Jedi agrees to become Sidious's apprentice after the Sith Lord promises him that **only** the powers of the **dark side can save her**. Once on the path to evil, there's **no turning back** for Anakin.

You know you're sliding to the dark side when you...

1. **Wipe out** the Tusken Raiders who kidnap your mother.
2. **Execute** Count Dooku after defeating him in battle.
3. **Destroy** younglings at the Jedi Temple.
4. **Massacre** Separatist leaders on Mustafar.
5. **Force choke** your beloved wife, Padmé.

In numbers

120kg (265lbs)
Darth Vader's weight in his armor

10 protective layers
In Vader's armor

4 artificial limbs
Attached to Vader

2.03m (6ft 8in)
Vader's height in his armor

2 lightsabers
Owned by Vader

STRANGE...

...BUT TRUE
Darth Vader **cannot eat normally** because he has been **injured so badly**. Instead, his life-support armor **feeds nutrient fluids** directly **into his body**. In his private chamber, Vader can **remove his helmet** and use a **feeding tube**.

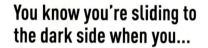

FAN FACT
Darth Vader's **breathing sound** was made by breathing through **scuba gear**.

Q: How does Vader try to lure Luke to the dark side?

A: Vader pleads with Luke to **help him defeat** his evil Sith Master, **Emperor Palpatine (Darth Sidious)**, so that they can **rule the galaxy together** as father and son.

THE SEPARATISTS

Fast Facts

NAME: Trade Federation
LEADER: Viceroy Nute Gunray
MEMBERS: Mostly Neimoidians
AFFILIATION: Wherever there's profit to be made
AIM: Control all galactic trade routes, ports, and freighters
PROTECTED BY: Huge army of battle droids

REALLY?!
Neimoidians are big **SHOWOFFS**! They dress in the latest fashions and wear the most expensive and bizarre robes and hats, no matter how **SILLY** they look.

BEST KNOWN FOR
COWARDICE AND ROLLING IN MONEY
Trade Federation

> "Is she dead yet? I am not signing your treaty until I have her head on my desk!"
> **GUNRAY TO THE SEPARATISTS ON SENATOR AMIDALA**

Tell me more!

THE SWINDLERS ARE SWINDLED
The Trade Federation are **duped** by scheming Palpatine (Darth Sidious), when he **goads** them into **blockading** the planet Naboo with their army of battle droid ships. It's all part of Palpatine's **secret plan** to **increase** his political powers and ignite a **galactic war**!

GREEDY GRUBS

The **powerful, corrupt Trade Federation** runs most of the galaxy's shipping routes. It will do anything to increase profit and avoid paying the Republic's taxes. Who leads it? Step forward grasping **Nute Gunray** and his **Neimoidian cronies**!

Peek behind the scenes
The actors who played Neimoidians wore mechanical masks that moved their mouths and eyes. Hats and headdresses hid the wiring and electronics.

THE SEPARATISTS

STRANGE

ONCE A GRUB...
Gunray was born a "**grub**," a **maggot-like larva** that grows into a walking, talking, cheating Neimoidian.

...BUT TRUE
For the first **seven** years of their life, Neimoidian larvae are forced to **compete** with each other over a limited food supply. Only those who learn to be **greedy** and **hoard the most food** survive—it's great practice for a life of **swindling**!

Battle droids—the gears of war
The Trade Federation prefers to rely on **battle droids** to save its skin, rather than hiring warriors for its security forces. Why? Battle droids are **cheap, disposable, easily mass-produced**, and will fight **without demanding payment**! What's more, the Federation has a business deal with the Geonosians to build **countless battle droids** in their huge **factories**, in preparation for war.

Q: Who are the Separatists?
A: Led by Count Dooku, this **influential movement** is made up of different groups of people **who want to leave** the Republic. One of those groups is the wealthy Trade Federation, who **secretly provide** the Separatists with battle droids, which become **soldiers** of the **mighty Separatist army**.

Who helps Nute Gunray in his dodgy trade deals with alien species?
This delightful job belongs to silver protocol droid **TC-14**, Gunray's **personal assistant**. Her memory banks are **wiped regularly** to stop her from developing a personality... or a conscience.

FEDERATION FLAGSHIP
Named *Saak'ak* • *Lucrehulk*-class freighter • 3,170m diameter (10,400ft) • Quad turbolaser cannons • Cloaking device • Orbits Naboo during the blockade and invasion

REALLY?!
In return for supporting the Separatists, Gunray **DEMANDS** that Count Dooku **SLAYS** Gunray's longtime nemesis, Senator Padmé Amidala of Naboo!

WOW!...

139,000

The number of battle droids that just one Trade Federation battleship can carry

STRANGE

...BUT TRUE
Nute Gunray **never** puts his own neck on the line. Why would he, when he can **trick** others into doing his **dirty work**? It's the Neimoidian way of doing business!

Fast Facts

OCCUPATION: Kaleesh warlord turned Supreme Commander of the droid army

AFFILIATION: Separatists

HOMEWORLD: Kalee

Peek behind the scenes
Sound designer Matthew Wood supplied the voice of General Grievous in Revenge of the Sith and Star Wars: The Clone Wars.

CYBORG FIEND

General Grievous is the **maniacal cyborg Commander** of the Separatist droid army. Most of his body has been **mechanically enhanced**, making him a match for even the strongest Jedi. But *never call him a droid*!

LUNAR HIDEOUT
Castle on the third moon of Vassek • Full medical facilities • Spare part storage • Defended by MagnaGuards

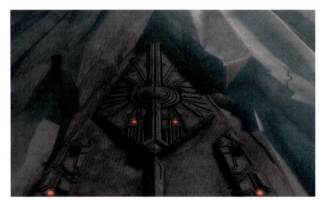

"This is the lair of General Grievous!"
KIT FISTO REALIZING HE HAS BEEN LURED INTO A TRAP

Q: Who maintains Grievous's mechanical parts?

A: Droid **A4-D** is Grievous's personal medical droid. **Part doctor, part mechanic**, he repeatedly repairs the cyborg's body after battles with the Republic.

Tell me more!

NEW, IMPROVED GRIEVOUS
General Grievous **chooses** to **upgrade his organic body** with synthetic parts. But with his **heart and lungs failing**, he has serious breathing problems and a **nasty cough**!

THE SEPARATISTS

BEST KNOWN FOR

KEEPING THE LIGHTSABERS OF DEFEATED JEDI

Grievous

WOW!...

95%

The amount of Grievous's body parts that are mechanical

STRANGE

...BUT TRUE
Grievous will **knock the heads off** his own battle droids when they **make him mad**—which is **most of the time!**

Grievous's **FACE MASK** must be painfully **PEELED FROM HIS FACE** with a fusion cutter when it needs to be replaced.

"*I do not care about your politics… (or) your Republic. I only live to see you die!*"
GENERAL GRIEVOUS TO THE JEDI COUNCIL

"*More machine than alive... though more dangerous for it.*"
YODA ON GRIEVOUS

AWESOME!!
Grievous can **WALK ON SIX LIMBS** like a crab when he needs to move quickly.

SPEED DEMON
General Grievous's **personal ground transport** is a modified Tsmeu-6 personal wheel bike. It is **swift and powerful**—strong enough to **crush soldiers in its path**.

REWIRED!

Even **bits of Grievous's brain** have been **cybernetically rebuilt** to make him a smarter, faster fighter.

Giant General
In his **cyborg body**, Grievous **towers over** his frequent foe, Obi-Wan Kenobi.

Height chart

Grievous 2.16m (7ft 1in) | MagnaGuard 1.95m (6ft 5in) | Obi-Wan Kenobi 1.82m (6ft) | Battle droid 1.91m (6ft 3in)

95

DEADLY WITCH

Asajj Ventress is a **lethal Nightsister witch** with a dangerously close connection to the **dark side of the Force**. Betrayed more than once by those she trusted, Ventress has learned that she can only **rely on one person: herself**.

Fast Facts

ALLEGIANCE: Separatists, Jedi, Nightsisters

PERSONALITY: Cunning, fierce, thirsty for success

HOMEWORLD: Dathomir

Dathomir

REALLY?!
Ahsoka Tano nicknames her sworn enemy, Ventress, a **HAIRLESS HARPY, BOG WITCH,** and **LOWLIFE**.

TOP 3
ASSASSIN SKILLS
1. **Stealth**—expertly ambushing unsuspecting enemies.
2. **Martial arts**—superior hand-to-hand combat with much larger foes.
3. **Force choke**—capable of lifting enemies by the neck, using only the Force.

Tell me more!

SISTERHOOD OF DARKNESS
The Nightsisters are a mysterious **sect of warrior witches** who tap into **ancient dark Force magicks** to help them **deceive enemies**. Ventress learns a great deal from their mystical leader, **Mother Talzin** (below center).

Résumé: Asajj Ventress

- **Student assassin**
  Trains as Sith Lord Count Dooku's apprentice throughout much of the Clone Wars.

- **Nightsister**
  Betrayed by Dooku, Ventress returns to Dathomir to fight alongside her witch sisters.

- **Bounty hunter**
  Works for herself as a bounty hunter after the Nightsisters are destroyed.

MISSION ACCOMPLISHED

THE SEPARATISTS

> "I don't fear you, Jedi."
> **VENTRESS TO YODA**

STRANGE ...BUT TRUE
Ventress is known to **kiss** her foes before **finishing them** with her lightsaber!

NO WAY!!
Ventress is strong enough with the dark side of the Force to **FORCE CHOKE MANY FOES AT ONCE!**

Top 4

Dangerous missions

1. **KIDNAPPING THE HUTT**
Ventress takes Jabba's son, Rotta, hostage and pins the crime on the Jedi.

2. **NEIMOIDIAN RESCUE**
The assassin must save Separatist leader Nute Gunray from the Jedi, or silence him before he spills secrets!

3. **ATTACK ON KAMINO**
Ventress tries to steal the original Jango Fett DNA from the Republic... and nearly succeeds!

4. **JOINING FORCES WITH THE JEDI**
Ventress teams up with Obi-Wan Kenobi to defeat the Nightbrothers Darth Maul and Savage Opress, who terrorize the galaxy.

Q: Is Ventress a Sith?
A: Ventress draws her power from the **dark side** of the Force and is mentored by Count Dooku, yet she is **not fully trained in the ways of the Sith**. Her skills are **undisciplined** and not perfect.

Peek behind the scenes
The name Asajj was inspired by the character "Asaji" in the 1957 samurai film *Throne of Blood* by Akira Kurosawa, one of George Lucas's favorite directors.

Ventress **TATTOOS HER HEAD, FACE, AND MOUTH** after embracing the **DARK SIDE**.

TEST OF FURY
Not one to take the easy way out, Ventress faces off against **six Nightbrother clan leaders** in the Test of Fury, a **trial she must pass** to **become a full assassin**!

Flirting with danger
Ventress **eliminates the bounty hunter Oked** when he tries to **flirt with her** at Mos Eisley Cantina!

Ventress's bounty hunter armor icon is a **snake**. She chose it because, like her, snakes are misunderstood creatures: They are thought to be evil **even when they are not**.

A CLOSER LOOK

THE EMPIRE

Fast Facts

AFFILIATION: Galactic Empire (some are former Republic officers)

OBJECTIVE: To maintain the Empire's grip on the galaxy and crush any rebellion

SPECIES: Almost always human

TRAINED AT: Imperial Academies around the galaxy

REALLY?!
Imperial officers live in **DREAD OF FAILURE**. Darth Vader Force chokes **ANYONE WHO MAKES A MISTAKE!**

IMPERIAL VETERAN
Hurst Romodi was one of the first generals in the Empire's Army. Tarkin brought him out of retirement to assist on the completion of the Death Star.

TOP 5
MOST PRESTIGIOUS POSTINGS
1. **The Death Star**—A posting to the new battle station is the ultimate honor.
2. **Super Star Destroyers**—The biggest ships get the finest crews.
3. **Coruscant**—Home to the Imperial government and the Emperor himself.
4. **Citadel Tower, Scarif**—A state-of-the-art facility with beautiful beachfront living.
5. **Weapons Factory Alpha, Cymoon 1**—The largest weapons factory in the galaxy runs all day and night.

TOP 4
IMPERIAL OFFICER TRAITS
1. Ruthlessness
2. Ambition
3. Intelligence and resourcefulness (occasionally)
4. Loyalty to the Emperor (especially when it's in their best interest)

NOT SO GLAMOROUS
Imperial officers who are **bad** at their jobs get assigned to **freighter duty** or posts in the **boring Outer Rim territories**.

COMMAND AND CONTROL

Who does Emperor Palpatine rely on to mercilessly enforce his **oppressive rule** across the galaxy? **Imperial military officers!** Their position gives them authority over most stormtroopers, and many senior officers hold **tremendous power in their hands**.

TOP BRASS ON THE FIRST DEATH STAR

DIRECTOR ORSON KRENNIC
Director of Advanced Weapons Research for the Imperial Security Bureau.

GRAND MOFF WILHUFF TARKIN
Governor of the Outer Rim Territories, Death Star Commander.

ADMIRAL ANTONIO MOTTI
Chief of the Imperial Navy, member of the Joint Chiefs.

GENERAL CASSIO TAGGE
Chief of the Imperial Army, survives to be named Grand General.

ADMIRAL WULFF YULAREN
Deputy Director, Imperial Security Bureau and Naval Intelligence Agency.

TAKING CREDIT
Though Orson Krennic is the officer who directly oversees the Death Star's development, that doesn't stop Grand Moff Tarkin from taking all the credit.

THE EMPIRE

Tell me more!

EMPIRE POSTER BOY
And the award for the Empire's **most talented military officer** goes to... Tarkin. Titled both Grand Moff and Governor, his career spans **naval service** in the Galactic Republic, a planetary **governorship**, and control of the **Death Star project**. Strategic skills and a love for scaring everybody into good behavior make Tarkin **one to watch**.

Peek behind the scenes
Peter Cushing, who played Grand Moff Tarkin, often wore **slippers** during filming, because the boots for his Grand Moff costume hurt his feet. He was usually filmed above the waist only!

IMPERIAL RANK GUIDE
You can tell an Imperial officer's rank by looking at the **plaques they wear on the left side** of their uniforms. Status is indicated by **red, blue, or yellow** plastic squares in rows that are attached to metal plates.

GRAND MOFF:

GRAND ADMIRAL:

ADMIRAL:

CAPTAIN:

> "Fear will keep the local systems in line. Fear of this battle station!"
> **— GRAND MOFF TARKIN ON THE FIRST DEATH STAR**

FUNCTION OVER FASHION
Designed by Tarkin himself, Imperial officers' uniforms are **functional, not fancy**. Different colors indicate the branches of service—gray for **Navy and Army**, black for **stormtrooper officers**, and white for **Intelligence**. No medals are worn, even by ambitious officers like Governor Pryce. They would clutter the uniforms' **clean lines**.

EMPIRE'S END
After the Empire is defeated at the Battle of Jakku, all remaining Imperial officers are declared war criminals. Many go into hiding.

WOW!...
2,000,000,000
Lives lost when Alderaan is destroyed in mere seconds by the Death Star, on Tarkin's order

Fast Facts

NAME: Mitth'raw'nuruodo, Grand Admiral Thrawn

AFFILIATION: Galactic Empire

COMMAND: The Imperial Seventh Fleet

SPECIES: Chiss

APPEARANCE: Blue skin, red eyes

COMBAT SKILLS: Blaster pistols, hand-to-hand combat

LANGUAGES SPOKEN: Basic, Sy Bisti

HOW TO THINK LIKE THRAWN

- **SET TRAPS FOR YOUR ENEMIES** You can capture them by letting them come to you.
- **BE PATIENT** Let a few rebels go in order to capture an even greater prize later.
- **USE THE BEST TECHNOLOGY** Upgraded droids, TIE fighters, and ships are best.
- **RESPECT YOUR ENEMIES AND THEIR CULTURE** Study them to understand what their next move will be.
- **LEAD FROM THE FRONT** Throw on some stylish white armor and lead the ground assault yourself.

BEST KNOWN FOR DEFEATING THE REBEL ALLIANCE AT ATOLLON — Grand Admiral Thrawn

THRAWN'S OFFICE

Located in Lothal's Imperial Factory • Houses the art and artifacts of his enemies • Pieces include Twi'lek portraits, Mandalorian art, Jedi armor, and rebel graffiti

"To defeat an enemy, you must know them. Not simply their battle tactics, but their history, philosophy, art."
— **THRAWN**

"I study the art of war. Work to perfect it."
— **THRAWN**

REALLY?! When Thrawn discovers that a worker is sabotaging Imperial speeder bikes, he makes him test one bike until it **BLOWS UP!**

Peek behind the scenes — The character Thrawn was first introduced in the 1991 novel, *Heir to the Empire* by Timothy Zahn.

THE EMPIRE

Tell me more!

SEARCH AND DESTROY

Thrawn uses **outlawed droid technology** to search and find the rebel crew of the *Ghost*. This **E-XD infiltrator droid** looks like a protocol droid, but transforms into a **terrifying murder bot**!

In numbers

94
Possible planets where the rebels are hiding

12
Squares on Thrawn's rank bar

7th fleet
Under Thrawn's command

6
Death troopers in his personal guard

2
Gold shoulder buckles on Thrawn's pristine uniform

TOP 5
KNOWN ASSOCIATES
1. **Ensign Eli Vanto**—A trusted aide.
2. **Arihnda Pryce**—Governor of Lothal.
3. **Rukh**—Noghri warrior who serves as Thrawn's assassin
4. **Kassius Konstantine**—Imperial Admiral.
5. **Death Trooper Squad**—Thrawn's personal guards.

CALCULATING COMMANDER

It's rare that an **alien** should climb through the ranks of the Imperial Navy, but Thrawn is not a typical leader. This **cold, calculating Chiss** ruthlessly rises to become Grand Admiral by being one step ahead of his enemies and **two steps ahead** of his fellow Imperials!

Thrawn has no time for **mystical Force beings**. He orders his troops to blast the ancient Force-wielding **Bendu** out of the sky over Atollon.

Fast Facts

OCCUPATION: Officer of the Imperial Security Bureau (ISB)

DEPARTMENT: Works in both Investigation and Internal Affairs

AFFILIATION: Rebel Alliance

HOMEWORLD: Coruscant

ABILITIES: Keen observational skills, bo-rifle expert

BEST KNOWN FOR
MUTTON-CHOP SIDEBURNS
Agent Kallus

SECRET SERVICE

Ruthless Agent Kallus is one of the Imperial Security Bureau's **best spies**. He is dedicated to tracking down enemies of the Empire—until he is marooned with Zeb Orrelios. The eye-opening experience motivates him to become a **secret rebel agent**!

How to speak in ISB spy slang

"AUDITING" — WHEN SUSPECTS KNOW THEY'RE BEING INVESTIGATED

"CRUSTBUSTING" — PROVOKING A SUSPECT TO COMMIT A CRIME

"SCATTERING" — INTERROGATING A SUPPOSED INNOCENT IN HOPES THEY REACT SUSPICIOUSLY

"JABBA" — FRAMING A WANTED SUSPECT FOR A CRIME TO MAKE SURE THEY ARE ARRESTED

Q: Who sets up the ISB?
A: **Cunning Palpatine** founds the ISB, a secret police organization, when he declares himself Emperor. It is dedicated to **rooting out enemies** of the New Order.

ISB CENTRAL OFFICE
Located on Coruscant • Huge building complex spans several city blocks • Houses personnel and equipment to analyze intelligence data

021 Kallus's ISB code number

WANTED: HAVE YOU SEEN THESE CRIMINALS?

WEDGE ANTILLIES — TIE fighter pilot and cadet at the academy on Montross who defects to Phoenix Squadron.

CHAM SYNDULLA — Twi'lek Resistance leader and icon—forges group to fight Imperial occupation.

TSEEBO — Worker at the Imperial Information Office—disappears with top secret Empire plans.

MART MATTIN — Nephew of Jun Sato. Flies a YT-2400 freighter and leads rebel Iron Squadron from Mykapo.

OBI-WAN KENOBI — Jedi General of the Clone Wars—rumored dead, but in hiding on Tatooine.

THE EMPIRE

> "I believe Agent Fulcrum will prove far more useful to the Empire than Kallus ever was."
> **GRAND ADMIRAL THRAWN TO COLONEL YULAREN**

STRANGE ...BUT TRUE
While on Lothal, Kallus uses **Ezra's old hideout** in the abandoned Imperial Communications Tower to send his transmissions as Fulcrum. Thrawn captures him there, though **Kallus escapes** and is rescued by Hera (before fleeing to Yavin).

REALLY?!
Kallus once defeated a Lasat Honor Guard in a duel. The Lasat gave Kallus his own bo-rifle in a warrior honor called **"BOOSAHN KEERAW."**

> "We all make sacrifices."
> **KALLUS TO EZRA**

Tell me more!

HIDDEN IN PLAIN SIGHT
Kallus's **former academy instructor, Colonel Yularen**, helps Thrawn investigate a suspected **spy in their ranks**. Kallus frames Yogar Lyste as the spy and convinces Yularen, but **Thrawn is no fool**! He quickly deduces the deception.

Did you know it's taken just 14 years for the ISB to grow from a handful of agents to a vast network double the size of Imperial Intelligence?!

Top 5
Powers of high-ranking ISB agents like Kallus

1. **COMMANDING** stormtrooper squads.
2. **OVERRIDING ORDERS** of civilian and military authorities.
3. **NOT FOLLOWING** standard Imperial rules.
4. **REPLACING SUSPICIOUS** military officers.
5. **TAKING CONTROL** of military vehicles and vessels, even Star Destroyers, if necessary.

Top 6 ISB branches

SURVEILLANCE—analyzes data for POTENTIAL THREATS.

INTERROGATION—claims to have a 95 PERCENT SUCCESS RATE in discovering useful data from questioned suspects.

RE-EDUCATION—BRAINWASHES suspects to support the Empire.

ENFORCEMENT—special operations units act as BACKUP for field agents.

INVESTIGATION—uses data to SUPPRESS rebel activity.

INTERNAL AFFAIRS—searches for TRAITORS within the Imperial ranks.

TOP 5

KALLUS OPERATES AS FULCRUM
1. Helps Wedge Antilles and Sabine Wren **escape from Skystrike Academy**.
2. Assists Kanan, Ezra, and Chopper's mission in Lothal's **Imperial Armory Complex**.
3. Warns Zeb, AP-5, and Chopper about an **E-XD infiltrator droid** at Chopper Base.
4. **Erases Atollon** from Thrawn's database and helps Ezra and the droids escape.
5. Warns the rebels that Thrawn has **discovered their base** and knows Kallus is a traitor.

Q: How does Galen help the Rebel Alliance?

A: By **secretly** building a **weakness** into the Death Star's main reactor! Galen then sends a **message** through ex-Imperial pilot Bodhi Rook to Saw Gerrera, letting the rebels know of this **fatal flaw**.

Fast Facts

NAME: Galen Walton Erso
HOMEWORLD: Grange
OCCUPATION: Scientist
AFFILIATION: Galactic Empire Tarkin Initiative
RELATIVES: Lyra (wife), Jyn (daughter)

 Love interest...

Galen meets his wife, Lyra, on Espinar during a field expedition.

TOP 5 GALEN'S TOP SUBJECTS
1. Math
2. Physics
3. Music
4. Chemistry
5. Energy Science

 **A CLOSER LOOK**

A fractured kyber crystal inspires the **logo** of the Tarkin Initiative.

Galen was held captive by the Empire for **13 YEARS** to develop the Death Star turbolaser!

Through the ages: GALEN ERSO

HOPEFUL SCIENTIST
Krennic tricks Galen into working on Project Celestial Power on Coruscant. Galen thinks it is a project to help rebuild the war-torn galaxy, but secretly it aims to power the Death Star turbolaser.

FUGITIVE FARMER
Realizing that he has been tricked, Galen flees the Empire with his family to hide on the faraway planet Lah'mu. Despite his best efforts, this brilliant scientist is a terrible farmer!

SCIENTIST IN CUSTODY
When progress on the Death Star stalls, Krennic forces Galen back into Imperial service. Galen has no choice but to lead a team of Imperial scientists on Eadu to help build the Death Star.

Q: How did they meet?

A: As **highly intelligent teenagers**, both Galen and Krennic were part of the Brentaal Futures Program for **gifted students**.

OPPOSING VISIONS

One is a **genius scientist** who seeks to make the galaxy a **better place**. The other is a **visionary leader** who will stop at **nothing** to achieve greatness. Galen Erso and Orson Krennic have **little in common**, but there is one thing in the galaxy that could bring them together: the **Death Star!**

THE EMPIRE

BEST KNOWN FOR
BEING BLOWN UP BY HIS OWN SUPERWEAPON!
Orson Krennic

EADU ENERGY CONVERSION LABORATORY
Secret site of Imperial energy research • Hidden in mountainous terrain • Home to Galen's 5-strong scientist team • Heavily defended by 975th stormtrooper garrison

KRENNIC vs. TARKIN
Krennic is **desperate to impress** the Emperor by building the Death Star. However, Grand Moff Tarkin is equally **driven to succeed**—and more than willing to **take credit** for the space station **himself!**

> "The power we are dealing with here is immeasurable."
> **KRENNIC**

REALLY?!
Darth Vader **FORCE CHOKES** ambitious Krennic for being so **SELF-CENTERED.**

STRANGE ...BUT TRUE
Krennic's **gloves** are made from **tee-muss leather**, an animal native to Onderon.

Fast Facts
NAME: Orson Callan Krennic

AFFILIATION: Republic (early career), Galactic Empire Tarkin Initiative

RESPONSIBLE FOR: Overseeing construction of the Death Star

FAVORITE TRANSPORTATION: Delta-class T-3c shuttle

PREFERRED WEAPON: DT-29 heavy blaster pistol

WOW!...
512,000,000
The capacity, in exonodes of data, of the datacapture cartridge containing the Death Star plans

Top 5

You know you're a Pau'an if...

1. **YOUR HOME IS A HOLE**
Pau'ans dwell in darkness.

2. **YOU LIKE YOUR MEAT RAW**
Hold the veggies! Pau'ans only eat raw, bloody meat.

3. **YOUR EARS ARE SENSITIVE**
Pau'ans have hypersensitive hearing and wear coverings to protect their ears.

4. **YOU'RE PALE AND WRINKLY**
Pau'ans have pasty skin with deep, vertical grooves.

5. **YOUR TEETH ARE POINTY**
That raw meat diet develops razor-sharp teeth!

WHO ANSWERS TO WHOM?

GOVERNOR TARKIN AND DARTH VADER Ruthlessly enforce the Emperor's orders

THE GRAND INQUISITOR Can commandeer required Imperial forces while on missions, aside from Governor Tarkin

STORMTROOPERS Obey all higher ranks without question

LESSER INQUISITORS Hunt Jedi independently or in small groups, always competing against each other

IMPERIAL OFFICERS Strictly comply with the Inquisitor's orders

Peek behind the scenes
The Grand Inquisitor is voiced by British actor **Jason Isaacs**, famous for his role as **Lucius Malfoy** in the *Harry Potter* movies.

WOW!...

10.6

The time it takes the Grand Inquisitor to identify a Jedi's fighting style, in seconds

Fast Facts

ORGANIZATION: The Inquisitorius

AFFILIATION: The Empire

SKILLS: Dark side Force-users

WEAPONS: Red, double-bladed, spinning lightsabers

Q: Are the Inquisitors Sith?
A: No! Darth Sidious can have only one apprentice at a time, and currently that is Darth Vader. The Inquisitors are merely **trained servants** and **assassins**, although they do possess **limited dark side Force powers**.

TOP 3

INQUISITOR ENDINGS

1. **Grand Inquisitor**—Falls into the *Sovereign*'s reactor core over Mustafar.
2. **Sixth Brother**—Ahsoka defeats him by pulling the kyber crystals from his blade with the Force.
3. **Seventh Sister**—Defeated by Maul after Ezra fails to eliminate her.

STRANGE ...BUT TRUE

The Grand Inquisitor was originally a **Jedi Temple guard** named the **Sentinel**! In a **vision**, Kanan meets him inside the temple on Lothal. The Sentinel **tests** Kanan before declaring him to be a Jedi Knight.

THE EMPIRE

Darth Vader orders the Inquisitors on an evil mission to **hunt down Jedi** and turn their **young apprentices** to the **dark side**—or **slay** them! They must also locate **Ahsoka Tano**, in hopes that she may lead Vader to Obi-Wan Kenobi.

Peek behind the scenes
Actress **Sarah Michelle Gellar**, star of *Buffy the Vampire Slayer*, voices the Seventh Sister. Her real-life husband, **Freddie Prinze Jr.**, plays Kanan Jarrus.

IS THAT A PROBE DROID ON HER SHOULDER? Not quite, but close! **ID9 seeker droids** are independent hunter-spies with shocker claws.

JEDI HUNTERS

Lean, mean, and **clad in dark armor,** the Inquisitors cut **sinister figures**. These loyal servants of the Empire will not rest until the last Jedi—or future Jedi—are **terminated**!

> "An excellent day's hunt."
> — SEVENTH SISTER

FLYING ACROBAT
The Eighth Brother is a male **Terrelian Jango Jumper**, with greenish-gray skin and four digits on each hand. His Force skills aren't advanced, so he relies heavily on his spinning lightsaber to **lift him up into the air** and make escapes from tricky situations!

TOP 4
GRAND INQUISITOR VS. KANAN BATTLE SITES
1. **Stygeon Prime**—Kanan and Ezra manage to outrun the Inquisitor.
2. **Fort Anaxes Base**—Ezra saves Kanan by using the Force to command a fyrnock that attacks the Inquisitor.
3. **Lothal Communications Tower**—Kanan surrenders to save his friends.
4. **Tarkin's Star Destroyer**—The Inquisitor interrogates Kanan for Tarkin. Later, the foes engage in one last duel before the Inquisitor meets his end.

REALLY?!
Even Imperials aren't safe from the Grand Inquisitor. He is ordered to **EXECUTE** officers Grint and Aresko as **PUNISHMENT** for their failures.

Tell me more!
SECRET IDENTITIES
The secretive Inquisitors are each given **numbers** and called **"brother"** or **"sister."** It is also a **secret** as to how many Inquisitors there are, though there may be **as many as twelve**. They come from a variety of species, but all use the Force.

BUCKET HEADS

Faceless in their iconic white helmets, **stormtroopers** are the **soldiers** of the Imperial military. Their **total loyalty** to the Empire and **boldness in battle** make them **feared** throughout the galaxy.

Fast Facts

LEADER: Stormtrooper commander
AFFILIATION: The Empire
AKA: Bucket heads (rebel nickname)

ENERGY SETTINGS
1. Sting 2. Stun 3. Lethal force

BlasTech E-11 blaster rifle
The stormtroopers' standard issue weapon is based on the clone troopers' DC-15a blaster.

Q: Why are they called "death troopers"?

A: It isn't just because they are **black and scary**, or even because they are associated with the **Death Star project**. The Emperor named these mysterious soldiers "death troopers" to capitalize on rumors of secret programs to create **zombie-like fighters**!

STRANGE ...BUT TRUE

Commandant Brendol Hux creates a **secret program** for raising children to become stormtroopers, much like the **Jedi train their Padawans**. His vision becomes a model for the **indoctrinated** stormtroopers of the **First Order**.

Tell me more!

YOUR EMPIRE NEEDS YOU
The Empire doesn't draft stormtroopers. Instead, it uses **propaganda** to attract recruits. **Posters** showing stormtroopers as brave peacekeepers have inspired **millions of volunteers** to sign up for training.

WOW!...

25,984

Stormtroopers are assigned to the Death Star

THE EMPIRE

BEST KNOWN FOR
RUTHLESSLY ENFORCING THE LAWS OF THE EMPIRE

Stormtroopers

The stun setting on blasters can knock a target unconscious.

Stormtrooper cadets who struggle in training are given the **most unpleasant jobs** to do around the Academy.

The stormtrooper helmet's plastoid shell protects its wearer from both **physical** and **energy attacks**.

In numbers

9,700+ stormtroopers
Can be carried on an Imperial Star Destroyer

19 years
Before the Battle of Yavin, the Stormtroopers Corps is founded

0 stormtroopers
The number who have turned traitor (according to Imperial records)

Sandtroopers patrol **pilgrimage routes** to Jedha City, riding **long-legged creatures** standing up to 4.9m (16ft) high! From there they can watch for **smugglers** and Saw Gerrera's **rebels**.

REALLY?!
Stormtroopers don't use their own **NAMES**. They are known only by **IDENTIFICATION NUMBERS**.

Talk like a trooper
STORMTROOPERS OFTEN LET THEIR BLASTERS DO THE TALKING. WHEN THEY DO SPEAK, THEY GET STRAIGHT TO THE POINT.

"BLAST 'EM!"

"FREEZE. DON'T MOVE!"

"SET FOR STUN!"

"STOP THAT SHIP!"

"ALL RIGHT MEN, LOAD YOUR WEAPONS!"

Peek behind the scenes
Concept artist Ralph McQuarrie's earliest illustrations for Star Wars showed stormtroopers carrying lightsabers!

IMPERIAL ACADEMY

Grueling training for stormtrooper cadets • Headed by Commandant Aresko and Taskmaster Grint • Located in Capital City on Lothal

"By the time you complete your training, you will be ready to serve your Emperor."
COMMANDANT ARESKO

PHASE I CLONE TROOPER
Basic plastoid body shell is used by early clone troopers. Cheap, but uncomfortable.

PHASE II CLONE TROOPER
More advanced armor used during the later stages of the Clone Wars. Easily adaptable.

STORMTROOPER
All-purpose shock trooper gear replaces clone trooper armor when the Empire is founded.

DEATH TROOPER
Armor of the elite death troopers includes specialized helmets that scramble verbal communications.

TROOPERS THROUGH TIME

These armored warriors have been marching across the galaxy for **decades**. Their armor has become a symbol of their **ruthlessness**, and they have worn many different kinds over the years. Whatever they're wearing, it's best to steer well clear—where **stormtroopers** go, bad things tend to happen!

FIRST ORDER STORMTROOPER
Updated, versatile armor design used by stormtroopers of the First Order.

THE EMPIRE

SHORETROOPER
Light armor is worn for shore duty, which includes guarding installations. Color bands identify rank.

DRIVER
Stormtroopers trained to drive tanks, walkers, and transports. Armor varies according to the vehicle.

SNOWTROOPER
Insulated thermal armor and helmet keeps the wearer's body warm in cold conditions.

SCOUT TROOPER
Light armor allows greater mobility for scouting missions and for riding speeder bikes.

Peek behind the scenes
When Luke says "I can't see a thing in this helmet!" while disguised as a stormtrooper, it was actually an *ad-lib* by Mark Hamill, due to the helmet prop not having **proper eyeholes**!

FIRST ORDER FLAMETROOPER
Specialized armor of First Order flame units. Helmet is designed to reduce glare.

FIRST ORDER SNOWTROOPER
Wind and waterproof fabric worn over body glove and covered in light armor plates.

FIRST ORDER EXECUTIONER
Tasked with carrying out the ultimate punishment on treasonous troops, using a laser axe.

THE FIRST ORDER

Q: Where did the First Order come from?

A: After the fall of Emperor Palpatine, Imperials fled into the **Unknown Regions**. They hid for almost **three decades** before revealing themselves as the First Order.

> "The First Order rose from the dark side."
> — LOR SAN TEKKA

Fast Facts

ORGANIZATION: The First Order

HOMEWORLD: [Classified] in the Unknown Regions

SPECIES: Almost entirely human.

AIM: To restore order to the galaxy by destroying the New Republic and the Resistance

COOL!! Phasma's armor is coated in **CHROMIUM** that was salvaged from Emperor Palpatine's **NABOO YACHT**. It reflects harmful radiation.

HOW TO BE LIKE CAPTAIN PHASMA

1. LEAD FROM THE FRONT
2. WALK EXTRA PATROLS JUST FOR FUN
3. MEMORIZE THE SERIAL NUMBERS OF ALL YOUR TROOPS
4. ALMOST NEVER REMOVE YOUR HELMET
5. TRAIN FROM CHILDHOOD

STRANGE ...BUT TRUE

First Order cadets must attend **morale sessions** twice a day. They are ordered to be happy!

In numbers

16 points On the First Order insignia

8x magnification On Phasma's blaster scope

4 hours In a typical First Order shift

Commanding Captain

Captain Phasma is a **commanding presence**. She demands total respect from her troops and from her peers.

	Captain Phasma	Kylo Ren	General Hux	Lieutenant Mitaka	Stormtrooper (FN-2187)
Height	2.0m (6ft 6in)	1.89m (6ft 2in)	1.85m (6ft 1in)	1.8m (5ft 11in)	1.78m (5ft 10in)

FIRST ORDER RULES

- Stormtroopers must not take off their helmets.
- Don't mention Supreme Leader Snoke's terrible looks.
- No laughing in uniform.

THE FIRST ORDER

RUTHLESS LEADERS

The First Order rises from the ashes of the Galactic Empire. With it comes a new generation of **shadowy leaders** who seek to restore their form of order to the galaxy. They have been **hidden for decades**, so few realize just how **dangerous** they are!

BEST KNOWN FOR
TURNING BEN SOLO TO THE DARK SIDE
Supreme Leader Snoke

"Silence!"
SUPREME LEADER SNOKE

STRANGE ...BUT TRUE
Supreme Leader Snoke speaks to his subjects through **holoprojectors**. This allows him to keep his command center **mobile**.

Tell me more!
THE FAMILY BUSINESS
General Armitage Hux is the son of Imperial Commandant Brendol Hux of the **Arkanis Academy**. The Hux family works to perfect the art of **stormtrooper training**. General Hux uses simulations to prepare those under his command for the fight against the New Republic and the Resistance.

REALLY?!
General Hux was a **WEAK**, quiet boy. His father was very hard on him.

Q: What is Snoke's goal?
A: He wants to **wipe out** the last Jedi, Luke Skywalker, before the Resistance can find him.

Officers of the First Order

LIEUTENANT MITAKA
Mitaka graduated at the top of his class, but he isn't prepared for Kylo Ren's temper.

CHIEF PETTY OFFICER UNAMO
Stationed aboard Kylo Ren's *Finalizer*, Unamo excels in communications.

PETTY OFFICER THANISSON
Thanisson spends almost his entire life stationed aboard warship the *Finalizer*.

COLONEL DATOO
This high-ranking officer has an important job leading the primary fire control room of Starkiller Base.

SENTRY DROID
First Order officers use **droid workers** to keep their base and fleet operating at peak efficiency.

Fast Facts

ROLES: Apprentice of Snoke, member of the Knights of Ren, First Order commander, former student of Luke

ALIASES: Kylo Ren, Ben Solo, "Jedi Killer"

SPECIES: Human

PARENTS: Han Solo and General Leia Organa

Peek behind the scenes
Kylo Ren's look went through numerous design changes. One rejected concept became the red-helmeted foot soldiers of the Guavian Death Gang.

TOP FOUR FORCE POWERS KYLO WIELDS
1. Uses Force-pulls on Lieutenant Mitaka and Force-pushes on Rey.
2. Senses the presence of others, such as Han Solo.
3. Probes the minds of his prisoners.
4. Immobilizes people

Top 5
Things that make Kylo Ren angry

1 HIS PARENTS
Poor Han especially disappoints him!

2 LIEUTENANT MITAKA'S FAILURE TO FIND BB-8
Kylo has a temper tantrum and attacks Mitaka.

3 NOT GETTING WHAT HE WANTS
Kylo craves Anakin's lightsaber, but Rey gets hold of it first!

4 ANNOYING PEOPLE GETTING IN HIS WAY
General Hux competes with Kylo for military authority.

5 LIGHT SIDE FAMILY REMINDERS
Kylo hates Lor San Tekka talking about any of his family, except Darth Vader.

Tell me more!
NEW LIGHTSABER, OLD DESIGN
Kylo's lightsaber is based on a design that dates back to the **Great Scourge of Malachor**. Its **rough look** is due to Kylo's inexperience when he built the weapon. The **cracked** kyber crystal inside is highly **unstable**—just like Kylo's **raging temper!**

REALLY?!
Kylo leads the **KNIGHTS OF REN**—a scary group of dark side users. They **DESTROY** Luke's Jedi academy and his students!

Q: Is Kylo Ren a Sith?
A: No. He is a **gifted apprentice** of First Order Supreme Leader Snoke. Snoke believes Kylo is the **perfect example** of the Force. He encourages Kylo to draw on the strengths of **both** the **light side** and **dark side**, but this creates a **great conflict** in Kylo's mind!

STRANGE ...BUT TRUE
Kylo admires his **grandfather** Darth Vader **so much** that he acquires his **melted helmet**, originally left at Vader's **funeral pyre** on Endor. Now Kylo **talks** to the helmet, looking for **guidance!**

THE FIRST ORDER

WHO DOES IT BETTER—
KYLO REN OR DARTH VADER?

- Both look frightening in long, dark clothing: **Tie**
- Each confronts a family member. **Winner: Kylo** (Vader fails to destroy Luke or turn him to the dark side.)
- Each hides their identity with a new name. **Tie**
- Both wear masks. **Winner: Vader** (Vader's more high-tech version keeps him alive.)
- Both try to deny their own light side past: **Tie**

RESULT: IT'S A DRAW!

In numbers

30cm (12in)
Length of Kylo's lightsaber hilt

4 silver stripes
On Kylo's mask

3 blades
Extend from Kylo's lightsaber

2 Masters
Luke Skywalker (former Jedi Master) and Supreme Leader Snoke

1.89m (6ft 2in)
Kylo's height

1 minute 30.5 seconds
Time that Kylo holds a blaster bolt suspended in midair with the Force

1 year
Between the Battle of Endor and Kylo's birth

WHAT'S IN A NAME?
Han and Leia originally named their son **Ben**—perhaps in **honor** of **Obi-Wan "Ben" Kenobi**. Ben changed his name to Kylo as part of his **fall** to the dark side.

RAGING STORM

Kylo Ren is a **dark side Force user** with a **terrible temper**. As grandson of **Darth Vader**, this **menacing warrior** believes he is destined to **rule the galaxy**!

> "Your son is gone. He was weak and foolish like his father, so I destroyed him."
> **KYLO TO HAN**

BEST KNOWN FOR

BETRAYING HIS FATHER, HAN SOLO

Kylo Ren

What makes Kylo a real menace when **chasing** the Resistance? His unique, angular **TIE silencer** (a Sienar-Jaemus TIE/vn space superiority fighter) boasts a **missile launcher** and laser cannons. Moreover, Kylo has **inherited** astounding piloting skills from his father, Han, a **cockpit legend**.

BOUNTY HUNTERS

Fast Facts

FATHER: Jango Fett
SON: Boba Fett
OCCUPATION: Bounty hunters
AFFILIATION: Highest bidder
AIM: To earn a good living by catching people with a price on their heads

Jango Fett

REALLY?! Boba shares the **GENETIC PATTERN** of his father, making him Jango's **TWIN** as well as his **ADOPTED SON!**

Boba Fett

FAMILY BUSINESS

For **two** generations, the name Fett **has struck sheer terror** into the hearts of wanted men. Few can escape capture from the **scarily skilled bounty hunters** Jango and Boba Fett.

HOW TO CLIMB THE CAREER LADDER BY JANGO

4. Make a lot of money and even gain a son in the bargain!

3. Sell your perfect genetic code to the Kaminoans so it can be cloned into an almighty army of identical troopers.

2. Be spotted by a two-faced secret Sith employer with an evil plan, like Count Dooku.

1. Build a reputation as one of the most ruthless warriors in the galaxy.

WHO TRAINED WHOM?

From an early age, Boba is taught how to fight by his father, who also supervises the flash-training of new clone troopers. After Jango comes to a grisly end, Boba learns more about bounty hunting from the assassin Aurra Sing.

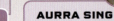
JANGO FETT
CLONE TROOPERS
AURRA SING

BOBA FETT

DON'T FORGET! Nobody knows how he came into possession of it, but Jango **wears the armor** of the legendary **Mandalorian warriors**. Boba **patches together** his own suit in **memory** of his father.

Peek behind the scenes

Concept artist Joe Johnson designed Boba's armor to look like Boba had **cobbled together pieces** taken from wanted men that he'd **captured or destroyed**.

BOUNTY HUNTERS

BEST KNOWN FOR

DELIVERING HAN SOLO TO JABBA THE HUTT

Boba Fett

Boba **blows up** his father's **Mandalorian helmet**! He rigs it with a bomb to lure Mace into a trap.

TOP 3
TARGETS PURSUED BY BOBA

1. **Mace Windu**—sliced off Jango's head with his lightsaber. Boba swears revenge!
2. **Wookiees**—a captured Wookiee is a big boost to a bounty hunter's status.
3. **Han Solo**—the most famous catch of all, wanted in every star system...

WOW!...

20,000,000

Credits paid by Kaminoans for Jango's genetic code

Q: What's that loop Boba is wearing around his shoulder?

A: Some say it's **hair** from an **unlucky Wookiee**, but others say the **braid** of a Jedi **Padawan**! No one dares ask...

"He's no good to me dead!"

BOBA TO VADER ON HAN SOLO BEING TESTED FOR CARBONITE FREEZING

Top 3
Special weapons in Jango's arsenal

1. **WRIST WHIPCORD THROWER**
Shoots out cord to tangle up his opponent and stop them from moving.

2. **MISSILE LAUNCHER**
Explosive missile on both jet pack models Jango owns.

3. **ZX MINIATURE FLAME PROJECTOR**
Casts a 5m (16ft 5in) cone of ferocious fire from gauntlet.

In numbers

200,000 clone soldiers
Of Jango produced in the first batch for the Republic!

70m (230ft)
Maximum vertical height of Jango's Z-6 jet pack thrusters

10 years old
Age that Boba is orphaned

1 blaster shot
All it takes for Jango to take out a giant reek beast in the arena

Special heirloom
Boba inherits *Slave I*, Jango's customized *Firespray*-class interceptor of the kind made to **guard prison moon** Oovo 4. If it's **good enough** to foil desperate criminals, then it's **good enough** for Jango!

123

HIRED GUN

Mad, bad, and dangerous to know, Cad Bane has been considered the best bounty hunter in the business ever since Jango Fett met a sticky end. Loyal to the highest bidder, he never lets morals get in his way.

BEST KNOWN FOR
WEARING HIS COOL WIDE-BRIMMED HAT
Cad Bane

TOP 3
BANE'S EMPLOYERS
1. **Darth Sidious**—Bane only ever deals with Darth Sidious's hologram form.
2. **The Hutts**—he regularly works for the bosses of these crime families, especially Jabba.
3. **Count Dooku**—Bane is hired by Dooku after successfully competing in "The Box."

STRANGE...
...BUT TRUE
Bane takes part in Count Dooku's competition on Serenno, in which **13 bounty hunters** enter a **deadly, maze-like device called "The Box."** Bane is one of the five bounty hunters who escape alive, and are then hired to **eliminate Chancellor Palpatine**.

REALLY?!
No job is too ghastly for Bane... he even **KIDNAPS CHILDREN** who may become future Jedi!

REPUBLIC JUDICIARY DETENTION CENTER
A prison on Coruscant • Inmates include Bane, Ziro the Hutt, Boba Fett, and Bossk • Bane breaks out with Rako Hardeen (Obi-Wan) and Moralo Eval

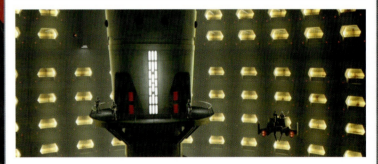

In numbers

1,000,000 credits
The price Separatists will pay Bane for one dead Jedi

75kg (165lbs)
Weight

51 years old
Equivalent age in human years

3x normal rate
Amount Bane is paid to steal a Jedi Holocron for Sidious

1.85m (6ft 1in)
Height

Peek behind the scenes
Bane's sidekick, Todo 360, is voiced by Seth Green, best known for his work on *Buffy the Vampire Slayer* and *Robot Chicken*.

> "Not the first time I've broken out of this stink hole."
>
> **CAD BANE TO MORALO EVAL AND RAKO HARDEEN (OBI-WAN IN DISGUISE)**

BOUNTY HUNTERS

> "I'm your worst nightmare, pal!"
> — CAD BANE

Fast Facts

OCCUPATION: Bounty hunter

HOMEWORLD: Duro

SPECIES: Duros

SPECIALTIES: Armed combat, maintaining a large network of bounty hunter contacts

HOW TO OUTFLY THE LAW
Bane is given a *Rogue*-class starfighter called *Xanadu Blood* by Darth Sidious, which he flies during several missions. Built by the Baktoid Armor Workshop, the ship is upgraded with **a cloaking device** and **superior weapons**.

NO WAY!! TODO 360 is Bane's very loyal service droid. So guess who he uses as a **BOMB** during the Senate **HOSTAGE CRISIS?**

WOW!...
2,500,000
The Republic's reward for Bane's capture, in credits

Top 6 Assignments

1. **HOLOCRON HEIST**
Bane sneaks into the Jedi Temple Archives to steal a Holocron.

2. **CHILDREN OF THE FORCE**
Bane kidnaps Force-sensitive children for Darth Sidious.

3. **SENATE PLANS**
Bane takes R2-D2 and C-3PO captive to steal their data about the Senate.

4. **SENATE HOSTAGE CRISIS**
Using the Senate as a diversion, Bane breaks Ziro the Hutt out of prison.

5. **HUNT FOR ZIRO**
Bane is hired to recover Ziro once again.

6. **CRISIS ON NABOO**
Bane tries to assassinate Chancellor Palpatine.

Fast Facts

HOMEWORLD: Most Hutts are from Nal Hutta

LEADERS: Jabba and The Hutt Grand Council

AFFILIATION: Gangsters and crime families

CLAIM TO FAME: Hutts are selfish, disloyal, and devious gluttons—and those are their good points!

> "Your mind powers will not work on me, boy."
> — JABBA TO LUKE SKYWALKER

How to speak Huttese

"CHUBA!" "HEY YOU!"

"PATEESA" "FRIEND"

"MOULEE-RAH" "MONEY"

"BOSKA!" "LET'S GO!"

"MEE JEWZ KU!" "GOODBYE!"

TOP 3 YUCKY THINGS HUTTS EAT

1. **Gorgs**—large amphibians that are sold in Mos Espa Market for the princely sum of seven wupiupi.
2. **Slime pods**—organisms bloated with gas that float in the swamps on Nal Hutta.
3. **Klatooine paddy frogs**—Jabba keeps an aquarium of fresh and tangy frogs by his throne at all times.

Top 5 Horrible Hutt Council members

1. **JABBA DESILIJIC TIURE** — A **gambler and slaver** who rules the council via hologram and through his representative, Gardulla Besadii the Elder.

2. **GORGA DESILIJIC AARRPO** — The council's **dishonest, dapper accountant**, who likes wearing a monocle with his fancy headgear.

3. **AROK THE HUTT** — Always-angry council member who **threatens to eliminate** Jabba's uncle, Ziro.

4. **ORUBA THE HUTT** — Ancient albino who **pampers himself** with fine clothing.

5. **MARLO THE HUTT** — A **deceitful dealer** in the slave markets of Zygerria.

Q: How do the Hutts pay for stolen goods?

A: With wupiupi, a type of **currency** used by the Hutts on Tatooine. **16** golden wupiupi coins equal **one** trugut, **four** truguts equal **one** peggat, and **one** peggat can get you around **40** Republic credits. So save your wupiupi!

REALLY?!

Hutts can't grow hair so some **WEAR** a small creature called a **SHA'RELLIAN TOOP** instead!

WOW!...

1,358

Jabba's weight in kg (2,994lbs)

SLIME LORDS

The **drooling, ruling** Hutts are a **slug-like** species who control the **criminal underworld** in the Outer Rim. These crooks avoid the wars of the Republic and the Empire—they only look out for themselves, and none more so than the **infamous Jabba!**

GRUESOME HUTT FATES
1. **Ziro** (Jabba's uncle)—shot twice by his love Sy Snootles on Teth, under orders from Jabba.
2. **Oruba**—sliced by Savage Opress's lightsaber on Nal Hutta.
3. **Jabba**—strangled by Leia Organa on Tatooine.

FAN FACT
The **slimy** sound of Jabba the Hutt was mainly made using a bowl of **melted cheese.**

TOP 3
HUTTS WITH TATTOOS
1. **Jabba**—the Desilijic crime family's tattoo is carved on his right arm.
2. **Arok**—his "kajidic" (crime gang) symbol is tattooed on his upper left arm.
3. **Ziro**—covered in bright tattoos indicating his connection to the Hutt world Sleheyron.

Tell me more!
SLIMY DOUBLE-CROSSING, NO-GOOD SWINDLERS

The Hutt crime gangs make money from illegal activities. Some buy and sell **slaves**, while others **smuggle goods**, or **gamble on podracing** and **gladiator matches**. Then there are those who lend money and charge **too much** interest. And if that's not bad enough, some Hutts even **hire pirates!**

In numbers

35,000 credits
The reward Jabba pays bounty hunter Boushh for capturing and bringing Chewbacca to his palace

604 years old
Jabba's age at his death

23 Sha'rellian toops
Stacked high on the head of Ziro's Mama!

15% interest
Charged by Jabba on the debt Han Solo owes him, after Han dumps the Hutt's illegal cargo from his ship

3.7m (12.1ft)
Gardulla's length, from head to tail

Hutts start out as **tiny Huttlets** like Rotta, at just 0.43m (1ft 5in) in height. With great age they reach **legendary sizes**, like Ziro's Mama at 4.52m (14ft 10in)!

HUTT GRAND COUNCIL
Ruled by the heads of the five Hutt crime families • Council Hall located on Nal Hutta, surrounded by murky swamps • Place for meetings and parties

Fast Facts

ORGANIZATION: Mandalorian Death Watch

LEADER: Pre Vizsla, governor of Mandalore's moon, Concordia

SPECIES: Human

AIM: To overthrow the peaceful New Mandalorian government

ABILITIES: Advanced combat training, weaponry expertise

Peek behind the scenes
Concept artists Ralph McQuarrie and Joe Johnston designed a supertrooper for *The Empire Strikes Back*, which became Boba Fett and later inspired Death Watch. The **original designs** finally appeared in *Star Wars Rebels* season 3.

Mandalore's moon, Concordia, is dotted with **disused mines**. Deep inside, the Death Watch wait, their minds fixed on the **violent glories of the past**.

> "We are the Death Watch, descendants of the warrior faith all Mandalorians once knew."
> — **PRE VIZSLA**

SHADOW ARMY

Conniving Concordia Governor **Pre Vizsla pretends to support** Mandalore's peace-loving Duchess Satine Kryze. Secretly, he **leads her greatest foes**—the **Death Watch warriors**.

REALLY?! Sabine Wren is a member of **HOUSE VIZSLA**—info she uses to impress the **PROTECTORS OF CONCORD DAWN!**

STRANGE...

...BUT TRUE
Pre Vizsla's Darksaber was created over a thousand years ago by **Tarre Vizsla,** the **first Mandalorian Jedi**. After his death, it was kept in the Jedi Temple, but members of House Vizsla stole it. They used it as a symbol to **unify and rule all of Mandalore**.

Tell me more!

GIVE PEACE A CHANCE?
Mandalorians were once **feared mercenaries** and **bounty hunters**. They even fought the Jedi—and **often won**. But constant war **ravaged the planet** and now Duchess Satine Kryze and her New Mandalorians want to **embrace peace**. However, not everyone agrees with them!

THE UNDERWORLD

BEST KNOWN FOR
REVIVING MANDALORE'S WARRIOR TRADITION
Death Watch

How to speak Mando'a

"AKAANIR" "FIGHT"

"NAAK" "PEACE"

"NAASTAR" "DESTROY"

"BESKAR'GAM" "ARMOR"

"NARUDAR" "YOUR ENEMY'S ENEMY"

"KYR'TSAD" "DEATH WATCH"

In numbers

4,000,000
Population of Mandalore

412,000
Population of Concordia

5,000 warriors
Rumored to be in the Death Watch

17.97m (58ft 11in)
Length of a Mandalorian shuttle

4 crew members
Needed to man the Death Watch *Kom'rk*-class fighter *Gauntlet*

OUCH!! The Death Watch **CAPTURES** Obi-Wan Kenobi on Concordia and tries to **SMASH** him in a **ROCK GRINDER!**

MANDALORE

Centuries of war have turned much of planet into desert • Citizens live in bio-cube cities • Capital Sundari City is home to Duchess and Ruling Council • Death Watch hides out in Mandalore's moon, Concordia

Mandalorian armor looks cool!
That's because it *is* cool! Mandalorian armor is packed with anti-Jedi gadgets, such as **missile-launching jet packs, armed gauntlets, magnetized boots,** and **helmets with tactical displays**. What's not to like?

Q: What's that symbol on Pre Vizsla's helmet?
A: It's the image of a **Mandalorian shriek-hawk** (or "jai'galaar") diving at its prey. The ancient symbol of Clan Vizsla, it is also used as the **insignia of the Death Watch**.

"Mandalore's violent past is behind us. Our warriors moved to Concordia. They died out years ago."
DUCHESS SATINE TO OBI-WAN KENOBI

Fast Facts

OCCUPATION: Pirates
AFFILIATION: Neutral
WEAPONS: Blaster pistol, electrostaff, sharp wits
SPECIES: Weequay

Q: What is Hondo's favorite ship?
A: Hondo's pride and joy is his **Personal Luxury Yacht 3000**. It's named *Fortune and Glory*—after his favorite things!

Peek behind the scenes
Flying saucers from 1950s' science-fiction stories inspired the design of Hondo's pirate ships!

MEET THE PIRATE GANG!
Hondo employs a gang of Weequay pirates. They're reliable as fighters, but as friends—watch your back!

TURK FALSO
Resents taking orders from Hondo. If he sees a chance to **betray his boss**, he'll grab it!

GWARM
Lieutenant in the pirate gang and a real bully. Dreaded by farmers all over Felucia.

PARSEL
Copilot on Hondo's ship. **Good pilot. Bad buddy**. His loyalties are always up for sale.

JIRO
Pirate lieutenant. Betrayed Hondo by joining Darth Maul. Then betrayed Maul.

PIIT
One of the few female pirates on Florrum. Noted for her purple-painted peg leg!

R5-P8
Not your regular astromech. He has a pirate blaster mounted on the top of his head.

PIRATE MENACE

STRANGE …BUT TRUE
Tough, leathery skin helps Weequay to endure the **harsh conditions** on their desert planet, **Sriluur**.

A **shrewd pirate** and **kidnapper**, Hondo Ohnaka leads a gang of **greedy bandits** on the Outer Rim planet of Florrum. He's chasing **fortune and glory**—in that order!

NO WAY!!
Pirates often blow their entire haul of **ILL-GOTTEN GAINS** on **DRINKS AND EATS** at Hondo's bar.

MARAUDING MOTHERSHIP
Hondo commands his gang from a *Corona*-class armed frigate. **No one** in the Outer Rim has **escaped their daring raids!**

Top 4 Most profitable missions

1 KYBER CRYSTAL THEFT
Pirates will even steal from Jedi. They find that younglings make the easiest victims.

2 ARMS DEALING
Selling weapons to mercenaries pays big. Who cares what they're used for?

3 STEALING CROPS
Local farmers can't defend themselves. Tough!

4 HOSTAGE-TAKING
Important hostages mean big paydays, so aim high!

MOTHER KNOWS BEST
Hondo's mom **sold him** when he was a boy, but luckily she taught him all about **hostage-taking** first! In Hondo's words: "As my sweet mother always said, 'Son, if one hostage is good, two are better, and three, well, that's just **good business**!'"

AWESOME!!
Weequay can be **GOOD GUYS**, too! Que-Mars Redath-Gom was a **JEDI KNIGHT** who fought for the Republic in the Battle of Geonosis.

THE UNDERWORLD

Failed friendships
Hondo eventually **loses his pirate crew** and must partner with **even less trustworthy** allies like Azmorigan and Terba the Ugnaught.

BEST KNOWN FOR ABDUCTING COUNT DOOKU AND STEALING HIS LIGHTSABER!
Hondo Ohnaka

HONDO'S PIRATE BASE
Marketplace for illegal trading • Full of listening devices and traps for hostages • Fleet of WLO-5 battle tanks • Fully stocked bar • Situated on Florrum

TOP 6
PIRATE VEHICLES
1. *Flarestar*-class attack shuttle
2. Pirate speeder tank
3. Starhawk speeder bike
4. *Broken Horn*, a stolen freighter
5. *Acushnet*, an armed frigate
6. *Last Chance*, a stolen Imperial shuttle

"But you know what I always say: Speak softly, and drive a big tank."
HONDO

"I smell profit. Nice, fat, juicy profits!"
HONDO

REALLY?!
Hondo tries to convince Ezra Bridger to be his **CRIMINAL PARTNER** and become a **PIRATE JEDI!**

Tell me more!

FRIENDS AND FRENEMIES
Hondo rubs shoulders with some of the most **infamous people** in the galaxy. He was a longtime **buddy of Jango Fett,** and bounty hunter **Aurra Sing is his ex-girlfriend**. Hondo often runs into **Jedi heroes** such as **Obi-Wan Kenobi, Anakin Skywalker,** and **Ahsoka Tano**. When he does, he will either **befriend or betray** them—whichever is most profitable!

STRANGE Almost everything Hondo owns is **stolen, including his snazzy red jacket!**
...BUT TRUE Pirates enjoy **betting** on Mukmuk fights—battles between Hondo's two Kowakian **monkey-lizards**.

In numbers

200 passengers
Capacity of a pirate frigate

6 parsecs
Distance between Florrum and the desert planet Vanqor

1.89m (6ft 2in)
Average height of a Weequay pirate

0.47m (18.5in)
Length of a typical pirate's peg leg

CRIMEWAVE!

In a galaxy filled with turmoil and war, **unsavory individuals** find plenty of opportunity to do **illegal deals**. These **vile criminals and gangsters** are known to fight the Empire, the Rebellion, and especially one another, as they scrape to be at the **top of the underworld!**

SPICE MARKET
The **Pyke Syndicate** is a powerful part of the **spice business**. They control the production of raw spice, used to create an **illegal drug**.

BEST KNOWN FOR
USING ILLEGAL BLACK MARKET WEAPONS
Guavian Death Gang

Q: Who is Bala-Tik?
A: He is the Guavian Death Gang's negotiator. He speaks on their behalf since they don't have mouths.

Tell me more!

SUPER SOLDIERS
Soldiers of the Guavian Death Gang have a **mechanical implant**. This pumps **secret chemicals** into their bloodstream to make them faster and more aggressive. The cybernetic central disk on their heads lets them **silently communicate** with each other.

REALLY?!
Azmorigan trades Lando Calrissian a **PUFFER PIG** in exchange for Hera Syndulla. She doesn't want to be Azmorigan's slave, so she hits him with a **DINNER PLATE!**

EVIL EXPERIMENTS
Dr. Evazan and Ponda Baba, also known as Roofoo and Sawkee, do terrible **medical experiments** by turning hapless victims into mindless **cybernetic slaves**. They have been known to work on Milvayne, Jedha, and Tatooine.

AZMORIGAN
SPECIES: Jablogian
HOMEWORLD: Nar Shaddaa
KNOWN FOR: Theft, a big appetite

DR. EVAZAN AND PONDA BABA
SPECIES: Human, Aqualish
HOMEWORLD: Alsakan, Ando
KNOWN FOR: Deadly experiments

GUAVIAN DEATH GANG SOLDIER
SPECIES: Human
HOMEWORLD: Varies
KNOWN FOR: Black market technology

THE UNDERWORLD

In numbers

50,000 credits
Loaned by Guavian Death Gang to Han Solo

8 pointed fangs
In a Pyke's smile

3 times
That Han Solo has failed to deliver on his promises to Kanjiklub

1.5 horns
On Cikatro Vizago's head

Kanjiklub were once **slaves** of the **Hutts**. They turned on their masters and now run their own **criminal organization**.

STRANGE ...BUT TRUE

When gangsters get caught, they are sent to **terrible prisons** like **Megalox Beta**. The **gravity** outside of the prison is so strong that it **crushes** anyone who goes outside!

Crime Does Pay
Wealthy **Falleen** head the vast **Black Sun** crime syndicate. They have dozens of high-paying **illegal trades**, including spice, slaves, and **illegal weapons**.

VADER'S NEIGHBORS
Like **Darth Vader**, the Black Sun operates a **secret fortress** on the lava planet **Mustafar**.

TOUGH TRADER
Cikatro Vizago, a Lothal-based crime lord, wears **earrings** and **metal spikes** on his horns to make himself look tougher.

Top 7 Gangs in the Galaxy

1. **HUTT CLAN** — A mob so powerful, even the Empire must work with it.
2. **BLACK SUN** — A vast network that employs bounty hunters.
3. **RED KEY RAIDERS** — A Tatooine-based gang that covers its illegal activities by pretending to be miners.
4. **PYKE SYNDICATE** — Spicers known to work for the Sith.
5. **GUAVIAN DEATH GANG** — Cybernetic gangsters who trade their humanity for enhanced abilities.
6. **KANJIKLUB** — Warrior criminals who train in martial arts.
7. **XREXUS CARTEL** — An organization that got more than it bargained for when members tried to auction a captured Padawan.

REALLY?! Tasu Leech refuses to speak BASIC because he thinks it sounds SOFT AND WEAK!

TASU LEECH (KANJIKLUB)
SPECIES: Human
HOMEWORLD: Nar Kanji
KNOWN FOR: Ruthless determination

CIKATRO VIZAGO
SPECIES: Devaronian
HOMEWORLD: Devaron
KNOWN FOR: Shady deal-making

BLACK SUN GUARD AND ZITON MOJ
SPECIES: Falleen
HOMEWORLD: Mustafar
KNOWN FOR: Use of martial arts

Who narrowly stops the **Ewoks** from **feasting** on the rebels **for dinner?**

WEIRD AND WONDERFUL BEINGS

Where do **rogues, smugglers,** and **alien misfits** settle their **debts** on Tatooine?

CHAPTER 3

Which **smart pets** can **understand** what their royal owner says?

WARRIOR TRIBE

Small? Yes. **Cuddly?** Maybe. **Tough?** Absolutely! The furry, forest-dwelling Ewoks may look like teddy bears, but the rebels couldn't win the **Battle of Endor** without them!

BEST KNOWN FOR
LIVING IN TREETOP VILLAGES

Ewoks

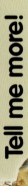

Tell me more!

BEATING THE EMPIRE—EWOK STYLE

Think you need high-tech weapons to trash **Imperial walkers** and bash **stormtroopers**? Ewoks don't! They **roll logs** to knock them over, pound them with **slingshots**, drop **rocks** on them from gliders, trip them up with **ropes**, and smash them with **log traps**! Take that!

Baby Ewoks, known as "**woklings**," sleep in baskets. When they get older, each receives a **hood** to wear and becomes **a full tribe member.**

How to speak Ewokese

"YAA-YAAH!" "GREETINGS!"
"YUB NUB!" "HOORAY!"
"EE CHEE WA MAA!" "WOW!"

Ewoks **don't build fast vehicles**, but they seem to like **driving other people's**! Paploo steals a **speeder bike** to distract Imperial soldiers, while two other Ewoks take charge of an Imperial walker.

THE SOUNDS OF MUSIC

1. **Drums**—Ewoks can beat a mean rhythm on their animal-skin-covered drums.
2. **Trumpets**—Animal horns make terrific trumpets, and create a **super loud blast**!
3. **Woodwind instruments**—Bird whistles and reed flutes flesh out the Ewok orchestra.
4. **Xylophones**—Not everyone can hit the right note on wooden slats or **stormtrooper helmets**!
5. **Voices**—Ewoks love singing and **burst into song** while preparing to cook the rebels!

Endor

Q: Do Ewoks have pets?
A: Yes! Chief Chirpa has a pet lizard that sits on his lap—or sometimes **his head**! Other animals must work for their keep. **Tip-yips** are like hens and are raised for their eggs. **Pulgas**, **bordoks**, and **gaupas** are used for riding.

140

INTELLIGENT BEINGS

Fast Facts

HOMEWORLD: Forest Moon of Endor

AFFILIATION: Side with the Rebel Alliance against the Empire

APPEARANCE: Cute, but appearances can be deceptive

SNEAKY SKILLS: Making traps and snares out of plants and rocks, ambushing unwary stormtroopers

REALLY?!
Ewoks will **EAT** almost anything! They are just about to **DINE ON SOME REBELS** when Luke and C-3PO stop them!

Peek behind the scenes
Wicket W. Warrick is played by Warwick Davis. His other character roles include the title character in *Willow*, and both Professor Flitwick and Griphook in the Harry Potter movies.

In numbers

200 Ewoks
Population of Bright Tree Village

42 seasons
Length of time Chief Chirpa has led his tribe before the Battle of Endor

15m (49ft 3in)
Bright Tree Village's height above the ground

13 teeth
Hang from Teebo's necklace

3 fingers
On an Ewok's hand

1m (3ft 3in)
Average Ewok height

"**Coatee-cha tu yub nub!**"
EWOKS SINGING "CELEBRATE THE FREEDOM!" AFTER THE BATTLE OF ENDOR IS WON

In Ewok tradition, chiefs are **always males**. However, Chief Chirpa's daughter, Princess Kneesaa, shows great **bravery and leadership**. She becomes the tribe's first female chief!

TOP 3
SKULLS WORN ON EWOK HEADS
1. **Churi**—this giant bird's cranium makes the tribe's shaman, Logray, **look taller than he really is**.
2. **Gurreck**—sharp tusks and fangs make it a bit **risky to wear** this predator on your head! Teebo doesn't seem to care.
3. **Forest beast**—a horned monster's head adorns the Elder Leektar's noggin.

WOW...
30,000,000+
Population of Ewoks on Endor

BUZZING SWARM

The insectoid Geonosians come from a desolate world where only the strong survive. Their exoskeletons match the planet's rocky surface—**rough, sharp,** and **hard to crack!**

BEST KNOWN FOR
BUILDING THE TRADE FEDERATION'S BATTLE DROIDS
Geonosians

Q: Who is the big boss?
A: **Archduke Poggle the Lesser** is the leader of all Geonosian hives (under Queen Karina). Poggle and his fellow aristocrats are **filthy rich** thanks to his decision to boost production—more droids means **more money!**

How to gesture in Geonosian

"WORK HARDER"
Click outer mandible twice

"10,000 CREDITS"
Rapidly click inner mandible 10,000 times

"DIE"
Loudly click both inner and outer mandibles together

"HELLO"
No such word exists!

In numbers

5,000,000 B1 battle droids
Sold to the Trade Federation before the Clone Wars began

8 seconds
The time it takes for the queen to lay one egg!

6 years old
Age that Geonosian soldier drones start their training

5% of population
Belong to the aristocracy

GROSS!!
Archduke Poggle's walking staff is made from the **LIMB BONES** of an unlucky political opponent!

Tell me more!

LIFE'S NOT FAIR...
Geonosians have a **caste-based society**. The upper classes enjoy a **life of luxury**, while poor lower classes **fight in the army** or **slave away** in the factories.

INTELLIGENT BEINGS

Fast Facts

HOMEWORLD: Geonosis
AFFILIATION: Trade Federation and Separatist allies
COOL FEATURES: Moth-like wings, toes that can cling to rocks

Peek behind the scenes
A termite infestation in filmmaker George Lucas's house inspired the Geonosians. He even collected some of the insects in a jar for his artists!

GRIMY FACTORIES
Dug into Geonosis's underground • Maze of polluted, dirty, stinky tunnels • Exhaust vents let out toxic gases to surface • Unsafe machines often squash Geonosian workers!

"We build weapons, Senator... that is our business!"
— POGGLE THE LESSER

WHY DOES KLIK-KLAK GUARD AN EGG?
He is protecting the last known queen egg. Hatching it is the only hope for his species.

STRANGE ...BUT TRUE
Geonosians **"get drunk"** by eating a **special fungus**. It reacts with their stomach fluids to create a **body odor** that produces **euphoria**!

NO WAY!!
Geonosians don't value life like some other species. They will **FIGHT EACH OTHER** for the best jobs building the Death Star.

PERILOUS PARTY
To **celebrate** the start of the **Death Star's construction**, the Geonosians host a 3-day arena fight. Tens of thousands of **drones are slaughtered** in battle!

CRAZY QUEEN
With her real **workers exterminated** and her ability to make new eggs ruined by the Empire, one Geonosian queen goes crazy and begins **"hatching"** droid workers. A queen's instinct to breed and rule is strong.

Fast Facts

THE GANG: Criminals, slaves, guards, assorted flunkies

THE BOSS: Jabba the Hutt

AFFILIATION: Money and power

LOCATION: Jabba's palace and wherever Jabba sends them

Slaves of fortune
As if being a slave for the hideous Hutt isn't bad enough, you also have to mind his **vile temper**! Jabba's **favorite performer** Yarna d'al'Gargan, and Barada, a **mechanic and skiff guard**, know the ropes. But Twi'lek dancer Oola, who is tricked into slavery, is less fortunate. After Oola rejects Jabba's slimy attentions, he feeds her to his **pet rancor beast**, and takes Princess Leia as a replacement—his **last slave and biggest mistake**!

Oola

BEST KNOWN FOR

BEING LUNCH FOR JABBA'S RANCOR!

Gamorrean Guard

Peek behind the scenes
For Jabba's palace, George Lucas wanted even more aliens than Episode IV's Cantina scene, so he spent over **$1 million** creating nearly 80 characters.

TOP 8
JOBS IN JABBA'S PALACE

1. **CHIEF OF STAFF**—Bib Fortuna is the Twi'lek who **runs** the palace.
2. **ACCOUNTANT**—Shasa Tiel is the **ambitious, amphibious** Ishi Tib in charge of the Hutt's fortune.
3. **HEAD OF SECURITY**—Ephant Mon is Jabba's Chevin security chief and friend, who **warns** that Luke is dangerous.
4. **JESTER**—Salacious Crumb, a despised, jumped-up Kowakian monkey-lizard, has to keep the Hutt constantly **amused**—or else!
5. **SKIFF GUARDS**—Wooof is a former smuggler who runs the skiffs and sail barge, and is **slain** by Luke above the sarlacc pit.
6. **DOG MINDER**—Ree-Yees is a Gran who looks after Jabba's frog-dog Bubo. Ree-Yees loathes Jabba, but Bubo hates Ree-Yees even more.
7. **PALACE GUARDS**—Gamorreans like Gartogg are dumb, thuggish "pig guards," who do the Hutt's dirty work.
8. **SPIES**—Saelt-Marae is a wily Yarkora who poses as a merchant to spy on Jabba's enemies inside the palace—a job for life!

Saelt-Marae

Ree-Yees

> **"Die wanna wanga."**
> **BIB FORTUNA GREETING C-3PO IN JABBA'S PALACE**

Tell me more!

JABBA'S MAIN MAN
Bib Fortuna is a **"big man" around the palace**. He manages staff, greets guests, organizes events, and even obtains **presents** for the Hutt, like Oola and the **rancor**. But that doesn't mean he likes his boss.

INTELLIGENT BEINGS

Top 5
Bounty hunters in Jabba's court

1. **BOBA FETT**
Jabba's best mercenary. Legendary pilot of *Slave I*, who captures the elusive Han Solo for the Hutt.

2. **BOSSK**
A brutish Trandoshan hunter of Wookiees, pilot of the *Hound's Tooth*, and Boba Fett's close friend.

3. **AMANAMAN**
Mysterious Amani headhunter, who prefers using traditional hunting weapons instead of blasters.

4. **DENGAR**
A Corellian mercenary who often works for the Hutts.

5. **SY SNOOTLES**
A glamorous Pa'lowick singer and spy, who executes her love, Ziro the Hutt, in return for a big reward from Jabba.

JABBA'S PALACE
Originally a B'omarr monastery • Jabba's headquarters • Located at the edge of the Northern Dune Sea on Tatooine

"Of course I'm worried. Lando and Chewbacca never returned from this awful place."
C-3PO TO R2-D2

JABBA'S CRONIES

Jabba the Hutt's palace gives shelter to the galaxy's **craziest criminals, bounty hunters**, and **lowlifes**. But don't mess around with Jabba—many who enter this hazardous **citadel of crime** are never seen again!

In numbers

100kg (220lbs)
Gamorrean guard's weight

4 tentacles
On Tessek's face

3 eyes
On Ree-Yees's head

3 fingers
On the hand of Hermi Odle, a Baragwin

2.2m (7ft 3in)
The height of Saelt-Marae

1 eye
On Jabba's TT-8L/Y7 gatekeeper droid

REALLY?!
YARKORA like Saelt-Marae eat all day long to fill their **TWO STOMACHS**. With all that food inside them, they also need their **FOUR KIDNEYS** and **THREE LIVERS**!

STRANGE ...BUT TRUE
Jabba has every good reason to be paranoid. Many of his **employees *are* out to get him**—even his right-hand man Bib Fortuna, his Quarren bookkeeper Tessek, and Gauron Nas Tal, a snarling Saurin combat trainer. That's why he has **spies everywhere**.

> "My forgotten, da bosses would do terrible tings to me, *terrible* tings if me goin' back dere."
> **EXILED JAR JAR ON OTOH GUNGA**

Gungans don't use blasters. Instead, they throw balls of energy they call "boomas."

Gungans can crack shellfish with their big teeth!

REALLY?!
Jar Jar was once mistaken for **A JEDI** when he wore a hooded cloak. His **CLUMSINESS** was mistaken for Force powers!

How to speak like a Gungan

"OKIE DAY!"
"OK!"

"LOOKIE LOOKIE!"
"LOOK!"

"MESA CALLED…"
"MY NAME IS…"

"BOMBAD"
"POWERFUL, GREAT"

Tell me more!
AMPHIBIOUS ALLIES
The **Gungan Grand Army** comes to the **rescue** of its **amphibious, squid-like** friends, the **Mon Calamari**, during the **Clone Wars**. Gungans are better suited to **underwater fighting** on Mon Cala than clone troopers.

Love interest…
Jar Jar and Queen Julia of Bardotta are in love. The two meditate together by locking lips!

Jar Jar tries to **eat a fresh gorg** at the Mos Espa market without paying for it!

INTELLIGENT BEINGS

Q: Why is Jar Jar banished from his home?

A: **Boss Nass**, the Gungan ruler, banishes Jar Jar **on pain of death** after the gawky Gungan **crashes Nass's personal submarine**. His banishment **doesn't last long**, however!

I LUV YOUS!

The Jedi Qui-Gon Jinn accidentally **saves Jar Jar's life** during the droid **invasion of Naboo**. Jar Jar pledges a Gungan **life debt** to him, swearing **never to leave his side**. Qui-Gon **quickly tires** of Jar Jar's **bizarre antics**, but as hard as he tries, he **can't get rid of him!**

Fast Facts

AFFILIATION: Republic
HOMEWORLD: Naboo
WEAPONS: Clumsiness
ABILITIES: Impossible to describe

TOP 3 GUNGAN SKILLS
1. Breathing underwater and on land.
2. Swimming long distances.
3. Throwing "booma" energy weapons.

COOL!! Gungan spit is waterproof and as **STRONG AS GLUE!**

Peek behind the scenes
Classic comedy actors like Charlie Chaplin and Danny Kaye inspired Jar Jar's goofy antics.

Naboo neighbors
The Gungans and the Naboo **haven't always seen eye to eye**. But when the Trade Federation blockades the planet, **the two civilizations must work together to defeat the droid army**! The Gungan Grand Army **distracts the droids**, while Queen Amidala **sneaks into the Naboo Royal Palace** to capture Trade Federation Viceroy Nute Gunray.

Naboo

In numbers
543 Gungans
Lost at the Battle of Naboo

75kg (165lbs)
Average weight of a Gungan

1m (3ft 3in)
Length of Jar Jar's tongue

CLUMSY GUNGAN

Deep in the **oceans of Naboo** live the **Gungans**, the most famous of whom is **Jar Jar Binks**. As **clumsy as he is loyal**, this **awkward amphibian** is an unlikely **army general** and **Senate representative**.

Fast Facts

HOMEWORLD: Tatooine

LEADERS: Clan chiefs, shamans

AFFILIATION: None—they're only interested in profits!

LANGUAGES: Jawaese, Jawa Trade Talk

SNEAKY SKILLS: Repairing anything so it works just well enough to sell.

COOL FEATURES: Who knows? No one's ever seen under a Jawa's robe.

Sandcrawlers really suck! They use a special suction tube to **load scrap and droids** into the cargo hold.

BEST KNOWN FOR
BRINGING C-3PO, R2-D2, AND LUKE SKYWALKER TOGETHER

Jawas

Q: How did Jawas get their sandcrawlers?

A: Mining companies originally brought sandcrawlers to Tatooine. When their mining projects failed, they **abandoned the sandcrawlers in the desert**. Jawas soon took them over, turning them into mobile homes and workshops.

"Jawa Juice" is a popular drink at Dex's Diner on Coruscant (but it isn't made from Jawas!).

SCRAP DEALERS

Jawas are the **scavengers** of Tatooine—they **roam the desert** in **giant sandcrawlers**, looking for scrap and faulty equipment to trade. These **dodgy dealers** have a reputation as **swindlers** and **thieves**!

WHAT'S UNDER THE HOOD?
No one really knows what a Jawa looks like, as they always fully cover themselves—even their faces! Some folk think they are related to the Tuskens, but others believe the Jawas are de-evolved humans, or that they may be even related to rodents!

INTELLIGENT BEINGS

WOW!...

1,500

Number of droids a sandcrawler can store

STRANGE

...BUT TRUE
The Jawaese language uses **scent** as well as spoken words! The Jawas' **stench** helps them **understand one another**—but also makes Jawaese impossible for others to learn. So Jawas use the simpler "Trade Talk" to **haggle over prices**. But **don't stand too close** when they **lose a deal**!

> "I can't abide those Jawas! Disgusting creatures!"
> **— C-3PO ON HIS LOVE OF JAWAS**

REALLY?! Jawas have a **VERY STRONG BODY ODOR**. They think washing is a waste of water!

TOP 4
DANGERS TO JAWAS
1. Deadly desert windstorms
2. Hungry Krayt dragons
3. Vicious Tusken Raiders
4. Unhappy customers

Want a special-purpose droid? For the right price, Jawas will build custom-made "monster droids" out of many standard droid parts.

Peek behind the scenes
Jawaese was developed from African languages, especially **Zulu**. Sound designer Ben Burtt wrote a script based on Zulu sounds, which were re-voiced by actors and sped up to create Jawaese.

Q: Why do Jawas look for scrap in the desert?
A: Not much technology or spare parts get to remote Tatooine. But over thousands of years, **crashed spacecraft and failed mining projects** have left plenty of wreckage and equipment in the desert, which Jawas salvage for reuse.

Say it in Trade Talk

"MOB UN LOO?"
"HOW MUCH?"

"MOMBAY M'BWA."
"THAT'S MINE."

"TANDI KWA!"
"GIVE IT BACK!"

"UTINNI!"
"COME ON!" OR "LET'S GO!"

"TOGO TOGU!"
"HANDS OFF!"

"OMU'SATA."
"SHUT UP."

In numbers

80 years
Average lifespan of a Jawa

36.8m (120ft 9in)
Length of a sandcrawler

30kph (18.6mph)
Sandcrawler's maximum speed

1m (3ft 3in)
Average height of a Jawa

Fast Facts

HOMEWORLD: Mon Cala

AFFILIATION: Rebel Alliance against the Empire, the Resistance

GOVERNMENT: Monarchy

FISHY FEATURES: Waterproof skin, ability to breathe on land and underwater

BEST KNOWN FOR
REUNITING QUARREN AND MON CALA

Prince Lee-Char

Ackbar practices martial arts with his **kar-shak** weapon to stay sharp and flexible.

STRANGE ...BUT TRUE
Mon Calamari starships have such **humid** environments that they turn human skin **damp** within **minutes.**

Tell me more!

UNDERWATER NEIGHBORS

Mon Calamari share their planet with the **aggressive Quarren**. During the Clone Wars, the Separatists **trick** the Quarren into fighting their neighbors, and **civil war** breaks out between the two species. The foes must **reunite** to **take their planet back** from the Separatist invaders.

Through the ages: GIAL ACKBAR

MON CALA CAPTAIN
Young Captain Ackbar is chief advisor to the Mon Cala royals. He is a loyal follower of Prince Lee-Char, and inspires him to take up the mantle of king.

REBEL ADMIRAL
Now an Admiral serving the Rebellion against the Empire, Ackbar commands the Rebel fleet from his flagship, *Home One*.

RESISTANCE LEADER
An aging Ackbar leaves retirement to join the Resistance against the First Order. He is a key strategist and naval commander for General Leia Organa.

AQUATIC ALLIES

Hailing from a planet almost completely covered in water, the Mon Calamari play a **pivotal role** in galactic military history! These aquatic beings first take up arms to **fight for their freedom**, and later venture to space to **defend peace and justice** in the galaxy.

COOL!
As Mon Calamari age, they grow **BARBELS** on their chin. This makes them look like they have **BEARDS!**

Q: Who designed the first rebel B-wing fighter?
A: The Mon Cala engineer named Quarrie designed the Prototype B6, known as the Blade Wing.

Mon Calamari take their **homes** into battle! They **convert** underwater buildings into spaceships for war.

INTELLIGENT BEINGS

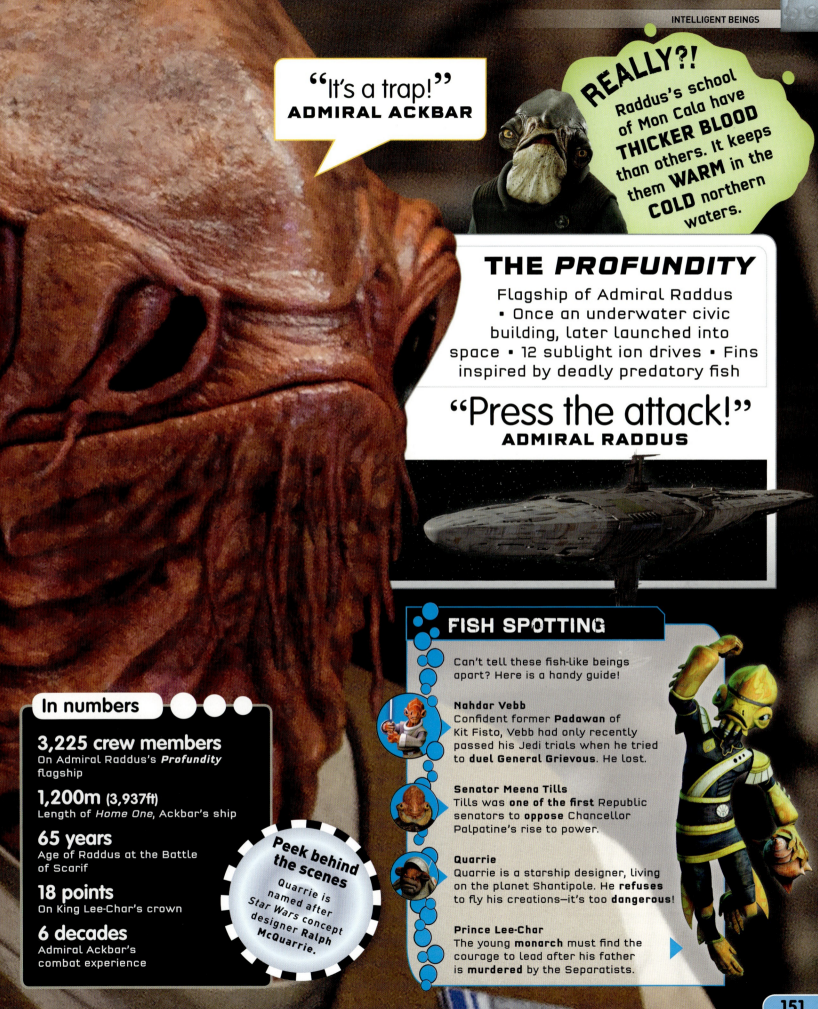

"It's a trap!"
ADMIRAL ACKBAR

REALLY?! Raddus's school of Mon Cala have **THICKER BLOOD** than others. It keeps them **WARM** in the **COLD** northern waters.

THE PROFUNDITY
Flagship of Admiral Raddus • Once an underwater civic building, later launched into space • 12 sublight ion drives • Fins inspired by deadly predatory fish

"Press the attack!"
ADMIRAL RADDUS

FISH SPOTTING
Can't tell these fish-like beings apart? Here is a handy guide!

Nahdar Vebb
Confident former **Padawan** of Kit Fisto, Vebb had only recently passed his Jedi trials when he tried to **duel General Grievous**. He lost.

Senator Meena Tills
Tills was **one of the first** Republic senators to **oppose** Chancellor Palpatine's rise to power.

Quarrie
Quarrie is a starship designer, living on the planet Shantipole. He **refuses** to fly his creations—it's too **dangerous**!

Prince Lee-Char
The young **monarch** must find the courage to lead after his father is **murdered** by the Separatists.

In numbers

3,225 crew members
On Admiral Raddus's *Profundity* flagship

1,200m (3,937ft)
Length of *Home One*, Ackbar's ship

65 years
Age of Raddus at the Battle of Scarif

18 points
On King Lee-Char's crown

6 decades
Admiral Ackbar's combat experience

Peek behind the scenes
Quarrie is named after Star Wars concept designer Ralph McQuarrie.

151

ROGUES' BAR

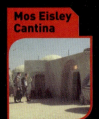
Mos Eisley Cantina

Mos Eisley Cantina is a raucous den of **smugglers**, **alien misfits**, and **renegade starship pilots**. Patrons from all over the galaxy flock to this turbulent tavern to enjoy **a drink** and **a brawl** over a few **dodgy deals**.

REALLY?!
Muftak is a snow creature with thick fur. He avoids **OVERHEATING** on Tatooine by hanging out at Mos Eisley's **SHADY BAR**, where he can also pick a pocket or two!

Fast Facts
LOCATION: Mos Eisley (major city on Tatooine)
BARTENDER: Wuher
WUHER'S ALLEGIANCE: Whoever pays their bill

DUROS
Duros have **no lips, no nose, green** or **blue skin, green blood**, and they fly a mean starship!

PONS LIMBIC AND BRACONNOR BAKISKA
The bar attracts a **strange crowd**. Pons Limbic (left) is a Siniteen nicknamed **"Brainiac"** because he can **mentally calculate hyperspace jumps**. Braconnor Bakiska (right), is **wary of strangers**, like many of his species, the Stennes Shifters.

ARLEIL SCHOUS
Defel **fortune-hunter** Arleil Schous is getting old. He's slowly losing his ability to **bend light around his body** and virtually **disappear**.

Q: Who runs Mos Eisley Cantina?
A: Wuher is the gruff human who works behind the bar at the cantina. He may not be the friendliest bartender in the galaxy, but his customers know that he never asks questions.

STRANGE ...BUT TRUE
Nabrun Leids must **wear a mask** on Tatooine, as his species has evolved to **breathe methane, not oxygen**.

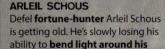

NO WAY!!
Gripped by madness, Dr. Evazan performs **ILLEGAL SURGERY** on Jedha. He leaves shortly before the city is destroyed—but starts up his **BAD BUSINESS AGAIN** on Tatooine!

Tell me more!
DON'T PICK A FIGHT WITH A JEDI
Doctor Evazan is **a wanted man** under a death sentence on **12** star systems, while his partner in crime, Ponda Baba, is **a bad-tempered thug**. When these dangerous criminals pull their weapons on Luke Skywalker and Obi-Wan Kenobi in the Cantina, the Jedi **cuts off Baba's arm** in one slice.

INTELLIGENT BEINGS

CANTINA SHOWDOWN
The Cantina is perfect for **settling old debts**. Eager to **collect the bounty** on Han Solo's head, Greedo foolishly fires at him... and misses. Han doesn't, shooting the bounty hunter dead with his hidden blaster. Cool as frozen juri juice, Han slips Wuher a coin to **pay for the mess**!

BEST KNOWN FOR REFUSING TO ALLOW DROIDS INSIDE
Mos Eisley Cantina

> "Most of the best freighter pilots can be found here. Only watch your step. This place can be a little rough."
> — **OBI-WAN KENOBI ON THE CANTINA**

HEM DAZON
Dazon is a **grouchy** Arcona stranded on Tatooine after blowing his credits on **salt and juri juice**. Dazon can't get enough juri juice—especially the rare stuff **made from Rodian blood**—even though it makes his **hands tremble** and has **turned his eyes a putrid yellow**.

Peek behind the scenes
Look closely at the bar behind Wuher on the opposite page and you'll see the **surplus jet engine parts** that were later used as assassin droid IG-88's head!

After the **Millennium Falcon** blasts its way out of Mos Eisley, the Empire sets up a permanent **garrison** there. Its presence is a real downer on the lively cantina!

BOM VIMDIN
An Advozse mercenary, Bom Vimdin is **a gloomy loner** obsessed with his credit balance. With a **sour face and a personality** to match, it's little wonder he's **universally disliked**.

MOS EISLEY CANTINA HOUSE RULES

- LEAVE YOUR DROIDS OUTSIDE. YOU DON'T WANT WUHER ON YOUR CASE.
- KEEP YOUR BLASTER HOLSTERED! WHY ASK FOR TROUBLE?
- FIND AN EMPTY TABLE OR BARSTOOL. CROWDING OTHER CUSTOMERS WILL ONLY END IN TEARS.
- BE FRIENDLY. BUY A DRINK FOR YOUR NEIGHBOR AT THE BAR.
- APPLAUD THE BAND—EVEN IF THEY'RE WAY OFF-KEY!
- MAKE PLEASANT CONVERSATION AND TRY TO LAUGH AT BAD JOKES.
- TIP THE BARTENDER, ESPECIALLY IF YOU MAKE A MESS.

STRANGE ...BUT TRUE
Momaw Nadon is an Ithorian. Like the rest of his species, he **can't speak Basic** without the help of a **vocabulator** to translate his voice.

GREEDO
Like most young Rodians, Greedo has **blue-green skin** covered with **lumps and warts**. Always up for **a scrap**, he scuffles with Anakin Skywalker after accusing the young pilot of cheating at podracing. **His mean streak** regularly lands him in hot water!

In numbers

473ml (16oz)
Size of a standard drink at the cantina

102 people
Maximum capacity of the cantina

12 drinks
Available on tap

2 Cantina owners
Since the Clone Wars

153

MAZ'S MENAGERIE

Maz Kanata is an **eccentric old adventurer** with a checkered past. She can be found in her **ancient castle**. This tavern hosts all sorts of **weird and wonderful guests**—as well as some **extraordinary secrets**.

BUCCANEER'S BOOTY
Perhaps it's no wonder that **pirate captain Sidon Ithano** pinches his gear from others. His helmet is stolen from the **Kaleesh** (General Grievous's species) and his blaster rifle is taken from a **Kanjiklubber**.

MAZ'S CASTLE
Thousands of years old • Possible connection to the Force • Previous battle site between Sith and Jedi • Once occupied by Jedi • Catacombs contain tombs of Jedi Knights

STRANGE ...BUT TRUE
Bounty hunter spy Bazine Netal wears a dress made with **Bafflewave** fabric, which **jams** scanners and allows her to pass **invisibly** through security systems. Now you see her... now you don't!

Ancient protocol droid ME-8D9 translates **shady deals** in Maz's castle. Rumors abound: Did ME-8D9 belong to the **Jedi Order**? Has she been in the castle since it was **first built**?

BIG GAME HUNTER
Grummgar is a **Dowutin huntsman** who tracks **exotic predators** on frontier worlds. He has **no respect for rules** and happily poaches on wildlife preserves. His most prized trophies are **endangered and rare creatures**.

Grummgar	Professor Allium	Laparo	Anophe Dengue
2.7m (8ft 10in)—when standing	1.9m (6ft 4in)	1.1m (3ft 7in)	0.5m (1ft 8in)—when sitting

A mixed party
Maz receives guests in all **shapes** and **sizes**. It's a wonder big lugs like Grummgar don't **squash** some of the smaller guests!

INTELLIGENT BEINGS

TOP 5
POPULAR GAMES
1. **Sabaac**—Card game played across the galaxy.
2. **Dejarik**—Chess game played on a holotable.
3. **Pazaak**—Ancient card game with a goal to reach 20 points.
4. **Deia's Dream**—The competitive Dengue sisters' favorite game.
5. **Droid Ball Fighting**—Colored spheroid droids combine for battle.

Tell me more!
GET TO KNOW MAZ
The **hospitality** in Maz Kanata's castle is renowned—new visitors get their **first night** of lodging, food, and drink for **free**! Maz is a **smart businesswoman** though, and she gets a **cut** of **any deals** made on the premises. She is highly regarded by some of the **biggest crime lords** in the galaxy.

In numbers

26 prayer beads
On Quiggold the pirate's necklace

25 years
Time passed since Maz last saw Han

7 strings
Strummed by Sudswater Dillifay Glon on his Hallikset instrument

5 towers
Rise up from Maz's castle

4 members
Play in the Shag Kava band

1 beloved Wookiee
Maz only has eyes for Chewie!

Q: Is Maz a Jedi?
A: Maz Kanata has a **strong connection** to the **Force**, but she is not a Jedi. She does possess some Jedi **antiques**, including a bust of ancient Jedi Master **Cherff Maota** and Luke Skywalker's lightsaber.

Services at Maz's castle include appraisals of valuable objects, forgery, gambling, navigational expertise, and plastic surgery.

MAZ'S STYLE
Maz Kanata wears variable lens corrective **goggles**, the **bracelet of the Sutro**, and clothing that she **knits herself**.

REALLY?!
A large, sentient **WORM** in Maz's castle offers free **SKIN-CLEANING** services, and **EAVESDROPS** on conversations.

Maz's Fast Facts

JOBS: Respected pirate, tavern owner

STARSHIP NAME: The *Epoch Swift*

HOMEWORLD: Takodana

SPECIES: Unknown

Peek behind the scenes
Maz Kanata—played by actress **Lupita Nyong'o** and motion-capture double, **Arti Shah**—is based on Rose Gilbert, the high school teacher of director J.J. Abrams.

WOW!...
1000+
Maz Kanata's age in years—though the exact number is a mystery

MADCAP MUSICIANS

From **dingy bars** to **crime palaces**, the galaxy's favorite **musicians** know how to draw a big crowd. As **bizarre** as they are **talented**, sometimes it's not just their instruments that are **highly strung**.

REALLY?!
Rappertunie spits **PARALYZING POISON** at anyone who threatens him.

Bith have such **sensitive hearing** that loud sonic grenades are said to make their **heads explode**!

Rappertunie plays a mean **Growdi Harmonique**—an instrument that's a **combo flute and water organ**.

Peek behind the scenes
Crew members playing Bith musicians in the Cantina moved to the beat of Benny Goodman's 1937 hit "Sing, Sing, Sing" while filming on set.

COOL!!
Droopy McCool's body releases a **VANILLA-LIKE SMELL**!

STRANGE ...BUT TRUE
Droopy McCool is a **stage name**. This Kitonak horn player's real name is a **series of whistles** that is unpronounceable by any other species.

LEADER OF THE BAND
"Fiery" Figrin D'an, king of the Kloo horn, is the **Bith leader of the Modal Nodes**—a regular act at Mos Eisley Cantina. What Figrin says goes... Well, he does **own most of the band's instruments**!

INTELLIGENT BEINGS

BEST KNOWN FOR BEING UNFAZED BY BAR FIGHTS
Modal Nodes

AWESOME!!
Max Rebo doesn't have arms, so he plays the organ **WITH HIS FEET!**

Tatooine's Greatest Hits

1. "MAD ABOUT ME" by Figrin D'an and the Modal Nodes
2. "LAPTI NEK" by The Max Rebo Band
3. "THE SEQUENTIAL PASSAGE OF CHRONOLOGICAL INTERVALS" by Figrin D'an and the Modal Nodes
4. "(THAT JOYOUS NIGHT) I ATE MY MATE" by The Max Rebo Band
5. "GOODNIGHT, BUT NOT GOODBYE (MAD ABOUT ME REMIX)" by Figrin D'an and the Modal Nodes

In numbers

82kg (180lbs) Weight of Droopy McCool

71+ years old Average lifespan of an Ortolan like Max Rebo

21 keys On Max Rebo's red ball organ

18 bells On a Hypolliope horn cluster instrument

7 band members In the Modal Nodes

4 band members In the Shag Kava band

SCRATCH AND SNIFF
Bith have **no nose or toes**. They sniff through special organs beneath the **skin flaps on their faces**! And their feet also smell—bad!

STRANGE ...BUT TRUE
The show must go on! Sy Snootles **steals** from her sweetheart and then **slays** him, but it **doesn't harm her later career** as The Max Rebo Band's **lead singer!**

Q: Who plays music at Maz Kanata's castle?
A: Maz gives free lodging to traveling musicians from across the galaxy, including the quartet Shag Kava.

Tell me more!

DOUBLE DUTY DRUMMERS
It takes **two** to beat out a rhythm on the **massive drum** in Jabba's palace! Drummers Ak-rev (below left) and Umpass-stay (below right) are the **crime lord's musicians**, and act as **his bodyguards**, too.

Fast Facts

HOMEWORLDS: Various—pilots come from all over the Outer Rim Territories

OBJECTIVE: To win the famous Boonta Eve Classic race and beat that cheat Sebulba!

MOST SUCCESSFUL PILOT: Sebulba—he always wins because he always cheats

YOUNGEST PILOT: Anakin Skywalker

MOS ESPA GRAND ARENA
Vast stadium for the Boonta Eve Classic Podrace • Holds more than 100,000 spectators • Features gambling, refreshment, and pit areas • Located at edge of Western Dune Sea on Tatooine

Fodesinbeed Annodue, the **two-headed Troig**, is the best-known race commentator at Mos Espa Arena. His red head, named **Fode**, calls the race in Basic, while his green head, **Beed**, reports in **Huttese**.

TOP 6 PODRACERS
(THE ONES WHO FINISH THE RACE!)

1. Anakin Skywalker: a human from Tatooine
2. Gasgano: a Xexto from Troiken
3. Aldar Beedo: a Glymphid from Ploo II
4. Ebe E. Endocott: a Triffian from Triffis
5. Elan Mak: a Fluggrian from Ploo IV
6. Boles Roor: a Sneevel from Sneeve

TOP 5
SNEAKY TRICKS SEBULBA USES TO WIN
1. Insulting rival pilots to rattle their nerves.
2. Sabotaging engines or other parts of podracers.
3. Swerving wildly to force competitors to crash into canyon walls.
4. Using a hidden flamethrower (illegal, of course) to roast an opponent's engine.
5. Tossing metal into a rival pilot's engine to cause it to blow up!

Tell me more!

THE GALAXY'S MOST FAMOUS PODRACE
Have a need for speed? **Professional and amateur** podracers enter the **annual nail-biting** Boonta Eve Classic, all hoping to win a fortune in prize money. Gamblers win (and lose) fortunes, too, as they **bet on the outcome**. Anakin's victory wins him another kind of prize—his freedom from **slavery**.

Q: How do you become a podracer champion?

A: Podracers must be **small and light**, with **nerves of steel** and **super-fast reflexes**. An **extra limb or two** helps, for operating the controls. If you're human, your chances of becoming a **podracing ace** and winning the Boonta Eve are slim—unless, like Anakin, **the Force** is with you!

Peek behind the scenes
The sequence featuring Sebulba and Anakin's battling podracers in *The Phantom Menace* was inspired by the chariot race in the epic movie *Ben Hur*.

DON'T crash in the Laguna Caves—the rescue teams won't come to help. They're going nowhere near the KRAYT DRAGON that lives there!

INTELLIGENT BEINGS

CHEATS AND CHAMPIONS

Thrills, spills, and spectacular crashes—that's what being a **podracing pilot** is all about! Pilots must be tough and competitive in this **dangerous sport**, as they chase their **dreams of glory**—and a **large pot of prize money**.

> "I don't care what universe you're from. That's gotta hurt!"
> **FODESINBEED, THE RACE COMMENTATOR, ON TEEMTO PAGALIES'S CRASH**

Peek behind the scenes
Most of the alien podracer pilots seen on screen were **digital creations** or **puppets**. Only Mawhonic was played by an actor in costume.

STRANGE ...BUT TRUE
Neva Kee, the Xamster pilot, **flies off course** in the second lap of the Boonta Eve Classic Podrace, while looking for a **shortcut**. He is never seen again and his fate **remains a mystery**!

REALLY?!
Ody Mandrell's podracer **EXPLODES** when a **PIT DROID** is accidentally sucked into its **ENGINE**!

How **embarrassing**! Pilot Ben Quadinaros is left on the **starting grid** when an **engine malfunction** destroys his podracer. He can only watch as his **rivals streak out of view**!

In numbers

947kph (588mph)
Maximum speed of Anakin's winning podracer in the Boonta Eve Classic

66% of podracers
Don't finish Anakin's winning race (18 start, 6 finish!)

18 contestants
In Anakin's winning race

9 years old
Anakin's age when he wins the race

7.47m (24ft 6in)
Length of the engines on Sebulba's podracer

3 laps
Number of times pilots fly around the Mos Espa circuit

0.79m (2ft 7in)
Height of Ratts Tyerell, the smallest podracer pilot

The **Boonta Eve holiday** on Tatooine is a **Hutt festival**. It honors the rise to godhood of famed Hutt **Boonta Hestilic Shad'ruu**.

Podracers have to **watch out** for Tusken Raider **snipers firing** at them. Teemto Pagalies **crashes** after a Tusken shot hits his fuel tank.

"Those Tuskens... are vicious, mindless monsters."
CLEIGG LARS, AFTER RAIDERS KIDNAP HIS WIFE, SHMI

WHAT DO TUSKENS DO FOR FUN?

- Ambush travelers in the desert
- ATTACK!
- Kidnap settlers and torture them
- Assault rival tribal groups
- Capture and care for their banthas
- Terrorize moisture farmers
- Take potshots at podracers

BEST KNOWN FOR
MURDERING SHMI SKYWALKER
Tusken Raiders

Talk like a Tusken

"AARRK! AARRK! AARRK!"
VICTORY CRY AFTER TAKING A CAPTIVE

"HUURRUGH!"
"RUN FOR IT!"

"ULI-AH"
"CHILDREN"

"URTYA"
"LIGHT TENT"

"URORRUR'R'R"
NAME OF A TUSKEN LEADER

AWESOME!!
The most **IMPORTANT TEST** for adult Tusken males is to **SLAY A KRAYT DRAGON** and **CUT OUT** the precious **PEARL** from its **STOMACH**.

Tell me more!

IT'S A WRAP!
Tuskens **dress to survive**. They wrap up from head to toe in **ragged cloth** to shield themselves from Tatooine's **blazing sun** and **ferocious windstorms**. They also wear mouth grilles and eye coverings to **retain moisture** and **keep out sand**.

FAMILY TIES

TUSKEN RAIDER
Male Tuskens are the **warriors and hunters** of the clan. Their rough wrappings and garments **provide protection** and **allow easy movement**.

FEMALE TUSKENS
Tusken women **look after the camps**. They wear heavy veils over their head and shoulders, with **elaborately decorated face masks**.

TUSKEN CHILDREN
All Tusken kids **wear the same style** of clothes. They cannot dress like males or females until they reach adulthood.

STRANGE ...BUT TRUE
Tuskens are **forbidden to remove their clothing** in front of others, except at childbirth, on their wedding night, and at coming-of-age ceremonies.

Peek behind the scenes
Tuskens' barking speech was created by sound designer Ben Burtt using the sound of donkeys braying. Bantha cries were produced from slowed down bear roars.

INTELLIGENT BEINGS

DESERT WARRIORS
AND THEIR BANTHAS

Primitive Tusken Raiders **terrorize settlers** on Tatooine. Riding **huge banthas**, these **hostile Sand People strike** out of the Jundland Wastes, **slaying** or, even worse, **kidnapping their victims**.

GROSS!!
"BANTHA POODOO" is slang for anything you HATE, because BANTHA CHOW smells absolutely REVOLTING!

Fast Facts

HOMEWORLD: Tatooine

LEADERS: Clan leaders, tribal chiefs, warlords

AFFILIATION: None—all non-Tuskens are targets

STRENGTHS: Desert camouflage, sneak attacks

STRANGE ...BUT TRUE
After Anakin Skywalker **slaughters a Tusken tribe** for taking the life of his mother, Shmi, the Tuskens fear him as a **vengeful desert demon**. So they use **ritual sacrifices** to ward him off.

Tusken country
Although mostly nomadic, many **Tusken clans set up camp** in an area of the Jundland Wastes known as The Needles—a frightening, **no-go zone for outsiders**.

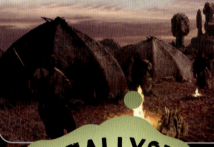

THE BANTHAS OF TATOOINE
Shaggy and elephant-like • Ridden and used for transportation • Tuskens cherish them and never harm or eat them (even if non-Tuskens do)

SACRED BOND
The **bond** between Tuskens and their banthas is **almost mystical**. Every boy has a male bantha to **train and ride** and every girl a female one. When Sand People marry, their banthas also mate, and should **its rider die**, a bantha usually **perishes soon after**.

▲ If a bantha dies before its rider, its body is placed in a **huge graveyard**, which Tuskens and other banthas treat with great respect.

REALLY?!
Though fierce, TUSKENS are easily SPOOKED into running away. But they'll SOON BE back on the ATTACK.

In numbers

20-30 Tuskens
In a clan group

15 years old
Age that a Tusken becomes adult

2.5m (8ft 2in)
Height of a bantha

1.9m (6ft 3in)
Height of a male Tusken

A GALAXY OF DROIDS

Droids of every shape, size, and service operate across the galaxy. From **menacing droidekas** and **efficient assassin droids** to **essential medical mechs** and **humble maintenance robots**, all droids have a role to play... even if it's not always in the best interests of their so-called "masters"!

AP-5 analyst droid
1.7m (5ft 7in)

TC-series protocol droid
1.67m (5ft 6in)

C1-10P astromech droid
0.99m (3ft 3in)

R2-M5 astromech droid
0.96m (3ft 2in)

BB-8 astromech droid
0.67m (2ft 2in)

R1-series astromech droid
1.94m (6ft 4in)

Imperial sentry droid
2m (6ft 7in)

Dismantler droid
3.1m (10ft 2in)

LEP servant droid
1.26m (4ft 2in)

IT-000 interrogator droid
1.5m (4ft 11in)

Viper probe droid
1.6m (5ft 3in)

PLNK-series power droid
1.37m (4ft 6in)

EV-9D9 supervisor droid
1.9m (6ft 3in)

SE-2 labor droid
1.79m (5ft 10in)

ID9 seeker droid
0.3m (0ft 12in)

2-1B surgical droid
1.5m (4ft 11in)

FX-7 medical assistant droid
1.7m (5ft 7in)

INTELLIGENT BEINGS

B2 super battle droid
1.93m (6ft 4in)

Droideka destroyer droid
1.83m (6ft)

DUM-series repair droid
1.19m (3ft 11in)

IG-88 assassin droid
1.96m (6ft 5in)

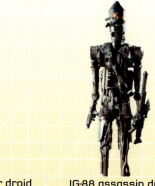
DSD1 dwarf spider droid
1.98m without antenna (6ft 6in)

LR-57 combat droid
2.58m (8ft 6in)

IT-O interrogator droid
0.3m (11.8in)

DLC-13 panning droid
1.5m (4ft 11in)

Huyang architect droid
1.8m (5ft 11in)

B1 battle droid
1.93m (6ft 4in)

Guardian police droid
1.82m (6ft)

LM-432 crab droid
1.49m (4ft 11in)

PZ-4CO protocol droid
2.06m (6ft 9in)

B-U4D starfighter
maintenance droid
1.75m (5ft 9in)

WED-15 Treadwell repair
droid 1.24m (4ft 1in)

RIC-920 labor droid
1.1m (3ft 7in)

K-2SO security droid
2.16m (7ft 1in)

NR-N99 Corporate Alliance
tank droid 10.96m (36ft)

WA-7 waitress droid
1.7m (5ft 7in)

RQ protocol droid
1.85m (6ft 1in)

4-LOM protocol droid
1.6m (5ft 3in)

J-1 proton cannon
6.46m (21ft 2in)

PK-series worker droid
1.46m (4ft 9in)

LIN demolition autonomous
minelayer mining droid
0.56m (1ft 10in)

Vulture starfighter droid
3.5m (11ft 6in)

OG-9 homing spider droid
7.32m (24ft)

163

MONSTERS

TOOTH AND CLAW

They don't carry blasters and they can't use the Force, but these beasts are amongst the most ferocious beings in the galaxy. Most people do their best to avoid these terrifying creatures, but some diabolical fiends like to keep them as pets!

Forget monsters—plants eat humans alive, too! Reeksa are giant carnivorous plants that grow on Iego. Their roots are used to create antidotes for the Blue Shadow Virus.

Big and bad!
All these beasts are larger than most species, but by far the biggest and most destructive is the gargantuan Zillo Beast.

How they size up

97m	Zillo Beast — 97m long (318ft 3in)
4.65m	Gor, the roggwart — 4.65m (15ft 3in)
3.7m	Gundark — 3.7m (12ft 2in)
2.74m	Krykna — 2.74m (9ft)
1.83m	Republic clone — 1.83m (6ft)

REALLY?!
Gutkurrs, native to Ryloth, like to SNACK ON TWI'LEKS using their sharp, curved claws to snare their prey.

Peek behind the scenes
The rancor is described as "a cross between a gorilla and a potato" by Monster Shop supervisor Phil Tippett.

"I wanna get off this planet now. This place is crawling with gundarks!"
BOUNTY HUNTER CASTAS ON THE PLANET VANQOR

COOL!
The Zillo Beast's SKIN is virtually INDESTRUCTIBLE— even a LIGHTSABER can't harm it!

Q: What's so special about the Zillo Beast?
A: There's only one! In ancient times, zillo beasts roamed freely on their homeworld, Malastare, where they devoured the local Dug population. The Dugs fought back and eventually destroyed all zillos, except for one.

Fast Facts

WATCH OUT FOR: Razor-sharp teeth

COOL FEATURES: Deadly claws and powerful arms to grab, scratch, and tear

FRIEND OR FOE: Everyone needs to beware of these beasts!

MONSTERS

STRANGE
...BUT TRUE
The Zillo Beast has **glowing green eyes** and can see in **total darkness**. It has lived underground for so long, the natives speak of it as a legend.

"I hate multi-leggers... more than two legs is just excessive!"
ZEB ORRELIOS

STRANGE
...BUT TRUE
General Grievous made his pet roggwart, **Gor**, even more dangerous by attaching sharp mechanical arms to the giant beast's back!

Q: Why should you run from a roggwart?
A: You need to ask? A roggwart has 20 piercing claws, a three-spiked tail, and a mouth rimmed with sharp teeth! And it's behind you!

REALLY?!
The role played by vicious, tentacled **RATHTARS** in the Trillia Massacre makes them **SUPER VALUABLE** to collectors throughout the galaxy!

Tell me more!
LOVE HURTS...
Jabba the Hutt's drooling rancor may love gobbling up **Gamorrean guards (armor and all)**, but the deadly beast is cherished by **his keeper**, Malakili. When Luke Skywalker eliminates the rancor, Malakili **weeps in sadness**!

In numbers
1,650kg (3,638lbs)
Average weight of a rancor

16 claws
On a gundark

8 eyes
On a krykna spider

2 horns
On a roggwart's head

WOW!...
60,000
Weight of the Zillo Beast in metric tons (132,277,357 pounds)

167

PETS

Fast Facts

- **BIG:** Anoobas—up to 2.7m (8ft 10in) long
- **SMALL:** Convor and Kiros birds—0.2m (8in) tall
- **FRIENDLY:** Convorees, Kiros birds, tookas, loth-cats
- **MEAN:** Anoobas, massiffs
- **POPULAR:** Monkey-lizards, Kiros birds, convorees

Queen Miraj Scintel's Kiros birds are highly **intelligent** and can understand **conversations**.

STRANGE ...BUT TRUE
Convorees are graceful little owls. Some see them as **omens of impending events** of importance—especially events **concerning the Force**.

Tell me more!

THE PERFECT PET...
Wild anoobas are dangerous, but some have been successfully tamed. Bounty hunter **Embo** has a pet **anooba** named **Marrok** who is very loyal to his master. It helps that Marrok is **small** and **lacks the deadly saber tooth** that juts out on the lower jaws of most anoobas!

Q: What is the difference between convorees and Kiros birds?
A: Convorees are **gold and brown**, and come from the **Wasskah moon**. Kiros birds are **purple and blue**, and live on the **planet Kiros**. Both have grabbing tails and are popular pets on many worlds.

WOW!...
119
The weight in kilograms that Jabba's frog-dog, Bubo, can pull with his tongue (262lbs)

Tookas are often kept aboard **starships**, where they are very handy for **hunting down pests** and **vermin**.

Peek behind the scenes
Tookas in The Clone Wars are named after "Tuuk," supervising director Dave Filoni's cat. They first appeared as toys in Season One.

Pets come in all **shapes, species, and personalities**. Kowakian monkey-lizards are **funny**. Tookas, Loth-cats, and convorees are **cute**. Frog-dogs are really **ugly**! But somebody loves them all.

MONSTERS

BEST KNOWN FOR HUNTING AHSOKA TANO ON CORUSCANT
Massiff

REALLY?!
Attark the Hoover looks like he wouldn't hurt a convor, but **AT NIGHT** he **STALKS** Jabba the Hutt's palace and **SUCKS PEOPLE'S BLOOD THROUGH HIS TRUNK!**

In numbers

60 credits
Selling price of a convor in Pons Ora, on Abafar

35kg (77lbs)
Weight of Bubo

28 teeth
In a tooka's mouth

12kg (26lbs)
Weight of a monkey-lizard

10-12 members
In an anooba pack

4 arms and 2 legs
On momongs and Hesten monkeys

Slobbering blarths
On Naboo, Gungans keep **lovable** pets called blarths. These fat amphibians have **long, grabbing tails** with **fine fingers** at the tip, which they use to catch their food in the **swamps**. Blarths have one really bad habit, however—they leave **large, slimy puddles of drool** all over the house!

Top 5 Pet foods

1. **WASSKAH CONVOREES** Eaten by **momongs** both in captivity and in the wild.
2. **PIKOBIS** Hunted by **tookas** in the Coruscant underworld.
3. **ESCAPED PRISONERS** Chomped on by **anoobas** at Osi Sobeck's citadel.
4. **GORGS** Gobbled up by **Bubo**—but he'd prefer to eat **Salacious Crumb**!
5. **ANYTHING THEY CAN STEAL** Nibbled by **monkey-lizards**, whenever their masters aren't looking!

MASTER AND PET

Hesten monkeys are caught by the **Balnab castaways**, who trap the **large-eared** critters in **nets**.

Kiros birds are raised by **Queen Miraj Scintel**. The Queen of Zygerria has a liking for **fancy, clever** pets.

Ryder Azadi, the former Governor of Lothal, keeps a loyal white Loth-cat. Its **wandering curiosity** leads Ezra to Ryder.

Massiffs are **powerful, dog-like reptiles** specially trained by **ARF clone troopers** as trackers.

Gwellis keeps a barghest named Izby. She looks **ghastly**, but she has a **sweet side**. Cookie agrees, and wants her on Maz's menu!

GROSS!!
SALACIOUS CRUMB sneaks **DRINKS** from **BIB FORTUNA'S CUP**, and sometimes **THROWS UP IN IT**, too!

Pilf Mukmuk
Pilf is pirate Hondo Ohnaka's **persistent pet**, who **eventually overcomes** Anakin and Obi-Wan after a crazy, failed first attempt.

Pikk Mukmuk
Pikk is Pilf's **brother** and also in Hondo's pirate gang. He **learns fast** and knows how to **drive a mean tank**.

FUNKY KOWAKIAN MONKEY-LIZARDS

Salacious B. Crumb
Salacious Crumb is Jabba's **gnarly court jester**. His **practical jokes** and **terrible table manners** win him few friends.

169

ARENA BEASTS

On the planet Geonosis, the vast Petranaki Arena is the main attraction. Crowds thrill to the sight of **ferocious beasts** unleashed on chained criminals, or forced to **fight each other to the death**.

The arena hosts plenty of **gruesome spectacles**! You can watch **gladiator-style combat** with beings pitted against beasts, **brutal sporting contests** between beasts, and **staged** battles to **show off** new military droids and weapons.

REALLY?!
Normally plant-eaters, arena reeks are fed **MEAT** to make them **AGGRESSIVE**!

Fast Facts

SPECIES: Acklay, reek, nexu, massiff, mongworst

ORIGINS: Some native, some offworld (bought or gifted and then bred on Geonosis)

VICTIMS: Criminals, guards, picadors—and other arena beasts!

UH-OH!
In the wild, the nexu uses its **INFRARED VISION** to track prey by body heat!

Top 3
Crowd favorites

1 NEXU
Agile, cat-like animal with four eyes, crushing jaws, vicious claws, and a whip-like forked tail.

2 ACKLAY
Part crustacean and part reptile, with sharp, claw-like legs. Tremendously strong!

3 REEK
Has long horns and a short temper. Charges victims and gores or tramples them.

STRANGE ...BUT TRUE
Reeks **change color** depending on what they eat! Arena reeks are **deep red** because of their rich meat diet. On other planets reek may be **brown, gray, or even yellow**.

MONSTERS

TOP 5
WAYS TO ESCAPE AN ARENA BEAST
1. Scramble to the top of an execution pillar.
2. Dodge its claws so it breaks your chains, instead of you. Then run like crazy!
3. Grab a picador's pike to fend off an attack.
4. Use the Force to control the beast.
5. Hope the Jedi sent to save you arrive in time!

PETRANAKI ARENA
Built in a natural rock hollow • Can be flooded for water battles • Named for an ancient art of combat • Tunnel links it to a secret droid factory

Executing criminals is cheaper than keeping them in prison. It's an electrifying spectacle for the crowd, too. You'll pay a fortune for a seat near the front!

"**Let the executions begin!**"
ARCHDUKE POGGLE THE LESSER

Q: Why are the heroes facing execution?
A: Anakin, Padmé, and Obi-Wan have been found **guilty of spying**—a crime that carries the **death sentence**! Obi-Wan is captured after following bounty hunter Jango Fett to Geonosis and **discovering the Separatists' plans**. Anakin and Padmé intercept his message to the Jedi Council and are caught as they **try to rescue him**.

Pick of the picadors
Picadors keep order in the vast arena, astride their **swift orrays**. These **powerful, reptilian** mounts are tamed by **removing their long stinger tails** and put to use **pulling carts** full of doomed criminals.

Peek behind the scenes
Obi-Wan's fight with the acklay was inspired by the 1961 movie *Mysterious Island*, in which a shipwrecked sailor battles a giant crab.

Lightly grilled **arch grubs** are a **popular snack food** at the execution arena. Yum!

WOW!...

100,000+
The number of spectators that the Petranaki Arena can hold

171

Fast Facts

HABITAT: Naboo swamps and wetlands
LARGEST: Fambaa
SMALLEST: Kaadu
MOST ORNERY: Falumpasets
ENEMIES: Separatist battle droids

BEST KNOWN FOR
"FAMBAA DELIGHT," AN OUTER RIM DISH MADE FROM... YOU GUESSED IT!
Fambaa

GREAT GRASS PLAINS

Site of conflict in Battle of Naboo • 40km (25 miles) from Theed • Fambaa-mounted energy shields enclose Gungan army • Nearby swamps provide cover for Gungans

Q: Which planet do fambaas and falumpasets come from?

A: Nobody knows for sure! Both species seem equally at home on **Naboo and Onderon**. Biologists think **Naboo traders** brought the beasts to Onderon long ago, though **fossil evidence** is thin on the ground.

Tell me more!

FROM MINUSCULE TO MIGHTY
Baby fambaas hatch from eggs laid in wetlands, emerging with **gills like a tadpole**. Believe it or not, these **plump, soft-bodied amphibians** will grow into the **scaly juggernauts** the Gungans rely on to carry their shield generators into battle.

The **stilt-like legs** of falumpasets help them to turn quickly, making them ideal for **hauling heavy artillery**.

STRANGE ...BUT TRUE

Wild **fambaas** don't stretch up to reach the **leaves they love to feed on**. They'd rather **pull down** the whole tree and munch away in comfort!

REALLY?!

Gungans LOOK AFTER their battle beasts *very* well, even housing them in BUBBLE-PROTECTED STABLES.

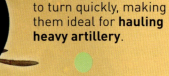

In numbers

1,000+ beasts
Estimated number of battle-ready animals in the Gungan Grand Army

100km (62 miles)
Echo distance of a falumpaset bellow

10-12 members
In a fambaa herd

6-8 eggs
Laid by a kaadu mother

2 fambaas
To generate an energy shield (each carries one of its parts)

Q: Why are these beasts so great in battles?

A: They **never back down**! The beasts of the famous Gungan Grand Army will **do anything** for their **masters**—even sacrifice their own lives. Raised from young hatchlings, they form very **strong bonds** with their owners.

WOW!...

100

Maximum number of kaadu in a flock (always single-gender)

COOL!!

CAPTAIN TARPALS of the Gungan Grand Army decorates his kaadu "Swamptoe" with **HUGE FEATHERS** it has won as race trophies.

TOP 3 USES IN BATTLE
1. **Fambaas**—carry shield generators and booma cannons.
2. **Falumpasets**—pull huge battle wagons.
3. **Kaadu**—make the most loyal cavalry mounts.

STRANGE ...BUT TRUE
Kaadu are **reptavians: part reptile, part bird**. These **duckbilled creatures** have **no wings**, but **long legs and sleek hides** to help them move swiftly on **land and in water**.

CHARGE!

The ground **rumbles under their feet** as they approach. These big, bad, and, to some, beautiful creatures, are trained in combat by the peace-loving Gungans for self-defense. So when war breaks out—bring on the **battle beasts**!

Peek behind the scenes
The kaadu snorts were created by slowing down a mix of **pig noises** with the sound of **whales** spouting water through their blowholes.

Fambaa — 4.3m (14.1ft)

Falumpaset — 3m (9.8ft)

Kaadu — 2.2m (7.4ft)

Combat creature lineup — Naboo's swamp beasts are **large and powerful**. Best not try to cuddle one—at least when it's **fired up for battle**!

NABOO ABYSS

Natural tunnels run from Naboo's surface to the core • The water-filled tunnels are used by Gungans for travel • Fearsome sea monsters lurk deep in the Abyss

Tell me more!

LEARN YOUR SCALEFISH
The waters around Otoh Gunga teem with **seven species of scalefish**—doo, ray, mee, faa, soo, laa, and tee. Some also **live in the depths of the Naboo Abyss**. Humans and Gungans feast on certain varieties, but the great **sea beasts are less fussy, and will eat any they catch**.

BEST KNOWN FOR
ALMOST SWALLOWING QUI-GON JINN'S SUBMARINE
Sando aqua monster

Peek behind the scenes
Early designs for the colo claw fish were based on an earwig. Later, features from a crocodile and a moray eel were added to the design.

Sando aqua monsters are more **terrifying myth than reality** for most Naboo. They have **never been seen** in the wild, and only **a few carcasses have washed up** on the planet's shores.

Q: Why do Jedi travel through the Abyss?
A: Gungan leader **Boss Nass** tells them that the Abyss tunnels are the **fastest way** to reach **Theed**, on the other side of Naboo. Nass hopes the **deadly monsters of the Abyss will devour the Jedi** and their navigator, Jar Jar Binks, to avoid Nass getting involved in the crisis on the planet's surface.

WOW!...

54,000

Average weight of a sando aqua monster in metric tons (119,049,622 pounds)

MONSTERS FROM THE DEEP

Take a big breath... we're diving deep into Naboo's **dangerous waters**. Here, **savage sea creatures stalk easy prey,** as Qui-Gon Jinn and Obi-Wan Kenobi quickly discover **to their peril!**

Tiny yobshrimp **live in the gills** of tee scalefish, but not for long. These tasty morsels are **licked out and eaten** by laa scalefish.

MONSTERS

STRANGE
...BUT TRUE
Opee sea killers **zip** through the water by **jet propulsion**! They **suck water** in through their **mouths** and **squirt** it out from small vents at the **rear of their bodies**, like a natural jet engine.

WHO EATS WHAT?

SANDO AQUA MONSTER eats...
↓   ↓
COLO CLAW FISH eats...   **OPEE SEA KILLER** eats...
↓
SCALEFISH: Doo, ray, mee, faa, soo, laa, tee. And the laa eats... → **YOBSHRIMP** Dish of the day!

The monstrous sando rules the Naboo Abyss. As the top predator, it eats anything it catches. And so it goes, as larger creatures eat smaller ones, all the way down to the tiny yobshrimp.

In numbers
160m (524ft 11in) Length of a male sando aqua monster
100 years Lifespan of a sando
40m (131ft 3in) Length of a colo claw fish
20m (65ft 6in) Length of an opee sea killer

A male opee sea killer **carries its mate's eggs in its mouth** for around three months. So, it **must not eat anything** until the young are born!

Top 3
Scary sea beast attacks

1 SANDO Grabs and holds prey in its huge, powerful arms, before tearing off its victim's head.

2 COLO Stuns prey with an intense hydrosonic screech, and then leaps from its lair to catch a meal with its vicious claws.

3 OPEE Clings quietly to rocky outcrops, and lures prey in with its worm-like antennae, before striking with its long tongue.

Fast Facts
HABITAT: Naboo Abyss
LARGEST: Sando aqua monster
SMALLEST: Opee sea killer
WATCH OUT FOR:
Sando: Huge mouth, strong arms
Colo claw: Lethal fangs, claws
Opee: Long, sticky tongue

REALLY?!
If eaten, young opees can **CHEW THEIR WAY** out of a colo claw fish's **STOMACH**, destroying the larger predator.

A colo claw fish can swallow prey **larger than its own head** by **unhinging** its jaw! It can also **expand its stomach** to enjoy a very big fish dinner.

"There's *always* a bigger fish."
QUI-GON, ON THE RUN!

GUNGAN STYLE
The tribubble bongo sub looks like a sea creature. Its hull is **grown from coral** using secret technology, and **tentacle-like fins** propel it along. **Organic bubble-shields**, like those around Gungan cities, keep the sub dry inside.

175

HITCHING A RIDE

REALLY?! DEWBACKS get their name because they **LICK** the **MORNING DEW** off their **BACKS**.

In peacetime or on the fields of battle, **beasts of burden** move people and goods throughout the galaxy. From **bountiful banthas** to **swooping rupings**, these creatures prove their strength, time and again.

Fast Facts

HABITATS: Deserts, frozen wastes, and swamps, to name a few
BEWARE OF: The ronto's nervousness
LARGEST: Ruping (counting wingspan)
SMALLEST: Eopie
SMELLIEST: Tauntaun
FRIEND OR FOE: Friend, if well fed!

Q: Why are rontos so easily spooked?
A: Although rontos have excellent hearing and a superb sense of smell, their **eyesight is poor**, which is why they are startled by **sudden movements**.

In numbers

12,000lbs (5,443kg) Average weight of an adult male happabore

90kph (56mph) Top speed that tauntauns can run on Hoth's icy plains

50-85 eggs Laid by a female dewback each year

20+ eopies Live in a herd

14.8m (48ft 5in) Wingspan of a ruping

5 Teedos Reasonable maximum luggabeast passenger load

BANTHAS—WASTE NOT, WANT NOT

Banthas are more than a reliable means of transportation—the whole beast is put to good use.

1. FOOD
Female banthas produce a **rich blue milk**, which is used in **ice cream, yogurt, and butter**. Their **meat** is also sought after for **dried jerky, steaks, and burgers**, often cooked using **fuel** made from **dried bantha dung**!

3. OTHER USES
The **rest of the hide** is tanned and turned into **clothes or furniture**.

Peek behind the scenes
Sandtroopers rode camels while filming *Rogue One* in Jordan. They were to be digitally replaced with tall striding beasts with long, flat heads. One is seen in Jedha City.

2. DRINK
Thirsty? Bantha-blood fizz is a sparkling beverage made from **purified bantha blood**! Bantha hides can also be **mashed** with fermented grains to create the bitter drink **Ardees**, aka "Jawa Juice."

Dewbacks are **large reptiles** native to Tatooine's Dune Sea. Well-suited to the planet's **harsh climate** and easy to tame, they are **highly dependable** beasts of burden.

MONSTERS

BEST KNOWN FOR

THROWING OFF RIDERS WHEN STARTLED

Rontos

Jawas **love to use rontos** for transportation. Valued for their **loyalty and strength**, these gigantic but jumpy beasts not only lug huge weights, but are also big enough to **scare off Tusken Raiders**—if they don't get frightened first.

Rupings are fast and nimble **reptile-bird creatures** used by rebels as **battle mounts** to help secure their victory at the Battle of Onderon.

WOW!...

90

The average lifespan of an eopie in years, if cared for.

Tell me more!

GROUCHY EOPIES

Eopies are grumpy critters that **snort and break wind** if their load is too heavy. Despite this, Tatooine's moisture farmers depend on eopies as pack animals to **carry them and their belongings** in the blazing desert sun, as they always **get the job done**.

Q: Why do tauntauns smell so bad?

A: These swift-footed snow lizards have **layers of fatty blubber** that allow them to **control their body temperature** and withstand the **intense cold** on Hoth. Unfortunately, the blubber's **strong odors** really **get up the noses** of their human riders!

STRANGE ...BUT TRUE

Luggabeasts are **cybernetically-enhanced** beasts that are used on harsh worlds like **Jakku**. They have **cyborg implants**, which mean that they can perform **beyond normal limits**. They do not need to eat or drink as they are fed nutrients through wires.

TOP 3

DEWBACK TREATS

1. **Tubers**—in the Dune Sea.
2. **Grass patches**—found in rare desert oases.
3. **Womp rats**—found in swamps, Beggar's Canyon, and the Jundland Wastes.

Fast Facts

HABITAT: Ice fields, snowy plains, mountains

FRIENDLY: Tauntaun, white bantha, mastmot

HOSTILE: Wampa, horax

UNPREDICTABLE: Narglatch, tibidee

> "I thought they smelled bad… on the *outside*!"
> **HAN SOLO ON SLICING OPEN A TAUNTAUN**

ICE BEASTS!

Wild **wampas** and tame **tauntauns** roam across the frozen wastes of **Hoth**. On snowy **Orto Plutonia**, a colony of furry Talz breed **fierce narglatch** to survive.

In numbers

150kg (330lbs 7oz)
Average weight of an adult wampa

25 members
In a average tauntaun herd

15 species
Of tauntaun known to exist

6.23m (20ft 5in)
Length of a narglatch, including tail

Top 4
Other creatures of frozen worlds

1. **HORAXES OF NELVAAN**
Giant blue reptiles with saber-sharp fangs and enormous horns.

2. **MASTMOTS OF TOOLA**
Massive, furry beasts of burden whose tusks are prized as necklaces.

3. **WHITE BANTHAS OF NELVAAN**
Large, hairy pack animals with long black horns.

4. **TIBIDEES OF STYGEON PRIME**
Flying critters that detect frequencies and once mistook the *Phantom*'s jamming signal as a mating call.

SCALES OF HONOR
The Nelvaanians make a **special elixir** from the **scales of a horax tail**, the smell of which can **repel the gigantic beasts** for a year. It becomes a perilous **initiation ritual** for young males to **obtain a horax scale** and join the ranks of their tribe's greatest warriors.

Q: How do tauntauns survive the cold?

A: Thick blubber! Plus, tauntauns live in **glacial caves** and **grottos**, where heat from the planet's core keeps them warm. Sunlight passes through the ice into their caves, **allowing lichen and small ice plants to grow**, which feed the tauntaun herds.

GROSS!!
Han crams an injured Luke inside **A DEAD, STEAMING TAUNTAUN'S BELLY** to prevent him from freezing to death!

MONSTERS

Tell me more!

MAKE THE MOST OF YOUR NARGLATCH
The primitive **Talz** of icy Orto Plutonia rely on their **narglatch** for nearly everything. Not only do they **ride them as transportation**, but they also use their **meat for food**, their **skins for clothing**, and their **bones for building shelter and tools**.

STRANGE ...BUT TRUE
Trandoshans are **great hunters** and keep **trophies** such as **stuffed narglatch** and **wampa hide** at their lodge on Wasskah.

HUNTERS AND COLLECTORS
Narglatch males and females only ever gather together in pairs to mate. Although **female narglatch are fiercer hunters than males**, they are **easily chased away** from their slain prey by opportunistic males.

REALLY?!
Jabba the Hutt keeps a **STUFFED TAUNTAUN HEAD** in his palace, beside a frozen Han Solo.

WOW!...
200
Maximum recorded weight of an adult wampa in kilograms (441 pounds)

Peek behind the scenes
For The Empire Strikes Back Special Edition, new shots were added with effects artist Howie Weed in a wampa costume. A scaled-down ice cave set gave the illusion that the wampa was huge!

SNOW LIZARDS
Tauntauns have **scaly skin** beneath their heavy fur and **secrete thick, smelly oils to attract mates**. They have **long claws** to help them **climb icy surfaces** and **scrape away lichen**. Their large **horns** are used for **combat** and their **tails** help them to keep **balance** when **running fast**.

BEST KNOWN FOR
HANGING LUKE IN ITS CAVE
Wampa

DEATH BY WAMPA
1. **ATTACK** Ambushes and stuns its unsuspecting quarry.
2. **DRAG** Lugs its prey's limp body back to its cave.
3. **HANG** Suspends its victim upside down to gnaw at later.
4. **EAT** Devours the prey at its leisure—frozen or fresh.

179

Fast Facts

HABITATS: Deep space, asteroid belts

SIZE: Ranges from enormous exogorth space slugs to tiny mynocks

FRIEND OR FOE: Foe, unless you know how to handle the Force

In numbers

10,000 years
Maximum lifespan of an exogorth

1,674m (5,492ft)
Wingspan of the largest neebray mantas

900m (2,953ft)
Length of the largest space slugs (big enough to swallow a starship whole!)

45 teeth
In an exogorth's mouth

3 babies
In a neebray litter

1.5m (4.9ft)
Average length of a fyrnock

Tell me more!

A FRIENDLY FYRNOCK?

While fyrnocks are usually hostile, Ezra Bridger uses his **Force affinity with animals**, and a hint of the **dark side**, to **summon and communicate** with a giant fyrnock at Fort Anaxes. He persuades it to **attack** the Inquisitor and his group of stormtroopers.

Peek behind the scenes
Huge slabs of beef fat and dozens of raw eggs being walked on were used to create the squelchy sounds of the Millennium Falcon crew's footsteps as they trudged through the insides of a space slug!

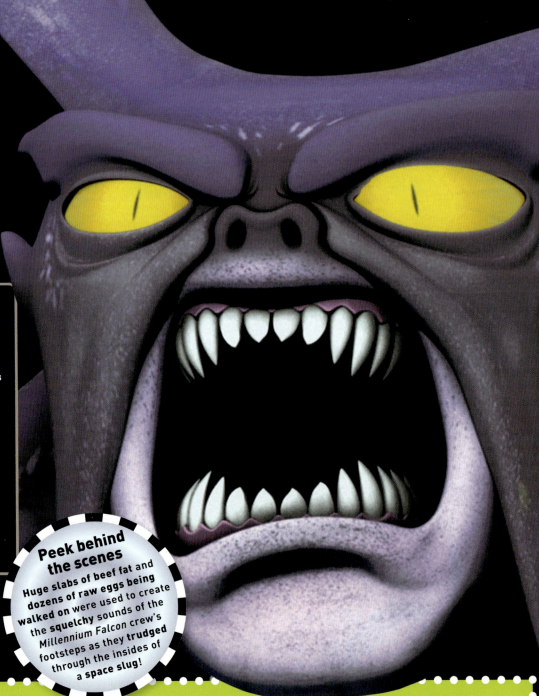

SPACE INVADERS

They say in space no one can hear you **scream**. Don't you believe it! Some of the **deadliest creatures** in the galaxy live in the **wilds of space**, where they **pounce on** unwary travelers.

MONSTERS

BEST KNOWN FOR ALMOST EATING THE MILLENNIUM FALCON
Exogorth space slug

The ever-hungry space slugs that lie inside asteroids with **their mouths open** can be mistaken for natural caves. But most pilots only **make that mistake once**!

Q: Do these monsters only live in deep space?
A: No. Some species, like **mynocks** and **neebray**, can live both **in space** and in the **atmospheres of planets**, where they fly around **like birds**. Only a few varieties of mynock live on planets.

TOP 4
BEASTS YOU DO NOT WANT TO MEET IN SPACE
1. **Exogorth space slugs**—sharp-toothed giants that will take a **big bite** out of your spacecraft.
2. **Giant neebray mantas**—don't fly through their nesting grounds, or you'll get **knocked silly** by them.
3. **Fyrnocks**—they hate sunlight, but are **ferocious night predators**.
4. **Mynocks**—these bat-like parasites chew through a spacecraft's power cables and drain the ship's energy.

> "This is no cave!"
> **HAN SOLO, WHEN HE REALIZES HE HAS LANDED INSIDE A SPACE SLUG!**

Top 5
Yummy space monster treats

1. **STELLAR RADIATIONS** Different types of radiation emitted into space by stars and absorbed through skin.
2. **INTERSTELLAR GASES** Invisible gases (like hydrogen) that float between the stars and are sucked through the mouth.
3. **ASTEROIDS AND SPACE ROCKS** Packed with tasty minerals and metals.
4. **OTHER SPACE MONSTERS** Space slugs need their daily dietary allowance of mynocks.
5. **PASSING SPACECRAFT** Always tempting as a last-minute snack or a full meal (depending on the ship's size).

REALLY?!
Mynocks **SWALLOWED** whole by space slugs can **SURVIVE INSIDE THEM** for years as **PARASITES**, before being digested.

Mynock on the menu
When properly prepared and seasoned, silicon-based mynocks can be eaten by carbon-based life-forms.

Mynock Cloud City and **Mynock Coronet City** are spicy dishes popular with Twi'leks.

Professional **mynock hunters stalk and slaughter** these flying pests, to supply space stations and colonists with regular meat rations. Mynock flesh tastes **strong and bitter** to humans, who only consume it when there's **nothing else left in the fridge**!

TODAY'S SPECIALS!

HOME AMONG THE STARS

HOTH ASTEROID BELT
Beware of mynocks and exogorths that live in this dangerous asteroid belt—it has become the graveyard of many different ships.

KALIIDA NEBULA
This magnificent interstellar cloud is one of the main nesting grounds for the giant neebray mantas. Disturb them at your peril!

FORT ANAXES ASTEROID
Fyrnocks and giant fyrnocks now run amok on this strategic asteroid, which once housed the Republic's Fort Anaxes listening post.

STRANGE ...BUT TRUE
Mynocks and space slugs reproduce by **splitting in two** and **growing new creatures from each half**!

RUPING

BEST KNOWN FOR
SENSITIVE EARS AND FOUR EYES
Rupings

In numbers

95 teeth
Inside a dactillion's mouth

24m (82ft)
Wingspan of a dactillion

9 x its own weight
The amount a bogwing can carry

6 eyes
On a xandu

0.8m (2ft 7in)
Wingspan of a carrier butterfly

Peek behind the scenes
Did you know the ruping is named after *The Clone Wars* concept artist Tara Rueping, who designed the creature?

Dactillions used to gobble up the native Utapauns—until they were tamed using fresh meat!

METALLIC MEALS
Steelpeckers found a perfect home on Jakku, where they **feast** on **scrap metal**. Their talons are **tipped with iron**.

XANDU USE THEIR GIANT EARS TO HEAR PREY AT GREAT DISTANCES.

Can-cells are attracted to the **buzzing sound** of Wookiee catamarans and gather near landing pads.

How do Zygerrian slavers **chase** their **runaway slaves**? By riding brezaks, of course!

REALLY?!
Banshees live on the planet Umbara, a world with little sunlight. The banshees themselves actually **GLOW GREEN**!

WHO KNEW?!
Carrier butterflies serve as **TINY MESSENGERS** on Maridun. They listen to their owners' instructions and **DELIVER** messages to allies.

Tell me more!

CUTE BUT LETHAL
Think convorees look harmless? Think again! These feathery birds **work in pairs** to lift their predators **high up into the air** and drop them crashing to the ground!

WINGED WONDERS

From the **tiny carrier butterfly** to the **nasty banshee**, these astonishing beasts **swoop through the skies** of strange planets in every corner of the galaxy.

Dactillions live in the **giant sinkholes** of Utapau, but fly to the surface when **looking for a mate**.

COOL!!
Gungans release bogwings into the skies to **SIGNAL HALF TIME** at **GULLIBALL GAMES**!

WOW!...
400
The top flying speed of a dactillion in kph (248mph)

STRANGE
...BUT TRUE
Xandu snatch up prey and **smash it against rock walls** using their two arms and two legs. They fly through the skies of lego using **four wings**.

BREZAK

STRANGE
...BUT TRUE
Brezaks are **giant flying lizards** from Zygerria. They don't have wings—instead they use **skin flaps** that help them glide long distances.

Tell me more!
GOOD LUCK CHARMS
Wookiees believe that seeing a **can-cell** brings **good luck**, and often keep them as pets. The odd-looking creatures are also the inspiration for the Wookiees' **fluttercraft** vehicle.

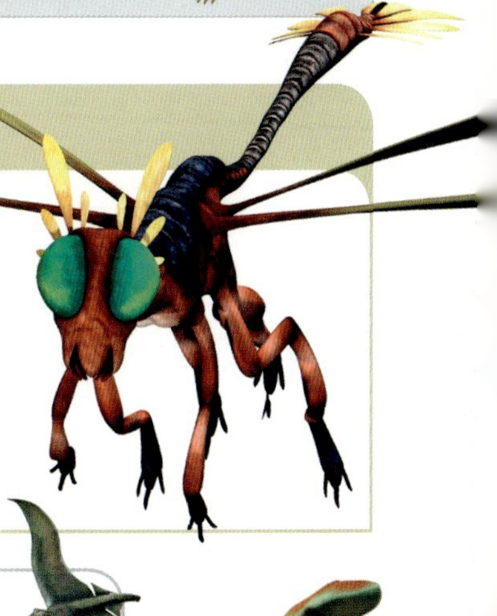

What can swim in the sea **and** zoom through the air? Aiwhas—their cool **wing-fins** allow them to **launch** straight from water to air.

MONSTERS

CREEPY-CRAWLIES

Bugs, slugs, worms, and warts: The galaxy teems with **creepy pests** that **crawl, slither, and slink** around, **spooking** all in their path!

Peek behind the scenes
The sound of the kouhun is partially made from squishing the inside of a grapefruit.

In numbers

20m (65ft 7in)
Length of a mature nightwatcher worm

10m (32ft 8in)
The largest duracrete slugs

8 legs
On a rock wart

4 eyes
On a rock wart

1 long, sharp stinger
On a kouhun

COOL!!
Duracrete slugs munch on sturdy duracrete used to make buildings, which then **OOZES** from their bodies and **HARDENS** to form their **ARMOR-LIKE SKIN**!

GROSS!!
Rock warts use their **POISONOUS BITE** to **KILL** a victim and then **LAY EGGS** inside their body!

REALLY?!
The bright blue slug-beetle from Naboo is a **GUNGAN DELICACY**! These chewy treats are only found under the perlote tree in Naboo's eastern **SWAMPS**.

MONSTERS

BEST KNOWN FOR
BEING JANGO FETT'S POISON OF CHOICE!
Kouhun venom

STRANGE
...BUT TRUE
Conduit worms have been known to **sneak onto starships** and **eat the electrical wiring** while the ship is still in flight!

NO WAY!!
Red-eyed nightwatcher worms lie deep under the sands of Jakku. Their stomachs contain ACID powerful enough to MELT METAL.

AWESOME!!
Geonosian brain worms **SQUIRM UP THE NOSES** of their victims —dead or alive— to **CONTROL THEIR MINDS!**

Fast Facts

HABITAT: These great survivors adapt to many environments

DEADLY FEATURES: Poison in rock warts and kouhuns, chomping teeth of womp rats

FRIEND OR FOE: Mostly just pests, but some can be deadly

STRANGE
...BUT TRUE
Womp rats **hunt in packs**, seizing prey with their **big, sharp fangs**. When alone, they are happy to **devour moisture farmers' garbage!**

Q: How do you stop a brain worm?
A: Freeze it! Brain worms **hate extreme cold** and can be **frozen** to stop their spread, even after they have infested someone.

On their swamp world Indoumodo, deep in Wild Space, kouhuns **HUNT CREATURES AS BIG AS DOGS!**

In numbers

5 or 6 pikobis
Travel in a group

4 arms
On a momong

2 sharp tusks
On a skalder

1 nuna
To feed a family of four

"Deep fried nuna leg! Mmm, delicious!"
SENATOR ORN FREE TAA, ABOUT TO DEVOUR A PLATE OF FRIED NUNA

REALLY?!
The armless nuna is the only animal used as a **BALL** in the aptly named **SPORT**, "nuna-ball"!

STRANGE

...BUT TRUE
Ikopi have **hollow tongues** two to three times longer than their heads! They use them like straws, to **suck up water and nectar** located in high places.

When angry or intimidated, the nuna can **inflate its body** to a larger size!

Motts give birth to **15 young at a time!**

Ikopi (not including its tongue) — 3.5m (11ft 6in)
Skalder — 3.5m (11ft 6in)
Shaak — 1.8m (5ft 11in)
Mott — 1.1m (3ft 7in)
Nuna — 0.5m (1ft 8in)

Size matters — When it comes to **survival**, it is often how big you are that determines whether you're **ridden, eaten, or both**.

Peek behind the scenes
Concept artist Terryl Whitlatch designed the shaak to be the Star Wars version of a sheep!

CRAZY CRITTERS

From the **hulking skalder** to the **waddling nuna**, the galaxy's land beasts are **weird, wonderful,** and full of **strange surprises!**

MONSTERS

BEST KNOWN FOR BLASTER-RESISTANT SKIN!
Skalders

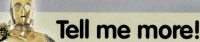

Tell me more!

MOUNT UP!
Wild skalders **aren't usually ridden as mounts**. However, when Jar Jar Binks and his clone trooper allies are stranded during a mission on planet Florrum, they ride the **surprisingly fast** beasts to reach civilization!

REALLY?!
Pesky dokma **SNEAK** onto the *Ghost* to hide from spider-like krykna—but they must run from Chopper instead, who makes it his mission to **REMOVE THE PESTS!**

STRANGE ...BUT TRUE
A shaak is **so plump** and its legs so weak, it can **barely stay upright!**

Q: What lives on the remote desert planet of Abafar?
A: Not much! Nimble **void striders** with **long necks and thin legs** are native to Abafar. They **run in large packs** across the featureless planet, searching for water.

Porgs are talented **mimics**. If someone is in an angry mood, they become very **scrappy**!

HUFF'N'PUFF
The placid puffer pig has a great **nose for precious minerals**... and trouble! Their amazing schnozzes make them a **prized item for smugglers**. Don't scare them though—if they sense danger, they can **puff up to three times** their normal size, and keep going depending on the level of threat!

[WHAT'S FOR DINNER?]

SHAAK—Slow-moving herbivore that grazes on the grasslands of Naboo.
NUNA—Armless omnivore that eats plants and, on rare occasions, fish.
MOTT—Horn-nosed herbivore from Naboo that eats swamp vegetation.
MOMONG—Carnivore that loves the feathered delicacy, fresh convor.
SKALDER—Lumbering herbivore that uses its tusks to dig up roots on Florrum.
IKOPI—Long-legged herbivore that elongates its tongue to slurp up water or nectar.
PIKOBI—Small, fast carnivore that eats tinier creatures in one gulp!

LOOK OUT BELOW!
Shaaks sometimes **slip into rivers** or get swept down Naboo's majestic waterfalls. Their **fatty bodies** help them **survive the fall and float** until they reach land!

Fast Facts
SPECIES NAME: Shaak
HABITAT: Grassy plains where food is plentiful
BEWARE OF: Being squashed by stampedes, when shaak herds are alarmed!
FRIEND OR FOE: Friend; these timid creatures are rarely dangerous to humans

A CONVOR IN THE HAND...
Momongs are **mischievous, monkey-like creatures** that live on the Trandoshan moon of Wasskah, where they **prey on yellow convor birds**—but not always successfully. On one memorable occasion, a greedy momong tries to snatch several convorees outside Ahsoka Tano's base on Wasskah. It fails— only to be **picked up** by its intended victims and **flung off the tree**!

Fast Facts

SURFACE FEEDERS: Sarlaccs and vixus wait for prey to come to them

TRANSPORTS: Milodons carry people and goods over long distances

WATER DWELLERS: Nos monsters live in deep, murky water

FEROCIOUS HUNTERS: Rishi eels stalk victims and pounce suddenly

REALLY?!
Joopas are the **TASTY MEALS** that bite back! A trio of clones use Zeb as bait to catch one!

Milodons muster in deep crystal caves on Quarzite.

Vixus vanquish prey during Umbara's endless nights.

Nos monsters nest in deep sinkholes on Utapau.

Sarlaccs survive in the harsh deserts of Tatooine.

Joopas are giant worms living beneath salt flats on Seelos.

WHO LIVES WHERE?

GROSS!!
Sarlaccs eat slowly. **THEY KEEP THEIR VICTIMS ALIVE**, gradually **DIGESTING** their **BODIES** for **1,000 YEARS!**

"Victims of the almighty Sarlacc: His Excellency hopes you will die honorably."
C-3PO TRANSLATING FOR JABBA

TOP 5
MONSTROUS HABITS
1. All grab food from above ground.
2. Most scavenge, hunt, or trap.
3. Most can sense vibrations.
4. Some can light up their bodies.
5. Many lack eyes or are nearly blind.

In numbers

100m (328ft) Average length of a female Sarlacc

80 teeth In a bonzami mouth

24 legs On a milodon (plus pincers and feelers)

19 eyes On top of a joopa's head

7 tentacles On a vixus (plus a long, taloned tongue)

3 pairs of mandibles Straddle a joopa's upper and lower jaw

Tell me more!

CATCHING TRAINS
The **Kage Warriors** of Quarzite ride **scampering, multi-legged milodons** through caves beneath the planet's surface. They even use a milodon to catch and board a racing subtram, or **underground train**, to rescue the captive warrior **Pluma Sodi**.

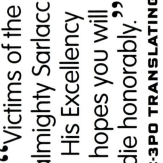

STRANGE ...BUT TRUE
Baby Sarlaccs stay on the surface and only dig below ground when they reach adulthood. While female sarlaccs are large, males are tiny and live as **parasites**, permanently attached to them.

MONSTERS

TERROR BELOW!

Monsters are everywhere—in the seas, the skies, or deep in the forest. But they also live just under your feet, ready to attack!

The Sarlacc is a terrifying, plant-like omnivore that becomes Jabba the Hutt's favorite pet.

Top 5
Sarlacc dinners

1. **POTE SNITKIN** Skrilling skiff pilot and weapons dealer.
2. **BOBA FETT** Human bounty hunter.
3. **BARADA** Klatooinian slave and mechanic.
4. **VELKEN TEZERI** Human guard and weapons dealer.
5. **VEDAIN** Nikto slave and skiff pilot.

WOW!...
50,000
Lifespan of a Sarlacc in years

Peek behind the scenes
The Sarlacc sounds were made by combining the noise of hissing alligators with a rumbling tummies of the film crew, after a pizza for lunch.

AWESOME!!
Clone troopers only DEFEAT THE VIXUS by dropping THERMAL DETONATORS into its STOMACH.

The vixus uses its **disguised, vine-like tentacles** to pull its victims into its **toothy maw**.

Bonzami are terrifying **armored beasts** living below the surface on **Bahryn** (a moon orbiting Geonosis). This nightmarish creature isn't all bad though—it actually inspires **Zeb and Kallus** to work together so they don't get eaten!

SPOT THE DIFFERENCE

VIXUS vs. SARLACC

VIXUS
- Long, thin, clawed tongue
- Opens and closes mouth
- Blue and purple tentacles
- Short teeth
- Glows from within the gut
- Rests mouth above ground
- Grabs prey and drops in mouth

SARLACC
- Stumpy, broad, beaked tongue
- Always has mouth open
- Brown and pink tentacles
- Long teeth
- Complete darkness inside gut
- Rests mouth on pit floors
- Lets prey mostly fall into mouth

Which **mysterious structures** can be found all over the planet of **Naboo**?

IN A GALAXY FAR, FAR AWAY.....

How does the Empire **damage** the **environment** on **Lothal**?

What is the *Millennium Falcon*'s **computer** made of?

CHAPTER 4

PLANETARY SYSTEMS ACROSS THE GALAXY

Fast Facts

INHABITANTS: Tusken Raiders, Jawas, Hutts, humans

MAJOR CITIES: Mos Eisley, Mos Espa, Anchorhead

LANGUAGES: Many, including Huttese, Basic, Bocce, Tusken, Jawaese

TOP 3
TRANSPORT FORMS
1. **Podracers**—very popular with locals and tourists alike.
2. **Beasts**—ridden in the city streets and deserts.
3. **Landspeeders**—hover above ground.

LAWLESS LAND

Tatooine

Life is tough on the **desert planet** of Tatooine. From market traders to moisture farmers, everybody faces **water shortages**, constant **sand storms**, and **intense heat**.

Q: What is Tatooine famous for?

A: **Gambling, crime, and slavery**, of course! Tatooine is controlled by **gangsters** known as the Hutts during the time of the Republic. Later on, the planet falls under the control of the Empire, but it is still **famous** for being **lawless!**

10 WAYS TO DIE ON TATOOINE...

1. Dehydrated in the Dune Sea
2. Swallowed by the Sarlacc
3. Gnawed on by anoobas
4. Blasted by bounty hunters
5. Run over by rontos
6. Chewed up by Jabba's rancor
7. Beaten by Tusken Raiders
8. Pulverized by Ponda Baba
9. Crashed in a podrace
10. Sunstroke in the Jundland Wastes

In numbers

43,000 light years
Distance from the Galactic Core

10,465km (6,503 miles)
Diameter of Tatooine

304 days
In a year on Tatooine

3 moons
Ghomrassen, Guermessa, and Chenini

2 suns
Tatoo I and Tatoo II

1%
Surface water

Peek behind the scenes
Tunisia, as well as Death Valley and the Buttercup Valley desert in California, stood in for Tatooine during location shoots on Episodes IV and VI.

Bantha — 2.5m (8ft 2in)
Dewback — 2.0m (6ft 7in)
Eopie — 1.75m (5ft 9in)

Native wildlife size chart
From monstrous to minuscule, Tatooine boasts an impressive array of wildlife!

PLANETARY SYSTEMS ACROSS THE GALAXY

WOW!...

800+

Maximum speed podracers can fly in kph (500+ mph)

MOS EISLEY
Famous starport town • 362 starship docking bays • Much of town lies underground

"...wretched hive of scum and villainy."
OBI-WAN KENOBI ON MOS EISLEY

Luke Skywalker isn't the only one with **Tusken troubles**. When Ezra Bridger comes looking for Kenobi, he and Chopper are attacked by Tuskens. Maul ends up **saving them**.

REALLY?! Bobbajo's Tatooine pet **WORRT** has venom strong enough to **SLAY A BANTHA!**

Top 6 drinks at the
Mos Eisley Cantina

BLUE MILK
(bantha milk)

TATOOINE SUNSET
(fermented fruit beverage)

JAWA JUICE
(aka Ardees: fermented bantha hide)

YATOONI BOSKA
(fermented dewback sweat)

TATOONI JUNKO
(powerful Hutt drink)

HUTT'S DELIGHT
(colorful slurry of aquatic organisms)

How to say "Hello!" on Tatooine

"ARRGH!"
TUSKEN

"H'CHU APENKEE!"
HUTTESE

"JETTOZ!"
BOCCE

"M'UM M'ALOO!"
JAWAESE

STRANGE

...BUT TRUE
Obi-Wan first catches a glimpse of Darth Maul while leaving Tatooine. Their story comes full circle **thirty years later** when Maul returns to the planet to face Kenobi **one last time**.

195

SERENE REALM

Wish you were here? Naboo is **an idyllic tourist spot** much praised for its **lush scenery** and **dazzling cities**, above ground and underwater. It's **peaceful** here, too—the Naboo **rarely fight unless threatened**.

Peek behind the scenes
The Theed Palace scenes were shot in Italy's **Caserta Palace**. To avoid damage, Italian regulators ordered that **no film equipment touch the palace walls**, so the filmmakers floated **helium balloons filled with lights!**

Fast Facts

INHABITANTS: Humans, Gungans (natives)
AFFILIATION: Republic
GOVERNMENT: Democratic monarchy (human), High Council (Gungans)
LANGUAGES: Basic, Gungan
MAJOR TERRAINS: Grasslands, swamps, vast and deep seas

BEST KNOWN FOR
SUPPORTING THE ARTS
People of Naboo

STRANGE ...BUT TRUE
Temple ruins and **broken statues** are found all over Naboo, though little is known about the **ancient civilization** that built them.

THEED
Stunning city of domed buildings • Set near majestic waterfalls • Queen resides in Royal palace • Capital of Naboo

"We can enter the city using the secret passages on the waterfall side."
— QUEEN AMIDALA

WOW!...
14
Padmé Amidala's age when she's elected to rule Naboo as Queen

REALLY?!
Naboo's people **VOTE** for their monarchs. Often they elect young women as **QUEENS**, believing they possess a **CHILDLIKE WISDOM** that is more pure than that of an adult!

PLANETARY SYSTEMS ACROSS THE GALAXY

> "If I grew up here, I don't think I'd ever leave."
> **ANAKIN TO PADMÉ**

Plasma from Naboo's core is a **reliable energy source**. Gungans collect and combine the plasma with **bubble wort extract** to grow their **gem-like cities** and chambers, while the Naboo use the plasma for **Theed's power supply**.

Tell me more!

KEEPING A SAFE DISTANCE
Otoh Gunga's **sparkling, bubble-like buildings** are hydrostatic force fields. They contain **breathable atmosphere** to keep water out, but have **special portals** to allow the amphibious Gungans to **enter and exit**. The city is built by the Gungans to **avoid contact** with their surface-dwelling Naboo neighbors, whom they consider quite **pompous** and **cowardly**.

Q: Why does the Trade Federation blockade and invade Naboo?
A: To **protest against the Republic's taxation** of their trade routes. Naboo is an **easy target** for them, because of its small military and the people's non-violent nature.

OTOH GUNGA
Underwater city in Naboo's Lake Paonga • Also known as "Gungan City" • Connected bubbles allow Gungans to live and breathe • One million inhabitants

In numbers

20,000 credits
The amount Qui-Gon offers Watto to replace the damaged hyperdrive on Queen Amidala's ship

847 years
The length of time Naboo has been a part of the Republic

327
Model number for Amidala's star cruiser, a J-type Nubian

85 sq km (34 sq miles)
Area of Lianorm Swamp

12 people
In Padmé's strikeforce that sneaks into Theed Palace to retake the capital

5 handmaidens
Work for Queen Amidala

> "Da moto grande safe place would be Otoh Gunga. Tis where I grew up... Tis a hidden city."
> **JAR JAR BINKS**

197

Fast Facts

INHABITANTS: Many species, including humans

LANGUAGES: Basic and thousands of other languages

TERRAIN: Planet-wide cityscape

GALACTIC COORDINATES: 0, 0, 0

REALLY?!
At a fancy restaurant in Coruscant, just one meal can cost **10,000 CREDITS**—which is almost the price of a **LOW-END** starship!

Coruscant air taxis fly up to 191kph (119mph). Their drivers have permission to **leave the skylanes** and take super-speedy **shortcuts** through the canyons of skyscrapers.

STRANGE ...BUT TRUE
Wealthy citizens in the city's **upper levels** breathe **rich, filtered air**. Undercity dwellers, however, are forced to inhale the **toxic fumes** from millennia of **vehicle** and **factory waste**.

In numbers
1 trillion+ beings Live on the planet

365 days In a Coruscant year

68% of population Is human

24 hours In a Coruscant day

Coruscant

Coruscant is always **growing upward**! As giant skyscrapers are **built on top of one other**, the levels below them get **cut off** from the surface. Some of the deepest layers have been **sealed up** for **thousands of years**!

Peek behind the scenes
As a tribute to the Yoda trick-or-treater in director Steven Spielberg's film E.T., George Lucas added aliens of E.T.'s species to the Senate scene in Episode I.

Q: Is Coruscant the capital of the New Republic?
A: No, it isn't. Instead the Senate **rotates its location across member worlds** according to elections. This reassures worlds that suffered during the Clone Wars and Imperial years. It doesn't work out well for Hosnian Prime though—a **capital seat destroyed by the First Order!**

WOW!...
5217
The number of megastructure levels that have been built on Coruscant (level one is the lowest)

LIVING A LIE
The **Erso family** lives in a stylish apartment on Coruscant after the Clone Wars. Galen researches kyber crystals for **Project Celestial Power**. He believes he is **helping people**, and has no idea he is actually **building a super-weapon!**

PLANETARY SYSTEMS ACROSS THE GALAXY

MEGA CITY

At the heart of the galaxy lies **vibrant, glittering** Coruscant. For millennia, **the fate of the galaxy** rests on the decisions made on this **sprawling, multi-leveled metropolis** of a planet.

BEST KNOWN FOR

BEING THE CAPITAL OF BOTH REPUBLIC AND IMPERIAL GOVERNMENTS

Coruscant

Top 5 Tourist traps

1. **DEX'S DINER**
   The food's so tasty in this greasy spoon that even Jedi can't resist!

2. **ENTERTAINMENT DISTRICT**
   Streets of shady-looking nightclubs where visitors can gamble and dance until dawn.

3. **JEDI TEMPLE**
   The Jedi Order's magisterial headquarters, which later becomes the Imperial Palace.

4. **GALAXIES OPERA HOUSE**
   Stages magnificent productions like "Squid Lake," at which even the Emperor has been spotted!

5. **MONUMENT PLAZA**
   Where the planet's only uncovered mountain peak can be glimpsed and even touched.

Coruscant's underworld cops are **covered from head to toe** and have **creepy mechanical eyes**. No one knows if they are droids or humanoids, but **everyone keeps their distance**!

Peek behind the scenes
The name "Coruscant" first appeared in Timothy Zahn's novel *Heir to the Empire* (1991).

GALACTIC SENATE BUILDING

Colossal statues outside commemorate Republic's ancient founders • Interior chamber is a bowl-shaped arena • Senators float on repulsorpods to speak to Senate

"The Senate is full of greedy, squabbling delegates. There is no interest in the common good."

SENATOR PALPATINE OF NABOO

Tell me more!

THE DARKEST DEPTHS
Sunlight never reaches the **lowest levels** of Coruscant, making them the perfect haven for **scum and villainy**. **Bounty hunters, criminals, and ghoulish monsters** haunt this murky realm. If you must travel here, **make the trip short**—or it may well be the **last** one you ever make!

CLONE WORLD

 On the edge of the galaxy lies the **water planet**, Kamino. It is home to the graceful, business-savvy Kaminoans: Great scientists who **manufacture clones to fight for the Republic**.

IT'S JUST BUSINESS
Kaminoans **think the Jedi are strange**! They usually **couldn't care less** about the tangled relationships between the Jedi, the Sith, and the Republic. They never question who is ordering the construction of the clone army—to them **the Republic is simply another paying client**.

BEST KNOWN FOR

PLACE WHERE THE REPUBLIC'S CLONE ARMY IS BUILT

Kamino

STRANGE ...BUT TRUE
The **genes** of one man, famed bounty hunter **Jango Fett**, are cloned by the Kaminoans to create an entire **clone army** for the **Republic**.

In numbers

463 days
In a Kaminoan year

100%
Water on Kamino's surface

12 parsecs
Distance from the dwarf satellite galaxy known as the Rishi Maze

11 years old
Age that Kaminoans reach adulthood

Aiwhas are also called "**air whales**" as they can swim and fly with equal ease. These **majestic creatures** are tamed by the Kaminoans, who **use them as mounts** to get around the planet.

Q: Why is Kamino not found in the Jedi archives?
A: All information about the planet was **removed from the archive**, in a plot to **hide** the clone army from the Jedi.

REALLY?!
Clones from Kamino are not born—they are grown in NUTRIENT-FILLED TANKS stacked MANY STORIES HIGH!

Fast Facts

INHABITANTS: Kaminoans, clone armies

MAJOR CITY: Tipoca City

LANGUAGES: Basic, Kaminoan

Tell me more!

SNEAKY SEPARATIST ATTACK
The Republic considers Kamino to be one of the most **important** planets to the war effort, and protects it with **a mighty blockade** in space. The Republic is taken completely by **surprise** when Asajj Ventress leads a sneak attack on it with **underwater assault ships**.

Kaminoans power their cities using the **limitless supply of hydrogen** taken from the seawater that covers the planet.

Kaminoan eyes **see ultraviolet light**, which is not visible to humans. To them, their **dull** white hallways actually look **bright and colorful**.

WOW!...

70,000
Light years from the Galactic Core

Top 5 Reasons to visit Kamino

1. **LEARN ABOUT GENETICS** The Kaminoans know everything about cloning.
2. **SHARPEN A SABERDART** Kaminoans make precision tools and weapons.
3. **BUY AN ARMY OF CLONES** Just make sure you have enough credits!
4. **WASH YOUR STARSHIP** There's more than enough rain to clean anything!
5. **UNDERWATER TOURISM** Take a journey under the stormy seas in a submarine.

Who's who?
Female Kaminoans have **bald heads**, while male Kaminoans have **a white crest** on the crown of their skull

TIPOCA CITY

Capital city of Kamino • Built on stilts above the ocean • Home to massive cloning facilities • Indoor walkways give shelter from frequent rainstorms

"If someone comes to our home, they better be carrying a big blaster."
CLONE CAPTAIN REX
ON THE SEPARATIST INVASION OF KAMINO

Fast Facts

INHABITANTS: Geonosians—made up of Queens, winged aristocrats, flightless drones

MAJOR CITIES (HIVES): Stalgasin, Gehenbar, Golbah (destroyed)

LANGUAGE: Geonosian

AFFILIATION: Separatists, Galactic Empire

6 ways to die on Geonosis

1. Savaged by Petranaki Arena beasts.
2. Devoured by the local wildlife like merdeths and massiffs.
3. Blasted by lethal solar radiation storms.
4. Swept away in frequent flash floods.
5. Crushed by plummeting meteors.
6. Trapped in a factory accident.

HIVES OF DEATH

Geonosis

Geonosis is a **dustbowl world** clinging to the Outer Rim of the galaxy. It is home to the **chittering, insect-like** Geonosians that hunker in vast underground cities to escape the planet's **brutal surface conditions**.

In numbers

43,000 light years
Distance from the Galactic Core

11,370km (7,065 miles)
Diameter of Geonosis

256 days
In a year on Geonosis

15 moons
4 major and 11 minor

5%
Surface water

1 sun
Named Ea

Building for battle

The **huge factories** on Geonosis build **battle droids, vehicles, and weaponry** for the Separatists, who are secretly preparing for war against the Republic. When their plans are discovered, a formidable force of **Jedi** and **clone troopers invade** the planet to take on the droid army. And so begins the first **fearsome clash** of the Clone Wars—the Battle of Geonosis.

PLANETARY SYSTEMS ACROSS THE GALAXY

STRANGE ...BUT TRUE
As an **insect race**, Geonosians are all born from a small number of **queens**, who dwell in the **deepest parts** of each hive. If a Queen dies, the hive is abandoned.

BEST KNOWN FOR
FIRST BATTLE OF THE CLONE WARS
Geonosis

Count Dooku, with the help of the Geonosian leader, Poggle the Lesser, establishes the Separatists' **secret stronghold** on the hive world.

STALGASIN HIVE
Spire-like termite mounds above ground • Vast network of caverns, tunnels, and shafts below • Capital of Geonosis and first capital of the Confederacy of Independent Systems • Site of major battle droid factory

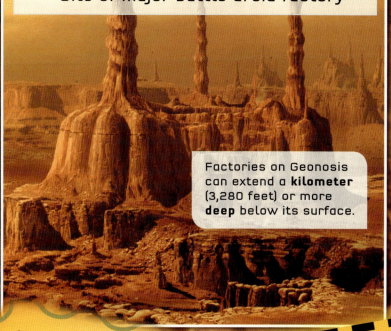

Factories on Geonosis can extend a **kilometer** (3,280 feet) or more **deep** below its surface.

The planet Geonosis is eerily silent during Imperial rule. After they helped build much of the Death Star, the Empire almost wiped out the species to keep the Death Star a secret.

DANGER ZONE!
During the Geonosian **rainy season**, the dry, dusty plains transform into an **acidic lake** that **smells terrible!**

REALLY?!
Geonosian **HIVE SPIRES AND BUILDINGS** are made from **STONE POWDER** mixed with **PHIDNA PARASITE DUNG** (poop)!

Tell me more!
A DEADLY BEAUTY
The **awe-inspiring** rings of Geonosis were created after a comet **crashed into one of the planet's moons**. The debris left thousands of **small asteroids** that rain down on Geonosis as **deadly meteor showers**. The raw materials from the rings are also used to build the Death Star.

"More happening on Geonosis, I feel, than has been revealed."
YODA TO MACE WINDU

Fast Facts

INHABITANTS: Pau'ans, Utai, Amani immigrants
MAJOR CITIES: Pau City (capital)
LANGUAGES: Utapese (Pau'an language), Utai, Basic
AFFILIATION: Neutral, then Confederacy of Independent Systems (enforced)

In numbers

51,000 light years Distance from the Galactic Core
12,900km (8,016 miles) Diameter of Utapau
351 days In an Utapaun year
9 moons
1 sun Utapau
0.9% Surface water

Utapau

SUNKEN CITIES

Utapau is a world of massive sinkholes. The **hyperwinds** that pummel the planet's surface are so deadly that its people build **underground cities** inside these holes to escape the winds' ferocity.

All shapes and sizes

Pau'an 1.9m (6ft 2in)
Utai 1.2m (3ft 1in)
Amani 2m (6ft 6in)

The Utai may be small, but they do all the mining and heavy work that keeps Utapau's cities running.

The Pau'ans live for **CENTURIES**, and are nicknamed **"THE ANCIENTS."**

The Utai, whose lives are **FAR SHORTER**, are called **"SHORTS,"** which has **NOTHING** to do with their height.

The Amani, many of whom are refugees from the planet Maridun, have **AVERAGE LIFE SPANS** of around **90 YEARS**.

Peek behind the scenes
The design of the tall Pau'ans was originally intended for a native race of the Pau'an the design was inspired face was inspired by an African tribal mask.

COOL!!
GANGLY AND SLIMY, the Amanis' really long arms reach the ground, so they can **CURL INTO A BALL** and roll along Utapau's surface!

Pau'ans once lived on Utapau's surface, while the Utai colonists dwelt deep underground. The planet's **worsening hyperwind storms** eventually drove the Pau'ans below ground to join their Utai neighbors and create **combined cities** that were built into the ledges lining the sinkholes.

PLANETARY SYSTEMS ACROSS THE GALAXY

Bone people The Pau'ans build homes with animal bones.

PAU CITY

Built within the Pau Sinkhole • 11 levels deep • Capital of Utapau • Major trade spaceport

"There's no war here, unless you brought it with you."
TION MEDON, PAU CITY PORT ADMINISTRATOR, TO OBI-WAN

Q: Where is all the water on Utapau?
A: Deep beneath Utapau's surface is a huge ocean where all **groundwater drained long ago.** Fresh water comes from naturally filtered seawater at the base of sinkholes or from **machines that extract valuable minerals** from the ocean.

The most infamous Pau'an in the galaxy is Darth Vader's henchman, the Imperial Inquisitor—a cold and merciless assassin, almost as feared as Vader himself.

STRANGE ...BUT TRUE
Utapau's raging winds have **stripped the planet of trees.** So Pau'ans build their sinkhole homes with all kinds of animal bones. Some of these structures have started to look like giant animal skeletons.

TASTY!!
Pau'ans prefer to **EAT RAW MEAT**, so freshly slain creatures are on the menu every day.

Top 5
Dangerous creatures

1. **RESPUTI** Live in deep sinkhole caves, and love snacking on Utai.
2. **NOS MONSTERS** Aquatic reptiles found at the bottom of sinkholes. They're not fussy and eat anything.
3. **WILD GINNTHOS** Giant spiders that wrap their victims in silk to ripen for a few weeks, before slurping down.
4. **ROCK VULTURES** One of Utapau's few surface dwellers. They can't wait for their prey to perish before eating them!
5. **UTAPAUN FLYING SQUID** A problem for anything airborne as it's always hungry and ready to strike.

TOP 2
WAYS TO GET AROUND

1. **Dactillion**—large, winged reptile used to fly within sinkholes or over the planet's surface.
2. **Varactyl**—very fast lizard-like creature that is ridden like a horse.

Fast Facts

INHABITANTS: Anyone who can handle the heat!

CAPITAL CITY: Fralideja

MAJOR EXPORT: Minerals and metal ore such as dolovite.

MAJOR IMPORT: Water. Lots and lots of water.

WILDLIFE: Lava eels, xandanks, lava fleas, roggwarts (imported to work in mines)

Peek behind the scenes
A real volcanic eruption on Mount Etna in Sicily, Italy, was filmed to create some of Mustafar's lava effects for Revenge of the Sith.

STRANGE ...BUT TRUE
Mustafar's buildings are held up by stem-like **gravity supports**. If you're inside one, just hope that nothing happens to **switch the gravity off**, or the building will **sink into the molten lava!**

HELL PLANET

Boiling lava, erupting volcanoes, and choking ash cover the **remote mining planet** of Mustafar. This **hellish world** is the setting for Darth Sidious's plan to **destroy** the Separatists.

REALLY?!
The Mustafarians' **UNDERGROUND BUILDINGS** are designed in the shape of **KAHEL CAVE FUNGUS!**

Lava fleas are well adapted to life on the planet's **fiery surface**, thanks to their tough exoskeletons. When tamed, these **six-legged beasts** make **obedient mounts**.

STRANGE ...BUT TRUE
Mustafarians make their **armor** from the **heat-resistant** shells of lava fleas.

Lava flea: 4.6m (15ft)
Northern Mustafarian: 2.3m (7ft 6in)
Southern Mustafarian: 1.5m (4ft 11in)

Mustafarians: Who does what?
There are **two species** of Mustafarian. **Southern** Mustafarians are **short and strong** and do all the **heavy labor**. **Northern** Mustafarians are **tall and slender**. They often become **guards** and **expert lava flea riders**.

The lava temperature is **800°C (1,500°F)**. Scorching!

PLANETARY SYSTEMS ACROSS THE GALAXY

BEST KNOWN FOR

VADER FALLING INTO A LAVA RIVER AFTER HIS DUEL WITH OBI-WAN

Mustafar

Tell me more!

CHILDREN OF THE FORCE
Darth Sidious **hires bounty hunter Cad Bane** to **kidnap Force-sensitive babies** and take them to a **hidden base** on Mustafar, where he plans to raise them as **spies**. The evil scheme is smashed by **Anakin Skywalker** and **Ahsoka Tano**, who save the babies and **destroy the base**!

"We should leave this dreadful place."
C-3PO TO OBI-WAN KENOBI

DLC-13 mining droids are made from **heat-resistant carbonite**. That's the same material in which **Han Solo** is frozen!

When a Mustafarian **speaks**, it sounds like an **insect buzzing**!

Top 6

Reasons to visit Mustafar

1. **IT'S WARM ALL YEAR ROUND**
The climate will be warm to boiling—guaranteed!

2. **IT NEVER GETS CROWDED**
Avoiding someone? Mustafar is the ideal place to hide out.

3. **TOUR A WORKING MINE**
Just don't go too near the lava.

4. **WEAR WHAT YOU LIKE**
As long as it's heat-resistant!

5. **SEE THE LAVA GEYSERS**
Gasp in awe as these natural wonders spew lava into the air.

6. **GO LAVA FLEA-SPOTTING**
Watch these majestic insects leap over molten chasms!

"...Mustafar is where Jedi go to die."
HERA SYNDULLA TO EZRA BRIDGER ABOUT MUSTAFAR

Falling Star (Destroyer)
Rebels destroy Grand Moff Tarkin's personal Star Destroyer, the *Sovereign*, over Mustafar. The massive ship is sent crashing into the fiery lava fields.

Q: Where do the Mustafarians live?
A: Mustafarians live in **underground caves**, which are created by lava fleas as they **munch through the planet's crust**. The Mustafarians venture onto the planet's dangerous surface only to collect **valuable minerals** from the lava flows.

DARTH VADER'S CASTLE
Vader's personal fortress • Soars above lava fields on Mustafar • Obsidian tower built upon ancient castle

BEST KNOWN FOR

THE DEFEAT OF THE REBEL ALLIANCE AT THE BATTLE OF HOTH

Hoth

FROZEN WASTELAND

The rebels think they've found the **safest place in the galaxy** to build their secret base—the **little-known, desolate ice world** of Hoth. But they're wrong! The Empire soon tracks them down and an **epic battle begins**.

Hoth

REALLY?!
Nighttime temperatures outside Echo Base reach **-60°C (-76°F)**—that's cold enough to **DECIMATE** even the native **TAUNTAUNS** that the rebel soldiers ride!

ECHO BASE
Secret Rebel Alliance headquarters • Carved from ice and rock • Protected by a planetary shield and v-150 ion cannon

Peek behind the scenes
Several scenes for Hoth were filmed on location near the tiny, isolated mountain village of Finse in Norway.

"We'd better start the evacuation."
— REBEL GENERAL RIEEKAN

Q: What is Blizzard Force?
A: It is an **elite Imperial stormtrooper unit** that specializes in cold-weather operations. In their fearsome AT-AT walkers, these snowtroopers spearhead the ground assault that **overruns Echo Base** during the Battle of Hoth. They are led by the **bold** and **ruthless** General Maximilian Veers.

TOP 5
DROIDS AT ECHO BASE
1. **2-1B**—Surgical droid who tends to Luke Skywalker's injuries.
2. **K-3PO**—Protocol droid with a memory bank full of battle tactics.
3. **R-3PO**—Moody, red protocol droid on the lookout for spies.
4. **EG-4**—"Gonk" droid that powers ships and machinery.
5. **R5-M2**—Black-topped astromech who helps evacuate the rebels.

STRANGE ...BUT TRUE
Fierce **wampas** often **sneak into Echo Base at night**. The rebels trap a few inside a room, clearly marked with **a warning sign**. During the battle, snowtroopers ignore the sign, enter the room, **and are slain**!

PLANETARY SYSTEMS ACROSS THE GALAXY

In numbers

50,250 light years
Distance from the Galactic Core

7,200km (4,473 miles)
Diameter of Hoth

526 days
In a year on Hoth

33% of Hoth's surface
Is covered by oceans

5 planets
Between Hoth and its sun

1 sun
Hoth's sun is blue-white

HEROES OF HOTH
When Echo Base is **attacked by Imperial forces**, Luke Skywalker leads the pilots of "Rogue Group," in a **snowspeeder assault**. Against the odds, they bring down giant AT-AT walkers, buying time for other pilots to **help the Rebel leaders escape**.

How do the rebels defend themselves against the Empire's overwhelming attack force?

With swift, agile, and well-armed snowspeeders.

Tell me more!

DANGER FROM ABOVE!
Hoth is **persistently pelted by meteors** from the asteroid belt that conceals the planet. This is bad news for the rebels. Not only do they risk getting flattened, but the meteors help disguise the arrival of **Imperial probe droids**.

> "There isn't enough life on this ice cube to fill a space cruiser!"
> **HAN SOLO ON HOTH**

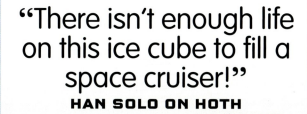

Top 5
Reasons for choosing Hoth

1 UNKNOWN
The planet is so remote it isn't on most star charts.

2 FROZEN SOLID
Ice and snow provide excellent cover for the base.

3 EMPTY
Great security because there are no other people on Hoth.

4 SMALL
Hoth is tiny enough to be fully protected by an energy shield.

5 HIDDEN
Shrouded from view by a dense asteroid belt.

 Imperial AT-AT walker — 22.5m (73ft 10in)

DF.9 Anti-infantry Battery — 4m (13ft 1in)

 1.4 FD P-Tower laser cannon — 2.8m (9ft 2in)

 T-47 Airspeeder (aka snowspeeder) — 1.4m (4ft 7in) tall, and 5.3m (17ft 5in) long

The bigger they are... During the Battle of Hoth, tiny rebel machines take on the towering Imperial AT-ATs.

Fast Facts

- **FLORA:** Gnarltrees, giant mushrooms, lahdia plants
- **FAUNA:** Dragonsnakes, swamp slugs, sleens, pythons
- **ATMOSPHERE:** Dense clouds envelop entire planet
- **INTELLIGENT INHABITANTS:** One
- **MAJOR CITIES:** Who would want to live out here?
- **TERRAIN:** Swamp, jungle, lakes, lagoons

Q: Why does Yoda say Luke is too old to train?

A: In the days of the Republic, **Jedi younglings** began their training as **infants**. However, Luke is all **grown up** before he learns of the Force from Obi-Wan Kenobi, so **he has plenty of catching up** to do!

Vine snakes on Dagobah will **squirm** and **squish** their way into anything, even the engine of an **X-wing**!

BEST KNOWN FOR
LUKE SKYWALKER'S JEDI TRAINING GROUNDS
Dagobah

Yoda renews his **connection to the natural world** on this wetland planet, which teems with **wildlife**. Here, he **meditates** on how the Jedi lost their way, and **prepares to train an apprentice** who may be **a new hope** for the doomed galaxy.

In numbers

180,000kg (396,832lbs)
Weight of Luke's X-wing lifted by Yoda using only the Force!

50,250 light years
Distance from the Galactic Core

20+ years
Length of time Yoda lives as a hermit on Dagobah before Luke arrives

8%
Surface water

1.2m (3ft 11in)
Ceiling height in Yoda's hut

> "Into exile I must go. Failed I have."
> **YODA**

REALLY?!
The **DAGOBAH PYTHON** that slithers around gnarltrees can swallow up to **15 TIMES ITS WEIGHT** in food!

SWAMP HIDEOUT

Dagobah

Shrouded in clouds, thick with fog, and far from the civilized galaxy, the Outer Rim bog world of Dagobah makes the **perfect refuge** for a Jedi Master in hiding after the catastrophe of Order 66.

Peek behind the scenes
It took more than **100 workers** to build the Dagobah swamp inside an Elstree Studios soundstage. The floor of Yoda's home was raised so that puppeteers could crawl underneath.

PLANETARY SYSTEMS ACROSS THE GALAXY

Top 6

Veggie delicacies in Yoda's pantry

1. **YARUM SEEDS** — Make a soothing hot tea
2. **MARSH FUNGI** — Mash into a creamy, sweet yogurt
3. **GIMER BARK** — Chew after meals for clean teeth
4. **ROOTLEAF** — Boil for 10 minutes to make a tangy soup
5. **GALLA SEEDS** — Provide a handy nutty snack
6. **DRIED FLOWER PETALS** — Add some crunch to salads

FEEL THE FORCE...

After failing to free his **crashed** and **sinking X-wing** from Dagobah's quagmire, Luke is stunned to see the diminutive Yoda **effortlessly raise the ship** using only the Force. A Force he learns to trust... and wield!

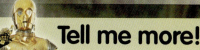

Tell me more!

CAVE OF FEARS

Yoda tests Luke by making him face his **deepest fears**. When Luke enters a **creepy cave** steeped in the dark side of the Force, he comes across **lizardy sleens**, **poisonous snakes**, and a **foreboding phantom of Darth Vader**—whose face is none other than Luke's own!

STRANGE ...BUT TRUE

The **swamp slug** that spits out R2-D2 has **thousands of teeth** in its esophagus—ideal for crunching up plants and animals, but **not metal droids!**

HOW DOES YODA TRAVEL IN SECRET TO SUCH A REMOTE PLACE?

In an E3 escape pod with a cloaking shield.

YODA'S HUT

Built against an ancient gnarltree • Constructed from mud, rock, and bark • Cramped for humans, perfect for Yoda-sized beings • Backup power supply from E3 escape pod • Tiny kitchen ideal for cooking rootleaf soup

"Mudhole? Slimy? My home this is!"
YODA TO LUKE

Fast Facts

PERMANENT INHABITANTS: Mainly humans and Ugnaughts

LANGUAGES: Basic, Ugnaught

MAJOR EXPORT: Tibanna gas

MOST FAMOUS ADMINISTRATOR: Lando Calrissian, responsible rogue turned rebel

AFFILIATION: Neutral, then Galactic Empire (enforced)

> "Lando conned somebody out of it."
> — HAN SOLO ON HOW LANDO BECAME ADMINISTRATOR

BEST KNOWN FOR
PLACE WHERE HAN SOLO GETS FROZEN IN CARBONITE
Cloud City

Peek behind the scenes
Lando's costume, with its dashing cape, was designed by Ralph McQuarrie and John Mollo. Mollo was the costume designer for Episodes IV and V and won an Academy Award for his work on Episode IV.

Q: Who runs Cloud City?

A: **Lando Calrissian** is its administrator, but day-to-day running of the facility is taken care of by **Lobot**, his cyborg aid. Lobot wears a **cybernetic implant** that allows him to connect directly to the city's **central computer**. Casino takings, gas mining statistics, and other data are **fed directly into his brain**!

UP, UP, AND AWAY

Cloud City floats high up in the atmosphere of the gas giant **Bespin**. Half-tibanna **gas mine**, half-**luxury resort** for the wealthy, Cloud City makes a unique **tourist destination**!

Tell me more!

HOW DOES EVERYBODY BREATHE?!
Cloud City doesn't need any airlocks or other life-support systems. It floats in a **layer** at the very top of Bespin's atmosphere, called the **"Life Zone."** Here, the atmosphere is **mostly oxygen** and the air pressure, temperature, and gravity are very close to normal for humans.

In numbers

6,000,000
Bespin's permanent population

118,000km (73,322 miles)
Diameter of Bespin

59,000km (37,000 miles)
Cloud City's height above Bespin's core

49,100 light years
Distance from the Galactic Core

16.2km (10 miles)
Diameter of Cloud City disk

HOW DO PEOPLE CRUISE AROUND THE CITY?

Twin-pod cloud cars are used for patrolling and as pleasurecraft.

PLANETARY SYSTEMS ACROSS THE GALAXY

TOP 5
TOURIST ATTRACTIONS ON CLOUD CITY
1. Watching the two-hour sunsets.
2. Gambling in the casinos.
3. Kicking back in the luxurious resort hotels.
4. Hiring a cloud car for a stunning scenic flight around the city.
5. Touring the mining operations (for the adventurous).

Yikes! Luke's life is saved by a **weather scanner vane** on the bottom of Cloud City, after he falls through a network of gas exhaust pipes to **escape Darth Vader**.

Q: Why is Bespin's tibanna gas so valuable?

A: Tibanna gas is vital to military technology and spaceflight. It produces **four times more energy** than other gases, when used in energy weapons such as **blasters**. It is also used in **hyperdrive** and **repulsorlift systems**. After all, there's got to be a **profit** in it for Lando!

REALLY?!
The **LUXURY** resort suite where Lando first places Leia, Han, and Chewbacca would cost a tourist **5,000** Imperial credits a night!

WOW!...
36,000
Number of respulsorlift engines and tractor beam generators needed to keep Cloud City aloft

STRANGE
...BUT TRUE
Work areas in Cloud City's mining and processing zones have **red lighting**. The **pig-like Ugnaughts**, who do most of the work, **prefer this color**, and it also improves their productivity.

Ugnaughts are **strong and tough**, and can live for up to **200 years**. They eat **genteslugs** and various types of **molds** and **fungi** grown in dark, dank side tunnels off their main living areas. Ugnaught kids are known as **"Ugletts."**

Peek behind the scenes
Ugnaught voices were created from recordings of the yips of **arctic fox pups** with their mother.

Cloud City has 392 levels • Top 50 levels are luxury resorts • Famous casinos include "Yarith Bespin" and "Pair O'Dice" • Lowest levels used for mining and processing gas

Fast Facts

NATIVE PEOPLE:
Ewoks (forest people), Yuzzum (plains people)

MAJOR CITIES:
None; inhabitants live in tribal villages

LANGUAGES:
Ewokese, Yuzzum

AFFILIATION:
Neutral, though occupied by Imperial forces

Bright Tree Ewok village

EWOK VILLAGE VISITOR GUIDE

GETTING AROUND
It's easy to get from A to B in an Ewok village, if you have a good head for heights. Just don't look down!

- Suspension bridges—hold tight, they can sway a lot.
- Rope ladders—strong but rough on the hands.
- Swinging vines—don't let go at the wrong moment!
- Wooden catwalks—often spiral around trees, so go slow or you could get dizzy.

FOREST MOON

Secluded and faraway, the "Forest Moon" of **Endor** is home to the **fierce, furry Ewoks**. This **leafy, low tech world** becomes the unlikely scene of the **Empire's downfall**, leading to the **destruction of Death Star II** and the **Emperor,** too!

The Ewoks use **booby traps** to snare the **huge, bear-like goraxes** that prey on them. They cleverly **adapt the traps** to **help rebel commandos** defeat the **Imperial forces** on Endor.

Peek behind the scenes
The Endor scenes were filmed in the giant redwood forests of northern California, in particular **Tall Trees Redwood Grove** and other forests near the remote town of **Smith River**.

Death Star shield

In numbers

43,300 light years
Distance from the Galactic Core

4,900km (3,045 miles)
Diameter of Endor

402 days
In an Endor year

8%
Surface water

2 suns
Endor I and II

Q: Why is Endor important?
A: The **Empire** is building **Death Star II** right above Endor, and protecting it with an **energy shield** generated from the moon's surface. Despite falling into a **trap set by the Emperor**, the **Rebel Alliance** succeeds in bringing down Death Star II and the Emperor, **freeing the galaxy** from Imperial control.

Ewok

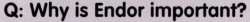

Hunting high and low

PLANETARY SYSTEMS ACROSS THE GALAXY

STRANGE ...BUT TRUE

Yuzzum use only the most **basic tools**. Ewoks, however, have an **advanced stone-age technology**. They even build **hang gliders** with **animal skin wings**!

Ewok glider

NO WAY!! Ewoks are **INTELLIGENT** beings, but that doesn't stop **OFFWORLD RAIDERS** from hunting them down to make **EWOK JERKY**, a popular snack on Outer Rim worlds.

SHIELD GENERATOR STATION

Imperial outpost on Endor • Deflector shield protects Death Star II while it is under construction • Bunker houses crew and power facilities

"The shield must be deactivated if any attack is attempted."
REBEL ADMIRAL ACKBAR

Yuzzum love **roasted "ruggers"**—rodents that hide in tall grasses—but first they have to catch them! To help them in the hunt, they tame and ride the **scary, swift,** and **spider-like rakazzak beasts**.

Yuzzum

Yuzzum are **taller** than Ewoks, thanks to their **rangy limbs**. On the plains, long legs help you **run fast** to catch prey, but in dense woodlands, **small is better**.

Boy, **can Yuzzum sing**! Joh Yowza's **gritty, soulful voice** delights **Jabba the Hutt** when Yowza performs at his palace as part of **Max Rebo's band**.

215

Fast Facts

INHABITANTS: Humans, Xexto, Ithorians, Rodians, Aqualish, Gotals, Ugnaughts

CITIES AND TOWNS: Capital City, Kothal, Jalath, Jhothal, Monad Outpost, Tarkintown

LANGUAGES: Basic, Huttese, Aqualish, Ithorian

Tell me more!

NEW SPECTRES RISE

After the *Ghost* crew leaves Lothal, a new rebel cell is formed. It includes Lothal's former governor, **Ryder Azadi**, Ezra's friend **Morad Sumar**, and the Ithorian **Old Jho**. They infiltrate the **Imperial factory** to sabotage assembly lines and help Kanan and Ezra steal plans for a new **TIE Defender**.

Lothal's loathsome leaders

- **Wilhuff Tarkin**—proud and heartless governor of the Outer Rim Territories (including Lothal).
- Lothal's governor, **Arihnda Pryce**, is rarely seen in public on the planet surface. Her ambitions keep her busy strategizing with **Imperial command**.
- **Maketh Tua**—government minister who meets a **tragic end** when she **defects** to the rebels.
- **Yogar Lyste**—Supply Master who **rises through the ranks** under Grand Admiral Thrawn's command—until Agent Kallus **frames him as a rebel informant**.

BLACK MARKET BLUES

The Empire's **cripplingly high taxes** create a **booming black market** in Capital City. Corrupt Imperial officials take advantage of the situation, **squeezing protection money** from Lothal's already hard-pressed citizens.

Top 5 Ways the Empire controls Lothal

1. **POLITICAL PRISONERS** — Anyone who publicly opposes the Empire is taken away.
2. **BLOCKADES** — Transportation offworld is screened and the import of products is tightly regulated.
3. **EVICTING CITIZENS** — The Empire forces farmers to leave so it can steal their land.
4. **EXPLOITING RESOURCES** — The Empire digs for metal and rare minerals, damaging the environment with filthy mines.
5. **MANUFACTURING SHIPS** — Sienar Fleet Systems' factories build TIE fighters—and also pollute the air and water.

WHAT'S THE EASIEST WAY TO TRAVEL TO NEARBY WORLDS LIKE GAREL?

Jump on a Star Commuter 2000 shuttle!

CAPTIVE TERRITORY

Lothal was a **quiet, green, and pleasant** backwater until the Empire arrived to **seize land** and **deny freedom** to the planet's citizens. Now anyone speaking out against the Empire is **arrested** by stormtroopers!

Peek behind the scenes

Disneyland's "Star Tours" ride inspired the shuttle between Lothal and Garel. The RX-24 droid who drives both is voiced by the same actor, Paul Reubens, best known as Pee Wee Herman!

BATTLE ON THE HORIZON...
When General Dodonna's **Massassi Group** joins **Phoenix Squadron** for an attack on **Lothal's Imperial Factory**, Thrawn catches them off guard. The rebel assault is aborted, but **only temporarily**.

STRANGE ...BUT TRUE
If you see **IG-RM droids lurking** around the streets of Capital City, then stay away. These **thug droids** are owned by local gangsters like Cikatro Vizago, and are sent to do their **dirty work**!

Tell me more!
FROM RICHES TO RAGS
Tangletown was a **thriving farming community** that grew fruits and vegetables. And then Governor Tarkin arrived, and forcibly took all the arable land for the Empire and its business buddies. The local people were forced to live in a **poor and dirty slum** they named "Tarkintown."

REALLY?!
Sometimes Lothal's Imperial Academy cadets **MYSTERIOUSLY VANISH**! Zare Leonis fears his sister has been taken from there by the Inquisitor!

In numbers

3258 LY
The year the Empire is founded (in the Lothal Calendar)

19,000 species
Grass types on Lothal's plains

624
Latest model of AVA Imperial speeders made on Lothal

125 credits
For the Meal of the Day at Bistro Lothal

20km (12 miles)
Distance from Capital City to Monad Outpost

17 varieties
Of wild Loth-cats

5 years
The timescale of the Empire's secret master plan for Lothal

4 credits
Cost of a single trip on Capital City's Empire Monoshuttle

2 moons
Orbiting Lothal

JEDI TEMPLE
Located in Lothal's wintery highlands • Surrounded by symbols of the dark side and the light • Walls display ancient symbols also found on Malachor • Lowest levels contain kyber crystals and drawings of wolf riders • Ransacked by Darth Vader and his Inquisitors

> "As you know, these temples can be tricky."
> **AHSOKA TO EZRA**

EZRA'S TOP 3
CAPITAL CITY HAUNTS
1. **Bazaar**—an open market where pockets are ripe for the picking.
2. **Sewers**—few Imperials will follow Ezra into these stinky tunnels, in case they mess up their uniforms.
3. **Imperial Academy**—no better place to snatch stormtrooper helmets!

Fast Facts

AFFILIATION: Empire

LANDSCAPE: Oceans and volcanic islands

NOTABLE FEATURES: Imperial Citadel and mining operations

REGION: Outer Rim Territories

NOT TO BE CONFUSED WITH: A peaceful place for a sunny holiday.

Peek behind the scenes
While director Gareth Edwards filmed some of Scarif's scenes on Gan Island, Addu Atoll in the Maldives, the tropical location was also recreated at Pinewood Studios in the UK.

Q: Why does the Empire choose Scarif?
A: Scarif is **far** from the **prying eyes** of the Senate, and it has a mantle of dense **metals** suitable for construction of **starships**. This makes it the perfect planet to undertake **classified military research projects**.

Tell me more!

INTRUDERS NOT WELCOME
Within the heart of the Citadel lies the **vault** holding the **Imperial archives**. This library of **top-secret datatapes** is disconnected from any network. It's protected by security doors, scanners, guards, and a screening tunnel to disable droids and computer equipment.

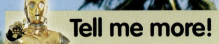

Tarkin **obliterates** the Citadel with the Death Star, to stop the rebels' mission. Sadly, Jyn and Cassian share the Citadel's **fate**—but not before they manage to **transmit** the Death Star plans to the **rebel fleet** above, **just in time**!

NATURAL HISTORY OF SCARIF

Stormtroopers stand guard beneath **areca palms**, scanning for **ravenous wildlife**. The fierce, semi-aquatic **Blixus drags** less vigilant officers and droids into lagoons to **eat** them! The islands are also full of other life—**colorful birds**, **reptiles**, and **insects**, too.

HOW TO MOVE CARGO ON SCARIF

SHUTTLES
Zeta-class cargo shuttles fly large shipments to and from Scarif via the shield gate.

AT-ACTS
Walkers move thousands of tons of processed and raw materials with the help of loadlifter droids.

RAIL SYSTEM
Transport containers of kyber crystals and other resources are moved via the repulsor rail system.

In numbers

475,000 humans
Population of Scarif

9,112km (5,622 miles)
Diameter of Scarif

1,500 known fish species
Swim in waters surrounding the Citdel

700kph (435mph)
Atmospheric speed of a *Zeta*-class shuttle

550m³ (19,423ft³)
Cargo space inside an AT-ACT

2 crew members
Pilot one TIE striker

Galen Erso codenames the Death Star plans in the vault **"Stardust,"** his nickname for Jyn.

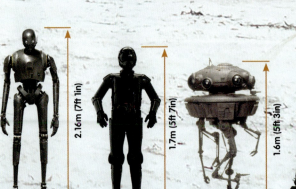

Droids of Scarif
Droid support—in all sizes—is crucial on Imperial bases.

- KX-series (security droid) — 2.16m (7ft 1in)
- 4D6-J-A7 (RA-7 protocol droid) — 1.7m (5ft 7in)
- Viper probe droid (Probot droid) — 1.6m (5ft 3in)
- C2-B5 (astromech droid) — 0.93m (3ft 1in)
- MSE-6 (mouse droid) — 0.25m (9.8in)

PLANETARY SYSTEMS ACROSS THE GALAXY

> "Scarif? They're going to Scarif? Why does nobody ever tell me anything, Artoo?"
> **C-3PO**

HOW DO YOU BREAK THROUGH AN IMPENETRABLE PLANETARY SHIELD WITH ONLY ONE ENTRY GATE?

COPY ADMIRAL RADDUS! SMASH ONE STAR DESTROYER INTO ANOTHER, MAKING IT CRASH STRAIGHT INTO THE GATE!

THE CITADEL
Above and below-ground facilities • Capped with command tower and communications relay • Surrounded by landing platforms and barracks

▶▶ UNUSUAL ARMOR
Shoretroopers (aka coastal defender stormtroopers) are **not a common** class of troopers, and their armor is **exclusive to Scarif**. Colored stripes indicate their rank.

PARADISE OF DOOM

Scarif

The **tropical world** of Scarif is covered by seas and island chains. It would be an idyllic place for a **holiday**—but the Empire values it for **top-secret military projects** instead!

Fast Facts

TERRITORY: Imperial
LOCATION: Mid Rim, Terrabe sector
ALSO KNOWN AS: The Pilgrim Moon, Cold Moon
ORBITS: NaJedha
CLIMATE: Cold desert
VEGETATION: Mostly barren

Q: Why does a Star Destroyer loom over Jedha City?
A: Because Saw Gerrera's rebels have been **attacking** the Imperial forces on the planet!

BEST KNOWN FOR BEING THE DEATH STAR SUPERLASER'S FIRST TEST
Jedha City

In numbers

25,000+ years
That the Force has been known to galactic faithful such as the pilgrims of Jedha

100 faiths
Represented by those who come to Jedha to connect to the Force

97% of the Imperial garrison
Evacuates Jedha after Krennic initiates Protocol 13

1 Death Star reactor
Used to destroy the entire city

Jedha

YUCK! Some residents of Jedha are known as the **DECRANIATED**. Their **BRAINS** have been replaced by cybernetics.

TRAVEL TIP Show **respect** to Jedha's locals and they will **welcome** you in return.

SACRED WAR ZONE

Jedha might look like a desolate rock, but this **mysterious moon** has a deep and intriguing connection to the **Force**. It boasts a volatile population: **pilgrims** searching for enlightenment, **Imperials** pursuing power, and **rebels** seeking revenge. This sacred place is now a fatal **battleground!**

TOP 9
PILGRIMS IN JEDHA
1. Cultists of the Huiyui-Tni
2. Order of the Esoteric Pulsar
3. Ninn Orthodoxy
4. Zealots of the Psusan
5. The Phirmists
6. Brotherhood of the Beautific Countenance
7. Disciples of the Whills
8. Clan of Toribota
9. Church of the Force
(Some locals believe anyone who is not a pilgrim is invading holy ground!)

PROPAGANDA! The Empire tells the Senate that Jedha City was destroyed in a **mining disaster**, not by the Death Star.

PLANETARY SYSTEMS ACROSS THE GALAXY

Tell me more!

PLUNDERED CITY

Jedha has **one** main notable resource: **kyber crystals**. Jedha City, also known as the Holy City or NiJedha, is its most **well-known landmark**. The city is built around the **Temple of the Kyber**, an ancient holy site. The Empire is **extracting** all of the temple's precious crystals to power their Death Star.

WARNING! Before the Death Star attacked the city, the Imperials enacted **"Protocol 13,"** which called for **immediate evacuation** of Imperial forces from the city.

STRANGE ...BUT TRUE

Most scholars believe the Jedi Order and Jedha are **somehow connected**, though it's not known exactly **how**. Mystifying...

Top 6

Must-see landmarks

1. **PATH OF JUDGMENTS**
Walk where thousands of other pilgrims have traveled.

2. **JEDHA CITY WALLS**
Ancient walls that are as breathtaking today as when they were first built.

3. **TEMPLE OF THE KYBER**
Towering temple containing magnificent kyber crystals. **CLOSED!**

4. **DOME OF DELIVERANCE**
A must-see architectural wonder, glistening with light.

5. **THE CATACOMBS OF CADERA**
See the bones of a people long forgotten.

6. **DESICCATED TABLELANDS**
Behold the massive table mountains in this barren region of Jedha.

Who used to protect the Temple of the Kyber?
The Guardians of the Whills, an order of dedicated warriors.

THE CATACOMBS OF CADERA

Secret base of Saw Gerrera's rebels • Far from Jedha City • Walls inlaid with monks' skulls • Locals believe it is haunted • Contains dungeon

221

Fast Facts

POPULATION: Native Teedos and Uthuthma, immigrant settlers and scavengers

NOTABLE SETTLEMENTS: Niima Outpost, Tuanul Village, Cratertown

NATURAL FEATURES: Goazon Badlands, Kelvin Ravine, Sinking Fields

EDIBLE PLANTS: Spinebarrels, Tuanulberry bushes, nightbloomers

BEST KNOWN FOR
BEING THE LONELY HOMEWORLD OF REY
Jakku

TOP 3 NOTABLE JAKKUVIANS
1. **Gallius Rax**—protégé of Palpatine, Imperial Fleet Admiral, and rebel spy.
2. **The Sitter**—human male silently keeping watch from atop a pillar.
3. **Constable Zuvio**—faithful law-keeper of Niima Outpost.

In numbers

25,000 inhabitants
Jakku's population (exact total unknown)

6,400km (3,977 miles)
Diameter of Jakku

352 days
Length of 1 Jakku year

2 moons
In Jakku's orbit

1 thirsty happabore
Doesn't want to share the drinking trough with Finn!

Settlers in Tuanul Village belong to the **Church of the Force**. It is home to **Lor San Tekka**—explorer and keeper of the **map** to Luke Skywalker.

Q: Why are there so many shipwrecks on Jakku?
A: Jakku becomes a ship **graveyard** when Imperial ships **crash** on the surface, and pull New Republic ships **out of orbit** with their tractor beams. The planet had hosted a **secret** Imperial research base until the Empire made its **last stand** and **battled** the New Republic there.

Top 3 You know you're a Teedo if...

1. **YOUR NAME IS TEEDO**
Teedos don't have individual identities—one name fits all!

2. **YOU WORSHIP A GODDESS NAMED R'IIA**
She is always cruel and usually angry about something.

3. **YOU BLAME BAD JAKKU STORMS ON R'IIA**
Her breath can create long days of wind and thunder. She never provides any nice, cooling rain, though!

NIIMA OUTPOST

Dusty spaceport settlement • Named after Niima the Hutt • Home to miners and scavengers • Location of Unkar Plutt's stall • Hotspot for unsavory people

> "Niima Outpost is that way. Stay off Kelvin Ridge. Keep away from the sinking fields in the north— you'll drown in the sand."
> **REY TO BB-8**

PLANETARY SYSTEMS ACROSS THE GALAXY

REALLY?!
Poor "Crusher" Roodown loses his **ARMS** in an argument with Unkar's thugs! He now wears mechanical **LOAD-LIFTER** arms and hauls junk for a living.

JAKKU FOOD CHAIN

Scavengers look for valuable ship parts and supplies, clean them up, and then sell them to Unkar Plutt in exchange for **food**. These **military rations** come in various sizes: quarter, half, and full portions. Unkar is always changing the exchange rate to his **advantage**!

1. Choose a wreck to search for goods. — **STAR DESTROYER**
2. Clean any parts that you can trade. — **CAPACITOR BEARING**
3. Haggle with Unkar for the best deal. — **STINGY BUYER**
4. Bon appétit! — **VEG-MEAT AND POLYSTARCH**

Q: What does Bobbajo carry on his back?

A: The Nu-Cosian crittermonger Bobbajo loves **creatures**. He carries a pet **worrt** named J'Rrosch, several **sneep**, **gwerps**, a pair of **zhhee**, and a **lonlan**.

Peek behind the scenes
Sound editor David Acord based the **Teedo** dialect on Thai, mixed with the names of Philadelphia Eagles sports team members!

STRANGE ...BUT TRUE
Scavenger and former bounty hunter Sarco Plank doesn't have any **eyes**! Instead, the Melitto "sees" using highly sensitive **cilia** hidden behind his faceplate. Cilia resemble tiny hairs and are sensitive to **scents**, **temperature**, and **sound waves**.

Tell me more!

DESERT DWELLERS
Jakku's **treacherous** environment suits some creatures **perfectly**. Birds include metal-munching **steelpeckers** and flightless **bloggins**. Among the reptiles are yellow-bellied **sand lizards** and winged **zhhee**. Three-tailed fire **scorpions** and **dune beetles** are pests, but **fantabu** and **dune zaywar** are valued for fur and tusks.

HOT PROPERTY: FINDING A HOME ON JAKKU

WATTLE AND DAUB — Tuanul villagers build homes with clay, sand, and animal dung, formed on a simple frame.

TENT SHELTERS — Vendors at the market in Niima Outpost set up temporary shops with tents and tarps.

SHIPWRECKS — Scavengers renovate New Republic and Imperial ships, turning ruins into liveable homes.

SHIP GRAVEYARD

Jakku is a **scorching desert world** of sand dunes, salt plains, and jagged rock formations. Though it appears desolate, Jakku harbors **important secrets**—and a **Force-sensitive girl** who could **change the fate** of the galaxy!

WORLD WRECKER

Deep within the Unknown Regions lies a terror unlike any other. Here, the First Order turns a cold, snowy world into a massive superweapon: Starkiller Base. Destruction is imminent...

Fast Facts

OWNED BY: The First Order

LOCATION: Various (the base is mobile). Hidden from the New Republic!

CLIMATE: Icy

BASE COMMANDER: General Hux

FIRST USE: Obliterating the Hosnian System

Q: How does the Starkiller destroy planets?

A: Lurking in the depths of space, it fires at planets across the galaxy using a **laser beam** that tunnels through **hyperspace**. Near its target, the laser **splits** into multiple beams, destroying **many** planet-sized targets **at once**.

MISSION FILE: THE RESISTANCE'S ATTACK

1. Snap Wexley leads a reconnaissance mission to scan the base.
2. Resistance leadership, with the help of Finn, identifies a weakness.
3. Han Solo, Chewbacca, and Finn penetrate the planetary shields by flying at lightspeed.
4. The ground team damage the thermal oscillator from inside with explosives.
5. Poe Dameron and his X-wing pilots attack the oscillator from the air.
6. The station is destroyed by its own power when the fuel cells rupture.

 SUCCESS

Before it was a base, the Empire **mined** the planet for **kyber crystals** to power its Death Star weapons.

PARADE GROUNDS

Serve as marshaling yard and landing platform • Large banners and long speeches inspire troops' loyalty • Perfect view of superweapon firing

"All remaining systems will bow to the First Order. We'll remember this as the last day of the Republic. Fire!"

GENERAL HUX

PLANETARY SYSTEMS ACROSS THE GALAXY

BEST KNOWN FOR

BLOWING UP THE GALACTIC SENATE

Starkiller Base

> "The weapon. It is ready. I believe the time has come to use it."
> **GENERAL HUX**

REALLY?! Han and Finn dump Captain Phasma down a **GARBAGE CHUTE** to the base's **TRASH COMPACTOR**!

STRANGE

...BUT TRUE
The superweapon charges by **draining** a nearby **sun** of its power until it **disappears**. To fire again, the whole base **moves** to the next star system to devour a **new** star.

TOP 4

BEST BASE DEFENSES
1. The "Tarkin's Revenge" fighter squadron
2. Snowtroopers on patrol in snowspeeders
3. Anti-aircraft tri-cannons
4. Anti-ship missiles

In numbers

660km (410 miles)
Diameter of Starkiller Base

16km (10 miles)
Diameter of the solarvac array to consume a sun

1 sun
Devoured in order to fire a single shot

½ Resistance fleet
Destroyed in the attack on Starkiller Base

The planet's **shields** have a fractional refresh rate that **stops** anything **slower** than **lightspeed** from getting in.

NO WAY!! When the base is wiped out, the superweapon explodes. The energy left behind forms a **BINARY STAR**.

Starkiller Base
660km (410 mi)

Death Star II — 200km (124 mi)
Death Star — 160km (99 mi)

Dwarfing the past Starkiller Base is more than **four times larger** than the Empire's Death Star space stations!

225

SPACE TRAVEL AND WEAPONS

FULL THROTTLE!

Have a **need for speed**? The galaxy is buzzing with high-powered spacecraft. From the **mighty but slow-moving Imperial Star Destroyer** to the **zippy and agile A-wing**, there's a starship to suit every mission!

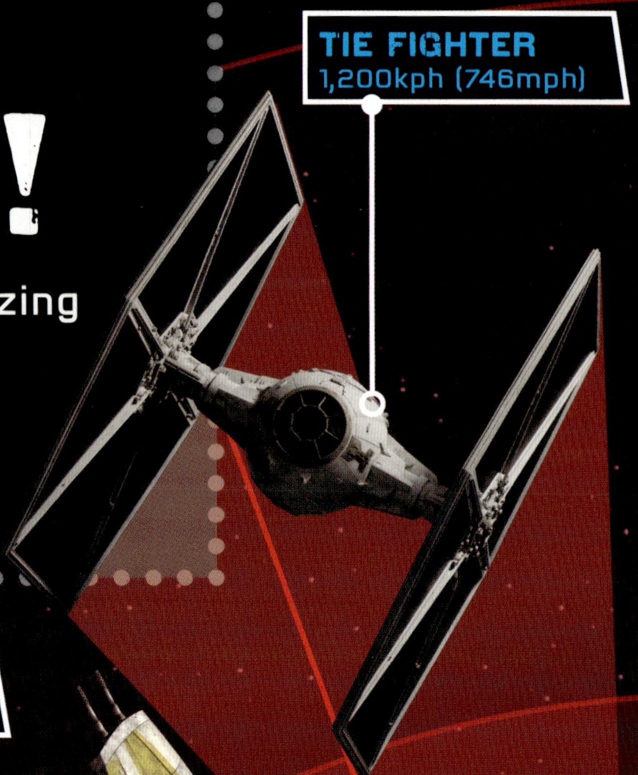

TIE FIGHTER
1,200kph (746mph)

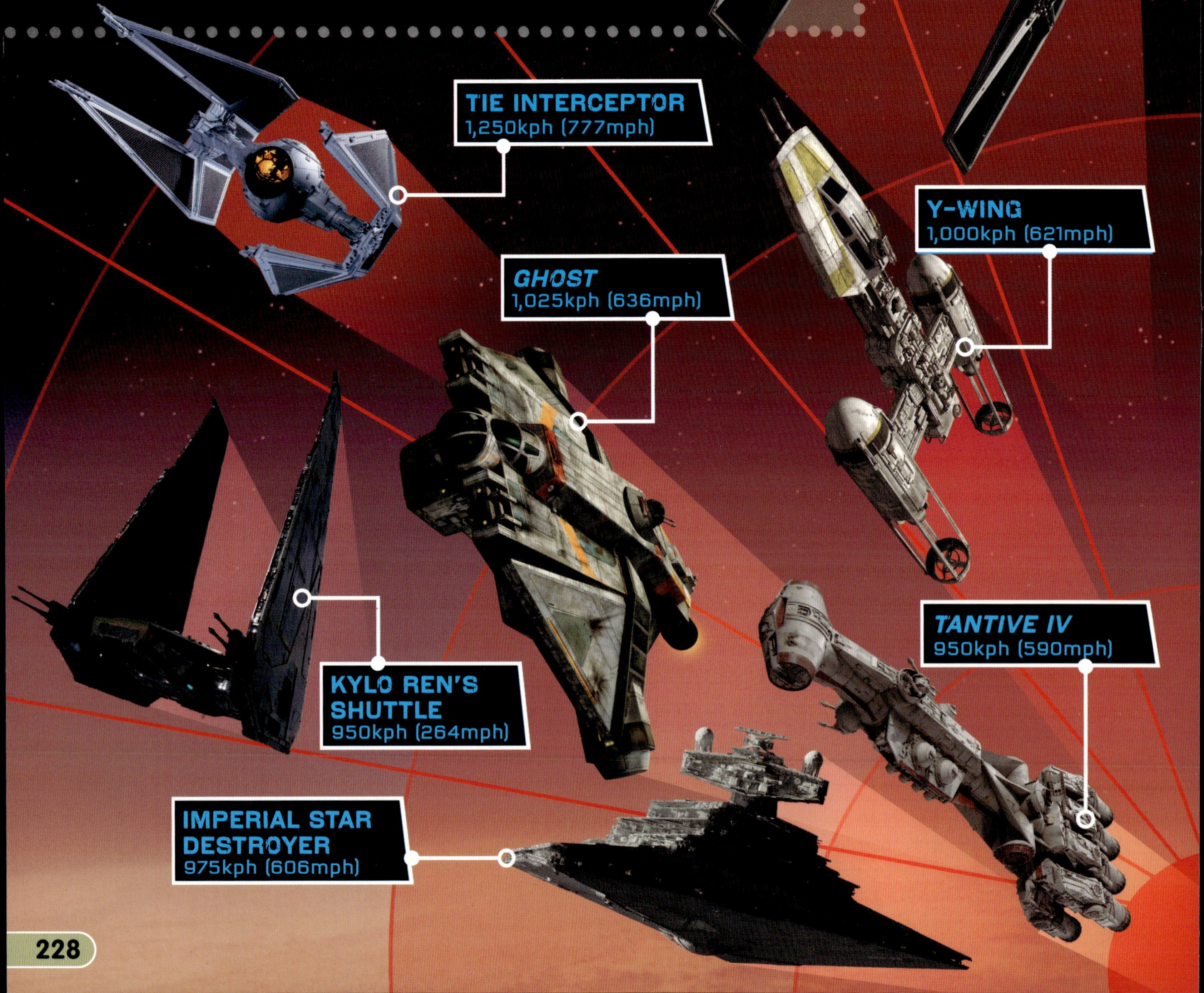

TIE INTERCEPTOR
1,250kph (777mph)

GHOST
1,025kph (636mph)

Y-WING
1,000kph (621mph)

TANTIVE IV
950kph (590mph)

KYLO REN'S SHUTTLE
950kph (264mph)

IMPERIAL STAR DESTROYER
975kph (606mph)

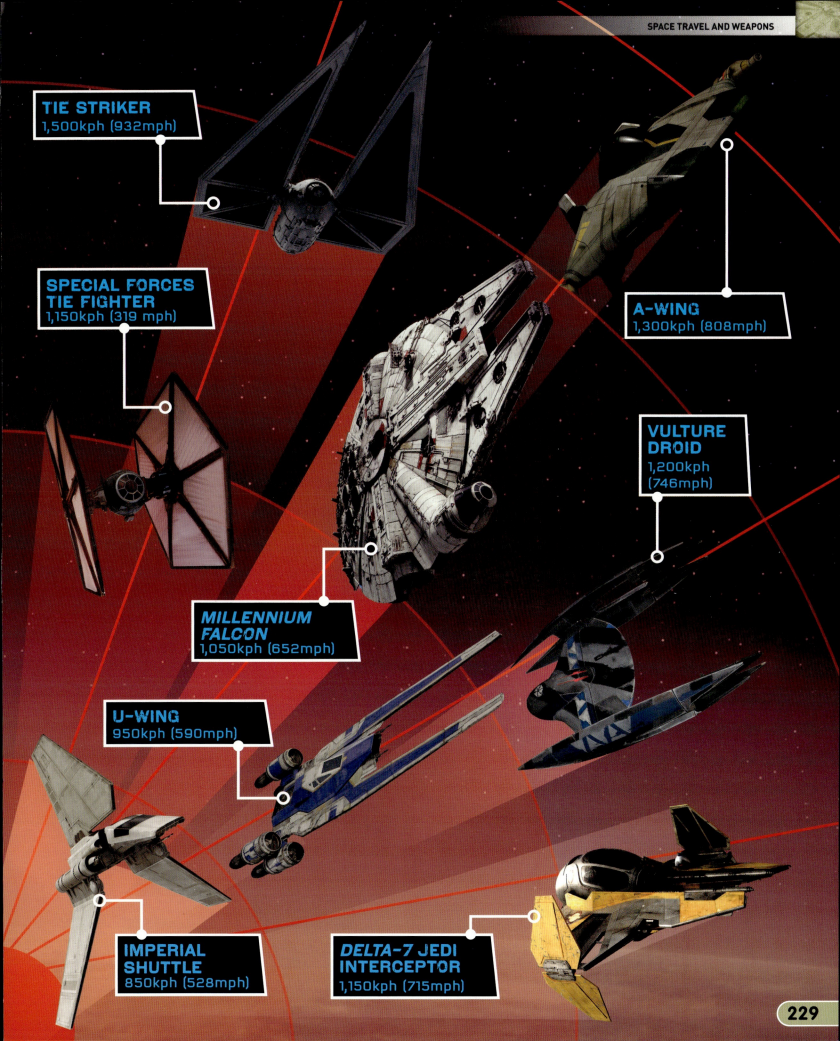

In numbers

150,000 light years
Travel range of a Jedi interceptor using a hyperdrive booster ring

3,600G
Maximum acceleration of a tri-fighter in open space

1,500 vulture droids
Carried on a Trade Federation battleship

192 V-wing starfighters
Carried on a *Venator*-class Star Destroyer

V-19 Torrent starfighter
6m (19ft 8in)
> Missiles with onboard targeting intelligence.

REALLY?!
The tri-fighter's three-armed design mimics the **SKULL FEATURES** of a **FEROCIOUS PREDATOR** native to the planet Colla IV.

Aggressive ReConnaissance (ARC)-170
12.71m (41ft 8in)
> **Hyperdrive equipped**, largest crew.

Droid tri-fighter
5.4m (17ft 8in)
> **Smallest** starfighter in either fleet.

Delta-7 *Aethersprite* Jedi starfighter
8m (26ft 2in)
> Interstellar travel with **hyperdrive**.

ARC OF AGGRESSION

Most Republic starfighters are single-pilot craft—small, nimble, and fast—but they lack heavy weapons, shields, and hyperdrives. The **ARC-170 is different**. Designed for **long-range solo combat**, it is large, well armed, lightspeed enabled, and requires a crew of three: a pilot, copilot, and tail-gunner.

HOW DO SMALL JEDI STARFIGHTERS CROSS INTERSTELLAR DISTANCES?
They engage the specially-fitted Syliure hyperdrive booster ring.

AERIAL COMBAT!

You're a Jedi pilot separated from your squadron and under heavy vulture droid fire. You're **outnumbered, outgunned,** and **almost out of luck**. Good thing you just serviced your **superfast Jedi interceptor**.

SPACE TRAVEL AND WEAPONS

Q: Why are Jedi starfighters the smallest ships in the Republic fleet?
A: The Jedi pilots' Force-enhanced abilities means they need **fewer controls, instruments, or sensors** than a regulation clone pilot. They also waste less ammunition, thanks to their precision targeting skills. Despite their size, they are just **as deadly as clone fighters**.

Buzz droid
0.25m (10in) (in sphere mode)
> **Sabotage droids** launched by **tri-fighters**.

Eta-2

Eta-2 Actis Jedi interceptor
5.47m (17ft 11in)
> **Fastest** starfighter in either fleet.

TOP 4
REASONS TO DEPLOY DROID STARFIGHTERS
1. Can make **extreme maneuvers** that would crush the sturdiest living pilot.
2. No life-support systems allows **more room for armaments and fuel**.
3. **No moral concerns** on certain death missions.
4. Designed for **multiple roles**, such as space fighter and ground walker.

Tell me more!

SMART SHIPS
Droid starfighters were **originally remote-controlled**, but later fitted with **artificial intelligence**. While tri-fighters are smarter than vulture droids and hyena bombers, no amount of droid programming can outthink a clone or Jedi pilot. Droid pilots rely on **speed** and **overwhelming numbers** to win the day.

Vulture droid
6.96m (22ft 10in) (flight configuration)
> Transforms into **walking patrol droid** to assist with ground operations.

Vulture droids are built in the **cathedral factories** of Xi Char, where precision manufacturing is an act of **religious worship**.

Peek behind the scenes
The design of the V-19 Torrent's engines and folding wings is based on that of the F4U Corsair aircraft flown in World War II.

STRANGE ...BUT TRUE
Some Separatist **missiles** don't hit their target. Instead they burst open to unleash the **brutal buzz droids** that **rip apart ships**—with the **pilot still inside!**

Buzz droid

Q: How do you defeat a buzz droid?
A: **Zap its center eye!** This sends a chain reaction through the whole droid that **shuts it down**.

231

RECKLESS REBELS

The *Ghost* isn't the only freighter fighting for the Rebellion. Calling themselves "Iron Squadron," Mart Mattin, Gooti Terez, Jonner Jin, and R3-A3 take on the Empire in their YT-2400, *Sato's Hammer*.

Q: Where does the *Ghost* get its name?

A: Hera equips the ship with **stealth systems** that reduce its energy emissions to make it **almost invisible**, like a ghost! Enemy sensors often **mistake** the freighter for cosmic radiation or a strange solar wave.

COOL!!
The *Ghost*'s weapons pack a **WALLOP**— enough to bring down a **LIGHT CRUISER**!

WOW!...
87
The number of illegal upgrades to the *Ghost*'s stealth systems

STRANGE ...BUT TRUE
Whenever Chopper sends commands to the *Ghost*'s navicomputer, the two machines get into **angry data arguments** with each other. The *Ghost* finds Chopper very **rude and pushy**!

TOP 5 PLACES EZRA HIDES ON THE *GHOST* AFTER PLAYING JOKES ON ZEB
1. Cargo bay locker
2. Inside the *Phantom II*
3. Interior air ducts
4. Under the common room's dejarik chess table
5. In Kanan's cabin

Common room

Fast Facts

MAIN FREIGHTER:
The *Ghost*

ATTACHED SHUTTLE:
The *Phantom II*

WEAPONRY:
Ghost: 1 dorsal laser turret, 2 forward laser turrets
Phantom II: 2 forward laser cannons, 2 swiveling aft laser cannons

CAPTAIN: Hera Syndulla

MANUFACTURER:
Corellian Shipyards

TOP 7 STARSHIP FEATS...

1. The *Ghost* uses its stealth systems to slip unnoticed into the Star Destroyer *Lawbringer*'s hangar bay.
2. The *Phantom* survives the fyrnock-infested Fort Anaxes asteroid—twice!
3. The *Ghost* provides cover fire during the rebels' rescue of Wookiee slaves on Kessel.
4. The *Phantom* infiltrates the Imperial prison on Stygeon Prime without being detected.
5. The *Ghost*, piloted by the mysterious Fulcrum, suddenly joins the fight above Mustafar in the nick of time to save the rebels.
6. The *Ghost* joins the space battle of Scarif, helping to steal the plans to the Death Star.
7. Guided by the Force, the *Ghost* discovers the mysterious planet of Lira San, thought only to be a legend.

SPACE TRAVEL AND WEAPONS

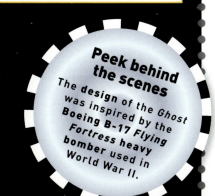

"Ghost to Spectre-5. We're in position."
HERA ABOUT TO PICK UP SABINE AFTER SHE WREAKS HAVOC AT A TIE FIGHTER BASE

Peek behind the scenes
The design of the Ghost was inspired by the Boeing B-17 Flying Fortress heavy bomber used in World War II.

HIDE AND SEEK

The **sneaky** *Ghost* and its **attack shuttle**, the *Phantom II*, can operate separately, but they work best together, as a **single starship**. This is ideal for its rebel crew, who need **all the options** they can get when **fighting** or **fleeing** the Empire!

THE SHOWDOWN: *GHOST* VS. *FALCON*
The *Ghost* may **not** be able to **outrace** the legendary *Millennium Falcon*, but it wins **sizewise**! The *Falcon* is 34m (112ft) long x 25.61m (84ft) wide, but the *Ghost* **punches in** at 43.9m (144ft) long x 34.2m (112ft 2in) wide.

Tell me more!

NO TIME TO CHECK THE MAP!
The rebels have escaped Imperial forces many times thanks to Hera **swiftly engaging** the *Ghost*'s hyperdrive. But this gives the navicomputer **no time** to chart a path through hyperspace, so they thank their lucky stars they haven't **run into an asteroid** or **bounced off a supernova** yet!

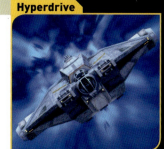
Hyperdrive

In numbers

1,025kph (636mph)
Ghost's maximum in-atmosphere speed

360 degrees
Swivel of the *Ghost*'s dorsal turret

100
Model number of VCX-class light freighter

4 personal cabins
On the *Ghost*

2 cockpit seats
For piloting the *Phantom II*

1 astromech socket
Added for Chopper in the *Phantom* and *Phantom II*

A CLOSER LOOK
The graphic on the *Phantom II* is a tibidee, a creature that once mistook the original shuttle's radio frequency for a mating call! Like the *Phantom II*, these massive space creatures can fly through hyperspace.

Q: Why have there been two Phantoms?
A: The original *Phantom* shuttle was lost on a mission to steal starfighters from the Empire's floating junkyard, Reklam Station. It was replaced with *Phantom II*, a **stolen** *Sheathipede*-class transport shuttle, once used by the **Separatist army**.

Fast Facts

CAPTAIN: Chewbacca
MANUFACTURER: Corellian Engineering Corporation
WEAPONRY: 2 quad laser cannons, 2 concussion missile launchers, 1 blaster cannon
MODEL: Heavily customized YT-1300 light freighter

BEST KNOWN FOR MAKING THE KESSEL RUN IN LESS THAN 12 PARSECS
The *Millennium Falcon*

"Well, you tell him that Han Solo just stole back the *Millennium Falcon* for good."
— HAN SOLO TO REY

MISSION FILE

1. **Providing transport to Alderaan** — Han tries to take Luke and Obi-Wan to Alderaan, but the planet has been destroyed. **FAIL**

2. **Rescuing the princess** — The crew rescues Leia from the Death Star and the *Falcon* carries her to safety. **SUCCESS**

3. **Battle of Yavin** — Piloting the *Falcon*, Han takes Vader out of the battle, while Luke blows up the Death Star. **SUCCESS**

4. **Escape from Jakku** — Rey, Finn, and BB-8 evade the TIEs and unexpectedly meet Han Solo and Chewbacca. **SUCCESS**

5. **Battle of Starkiller Base** — Rey is rescued and the base is destroyed, but Han Solo is lost. **SUCCESS & FAIL**

Peek behind the scenes
New films use several versions of the *Falcon*. There are digital models, but also physical scale models, an isolated cockpit on motion supports, and a life-size model (about 2/3 complete).

A PIECE OF JUNK?

In its long service, the *Millennium Falcon* is many things—a **freighter, a smuggler's vessel, and a warship**. To Han Solo and Chewbacca, it's also **home**... not to mention the **most important starship** in the Rebellion!

REALLY?! The *Millennium Falcon*'s computer is entirely **UNIQUE**. It is made of elements from a variety of **DROID BRAINS**.

STRANGE ...BUT TRUE
Other owners make **small changes** to the Falcon—**none** of them good! Unkar Plutt installs a fuel pump that must be **primed** to start the ship, and an ignition line compressor that causes **constant problems**!

SPACE TRAVEL AND WEAPONS

Q: What is dejarik?
A: The *Millennium Falcon* has a checkered **dejarik (chess) hologame table** that Chewbacca enjoys playing with. The game includes characters of eight different species, including a **Ng'ok, Houjix, Mantellian Savrip, Ghhhk, K'lor'slug, Kintan strider, Monnok,** and **Grimtaash the Molator**.

FREIGHT PUSHER
The *Millennium Falcon* is a YT-1300 light freighter. Its original purpose would have been to transport cargo, which was pushed by the two **front-facing prongs**.

STRANGE ...BUT TRUE
Han didn't buy the *Millennium Falcon*. He **won** the ship from **Lando Calrissian**, who **bet** the *Falcon* in a high-stakes game of **Sabacc**!

A number of owners
The *Millennium Falcon* has had many owners. Ducain steals it from Han Solo, before the Irving Boys steal it from Ducain. Unkar Plutt steals it from them, but Rey and Finn steal it from Unkar. After Han's death, Rey and Chewbacca take it to look for Luke Skywalker.

Top 3
Repairs and enhancements

1. **SCANNER-PROOF COMPARTMENTS**
Good for hiding people and cargo from Imperial inspections.

2. **WEAPONS UPGRADES**
Modified laser and blaster cannons to take out pirates and TIE fighters.

3. **HYPERDRIVE FIX**
Rey corrects an electrical overload and a coolant leak, and shuts off the alarms.

TOP 8
MOST DANGEROUS MOMENTS
1. Surviving Jakku's junkyard maze run.
2. Being chased by Star Destroyers.
3. Being pulled aboard the Death Star.
4. Crash landing on Starkiller Base.
5. Getting swallowed by a space slug.
6. Being chewed on by mynocks.
7. Being chased by bounty hunters.
8. Zooming through Death Star II.

In numbers

3720 to 1
The odds of the *Falcon* safely navigating Hoth's asteroid belt

100 metric tons (220,462lbs)
Cargo capacity

6 passengers
The number who can be comfortably accommodated onboard

5 escape pods
Model CEC Class-1

1 Jedi training remote
Left behind by Luke Skywalker

0.5 hyperdrive class
The *Falcon*'s lightspeed rating—twice as fast as most Imperial warships

235

FAMOUS X-WING PILOTS

Luke Skywalker
Red Five and later Rogue Leader, the X-wing is his ship of choice.

Wedge Antilles
Former Imperial cadet turned rebel. Veteran of two Death Star attacks.

Garven Dreis
Led Red Squadron at the Battles of Scarif and Yavin.

Jek Porkins
Lost in the Battle of Yavin. Jek's Belly Run maneuver is standard pilot training in the Resistance 30 years later!

Poe Dameron
The best pilot in the Resistance. Trusted by General Leia Organa.

Snap Wexley
Trained as a pilot at a young age. Considered the Resistance's best recon pilot.

WHY IS IT CALLED AN "X-WING?"
In combat, the wings spread apart to form an "X." This makes the ship less speedy, but easier to navigate.

TAKING FIVE
Red Five pilot Pedrin Gaul lost his life in the Battle of Scarif. His death leaves a space on the roster for Luke Skywalker.

Peek behind the scenes
ILM's visual effects team found 40-year-old unused footage of Red Leader and Gold Leader to bring their classic characters back in Rogue One.

STRANGE ...BUT TRUE
Luke does **not need** his **targeting computer** to destroy the Death Star. He uses the **Force** to judge **when to fire** his torpedoes, landing a perfect shot.

Rebel X-wing pilots are allowed to **customize** their Koensayr K-22995 helmets. Each is a **statement** of the pilot's experience and personality.

Q: Who is the X-wing's designer?
A: **Incom Corporation** originally designs the X-wing for the **Imperial Navy**. But when the Empire chooses **TIE fighters** to be the backbone of their fleet, the mighty X-wing finds a home in the **Rebel Alliance**.

FAST FLYERS

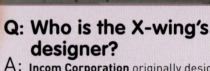
T-65 X-WING (REBEL ALLIANCE)

They have four wings, one pilot, and a seemingly **endless** ability to **ruin** the plans of **bad guys** everywhere. With heroic pilots at the stick, X-wings have the power to change the course of galactic history. Dive in **full throttle** and take a closer look at these space superiority fighters!

SPACE TRAVEL AND WEAPONS

T-65		**T-70**
Incom	Manufacturer	Incom-FreiTek
1,050kph (652mph)	Atmospheric speed	1,150kph (715mph)
Four KX9 laser cannons; two proton torpedo tubes	Typical weaponry	Four KX12 laser cannons; two proton torpedo tubes
Fixed	Armament options	Quick-change magazine to swap torpedoes with other weapons, such as concussion missiles
Incom 4L4 fusial thrust engine	Engines	Incom-FreiTek 5L5 fusial thrust Split-engines
Yes	Deflector shields	Yes
R-series	Astromech	Variable: R-series or BB unit

T-70 X-WING (RESISTANCE)

Poor rebel astromech droid D4-R4B has a programming **flaw**—he's **afraid** of **flying**!

REALLY?! A T-70 X-wing is **PRECISE** enough to hit a single stormtrooper-sized target while flying at **TOP SPEED**.

Q: What does an astromech do in an X-wing?

A: Droids act as **copilots** and **flight engineers**, flying when needed or maintaining the ship's **systems** during combat.

X-WING vs. TIE FIGHTER
Deflector shields, hyperdrives, more cannons, and onboard astromech droids make Rebellion X-wings **superior** to Imperial TIE fighters. In battle, Imperials must rely on **maneuverability**, **speed**, and **numbers** to defeat the rebels' X-wings.

TOP 6 X-WING MISSIONS
1. **Battle of Scarif**—attacking the planet's shield gate and Empire forces.
2. **Battle of Yavin**—destroying the first Death Star.
3. **Battle of Endor**—destroying the second Death Star.
4. **Attack on Starkiller Base**—destroying a weapon even bigger than the Death Star space stations!
5. **Battle of Jakku**—the New Republic fighting the final stand of the Empire.
6. **Rescue at Takodana**—saving Han Solo and Finn from the First Order.

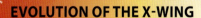

EVOLUTION OF THE X-WING

Z-95
This single-wing fighter is built for the Republic, and is used during the Clone Wars.

ARC-170
This three-person fighter is an ancestor of the X-wing's S-foil, or moveable wing, design.

T-65
The primary fighter of the Rebel Alliance, this vehicle is well known for its incredible speed.

T-70
Supporters of General Organa donate unneeded New Republic X-wings to the Resistance.

The development cost of the T-70 prototype produced prior to the Battle of Jakku is **1,499,999** credits!

237

MIGHTY FLEET

With its massive **Star Destroyers**, sleek **shuttles**, and swarming **TIE fighters**, the powerful Imperial Navy is a constant reminder of the Emperor's **iron grip** on the galaxy.

Fast Facts

BIGGEST VEHICLE: Super Star Destroyer

SMALLEST VEHICLE: E-XD infiltrator droid landing pod

WEAPONRY: Turbolasers, ion cannons, tractor beams

Tell me more!

IMPERIAL TRAP
Imperial interdictors have four massive **gravity wells**. When in the right position, they can pull a ship out of **hyperspace** and blast it into oblivion.

Peek behind the scenes
The sound of diving German World War II Stuka bombers inspired the iconic scream of the TIE fighter engine.

Q: Where are TIE fighters manufactured?
A: The Empire builds TIE fighters at **Sienar Fleet Systems** factories across the galaxy. This includes the advanced facility on the **planet Lothal**.

WHAT MAKES A STAR DESTROYER?

All Star Destroyers are **gigantic warships** with **pointed hulls**, but that's where their similarities end. The *Acclamator*-class assault ship (1) is mainly a **troop transport**. The *Venator*-class (2) is more heavily armed than the assault ship and is also a **fighter carrier**. The giant *Imperial*-class Star Destroyers (3) are self-contained **mobile bases**, and all are dwarfed by the colossal Super Star Destroyers (4).

1.
4.
2.
3.

REALLY?!
Only **10 PERCENT** of Imperial Navy cadets **GRADUATE** to become pilots. Their pride in this accomplishment makes them **ARROGANT** and **BOSSY**.

Small but lethal

Zeta-class cargo shuttle — 28.74m (94ft 4in)

TIE defender — 8.94m (29ft 3in)

TIE interceptor — 4.9m (16ft 1in)

TIE striker — 2.95m (9ft 8in)

From the well-armed **TIE interceptor** to the high-speed **TIE striker**, the Imperial Navy uses a range of smaller craft to maintain order in the galaxy.

SPACE TRAVEL AND WEAPONS

In numbers

1,600m (5,249ft)
Length of an *Imperial*-class Star Destroyer

1,200kph (745mph)
In-atmosphere speed of a TIE fighter

60
Turbolaser batteries on a Star Destroyer

32
ArmaTek VL-61/79 proton bombs in a TIE striker

13
Engine clusters on a Super Star Destroyer

2
Refreshers (toilets) in *Sentinel*-class landing craft

Star Destroyers carry enough supplies to travel for two years without restocking.

STRANGE ...BUT TRUE
Standard Imperial protocol requires that a Star Destroyer **dump its trash into space**, before jumping to hyperspace.

> "There's too many of them!"
> — REBEL PILOT TELSIJ ON THE OVERWHELMING SIZE OF THE IMPERIAL NAVY

Imperial Insults!
TIE striker pilots often call regular TIE pilots **"vac-heads,"** implying that flying in space makes them **stupid**.

WHAT IS THE MOST COMMON SHIP IN THE IMPERIAL NAVY?
→ The TIE fighter

When the Imperials need to move small cargo, groups of prisoners, or a squad of troops, they use the *Gozanti*-class freighter. Boasting serious firepower, the freighter carries four TIE fighters for protection.

Q: How does the Emperor travel?
A: Emperor Palpatine uses his own personal **Imperial shuttle**, staffed with Royal Guards and **heavily armed** with **five sets of laser cannons**.

WOW!...

9,700
Stormtroopers stationed on a single Star Destroyer

Luke Skywalker's lightsaber

Anakin Skywalker's lightsaber

Qui-Gon Jinn's lightsaber

Obi-Wan Kenobi's lightsaber

Yoda's lightsaber

Ezra Bridger's first lightsaber

Kanan Jarrus's lightsaber

Mace Windu's lightsaber

Ahsoka Tano's duel lightsabers

SPACE TRAVEL AND WEAPONS

Darth Vader's lightsaber

Darth Sidious's lightsaber

Asajj Ventress's lightsaber (one of a pair)

Count Dooku's lightsaber

Kylo Ren's lightsaber

Darth Maul's lightsaber

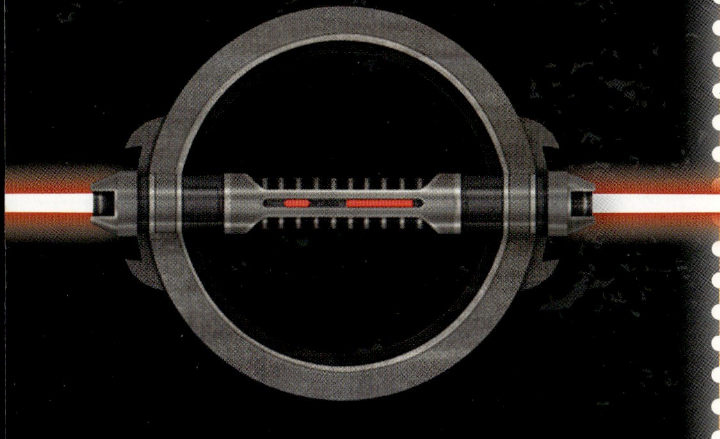

Grand Inquisitor's lightsaber

DEADLY BLADES

Lightsabers are handmade by their owners. Jedi lightsabers are mostly powered by blue or green kyber crystals. Evil Force users like the Sith wield red blades, with crystals tainted by the dark side.

Fast Facts

NAME: Death Star
AFFILIATION: The Empire
ROLE: Planet-smashing battle station
WEAPONRY: Superlaser, turbolasers
DEFENSES: Tractor beams, TIE fighters
FIRST TESTED: Jedha City

REALLY?! Using just one reactor, the Death Star can destroy a **WHOLE CITY**. With its full power, the weapon wipes out an **ENTIRE PLANET!**

STRANGE ...BUT TRUE Tens of thousands of Geonosian drones from the Stalgasin hive **build** the Death Star. Soldier Geonosians **zap** or **blast** workers who don't work hard enough!

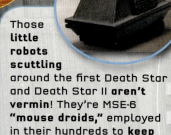

Those little robots scuttling around the first Death Star and Death Star II aren't vermin! They're MSE-6 "mouse droids," employed in their hundreds to keep the floors clean.

BEST KNOWN FOR

OBLITERATING THE PLANET ALDERAAN

Death Star

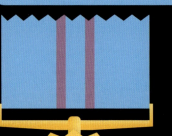

DOOMSDAY WEAPONS

Q. What's the size of a small moon and has enough firepower to blast a planet to bits? A. One of the Empire's **mighty Death Star battle stations**, built to keep rebellious star systems in line—or else!

BATTLE STATIONS!

Both boast massive firepower, but Death Star II has more advanced weaponry • Both carry huge numbers of Imperial Navy, Army, and stormtroopers

"That's no moon. It's a space station."
OBI-WAN KENOBI ON THE DEATH STAR

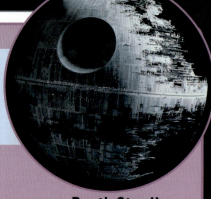

Death Star		Death Star II
160km (99 miles)	Diameter	200km (124 miles)
Director Krennic (construction)	Commander	Moff Jerjerrod
342,953	Total crew	637,835
15,000	Turbolaser batteries	30,000
24 hours	Superlaser recharge time	3 minutes
768	Tractor beam emplacements	768

SPACE TRAVEL AND WEAPONS

GROSS!!
A **DIANOGA SQUID** lurks in the Death Star's garbage compactor. Its usual diet is **ROTTING TRASH**, but Luke looks **PRETTY TASTY**, too!

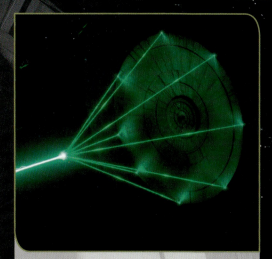

In numbers

2,471,647 passengers and crew
On Death Star II

7,500 laser cannons
On Death Star II

5,000 ion cannons
On Death Star II

10x the firepower
Of a Super Star Destroyer

DESTROYER OF WORLDS
At the heart of the Death Star lies a **devastating weapon of doom**— the **superlaser**. Powered by hypermatter reactors, it magnifies energy through kyber crystals harvested from across the galaxy into one **planet-shattering beam**.

Peek behind the scenes
The sound of the giant Death Star ray that blasts Alderaan is taken in part from the buzzing of spaceships in the 1930s Flash Gordon science fiction serials, favorites of George Lucas.

Tell me more!

FATAL FLAWS
Both Death Star battle stations prove to have significant **faults**—and the rebels exploit them! **Luke Skywalker** fires **torpedoes** from his X-wing into an open **exhaust vent** to blow up the first Death Star. The Death Star II falls when rebel teams disable its **shield** and explode its **reactor core**.

TOP SECRET
The Empire build the first Death Star in **secret**. They don't want the Imperial Senate to **find out** about the terrible weapon they are building. Without proof, most people in the galaxy **don't believe** such a mechanical marvel is even **possible**!

Top 5
Locations on the Death Star and Death Star II

1 EMPEROR'S THRONE ROOM
Never used on the first Death Star. Evil emperors have little time to sit and give orders.

2 OVERBRIDGE
Command center and commanders' headquarters.

3 SUPERLASER CONTROL STATIONS
Prepare and fire the weapon.

4 DETENTION BLOCKS
Section where prisoners are interrogated and executed.

5 HYPERMATTER REACTORS
Generate huge amounts of power. When these are wiped out, so are the Death Star battle stations!

WOW!...

1,000,000,000,000+
Cost of building a Death Star in galactic credits (one trillion plus)

How does Luke Skywalker **survive** in **exile** on Ahch-To?

THE BATTLE CONTINUES...

What types of **weapon** do the menacing **Praetorian Guards** wield?

Which **animal** decorates the windows of Canto Bight's **casinos**?

CHAPTER 5

HERMIT'S HIDEOUT

Q: What's it like to live here?
A: Luke lives a humble way of life on the island. He survives on what nature provides for his food and shelter.

Towering cliffs and stone ruins dot the **secluded island** that **Luke Skywalker** calls home, located on the planet Ahch-To. Troubled by the **tragic** events of the past, **weary** Luke lives here in **quiet exile**—until **Rey** arrives in search of **help** for the stricken Resistance.

> "Breathe. Just breathe. Now, reach out. What do you see?"
> **LUKE TO REY**

MEETING THE LOCALS
Chewbacca doesn't just wait around while Luke and Rey **explore** matters of the Force. The Wookiee gets to know the **wildlife** of this remote island—such as the **feathery winged porgs**!

Peek behind the scenes
The design for the porgs is a mixture of **puffin** meets **penguin** meets **guinea pig**!

STRANGE ...BUT TRUE
Flocks of **adorable porgs** roam and roost in the island's craggy rocks and cliffs. These flat-muzzled avian creatures are **very inquisitive** by nature.

THE BATTLE CONTINUES...

Tell me more!

PRIME PARKING SPOT
Rey is not alone on her journey to Ahch-To. The ever-faithful **R2-D2** and copilot **Chewbacca** accompany her in the *Millennium Falcon*. The ship is left docked on low rocks beneath a set of **stone steps** that scale the steep cliffs. Chewie and R2-D2 wait by the *Falcon* as Rey climbs the winding steps to **find Luke**.

Top 4

Extreme spots to spend in exile

1 AHCH-TO
Luke lives for many years on this bleak, hostile island surrounded by seas.

2 TATOOINE
Obi-Wan Kenobi's hermit hut in the desert is the perfect place to hide from the Empire and keep an eye on the young Luke.

3 LOTHO MINOR
A badly wounded Darth Maul survives years in exile on this trash-covered planet, searching the junk for resources.

4 DAGOBAH
The lonely, murky swamps of this planet become Yoda's home for more than 20 years after the horror and chaos of the Jedi Purge.

LOST AND FOUND
Rey travels to Ahch-To on a quest to find **Luke**, who may be the Resistance's **only hope** to defeat the terrifying First Order. Rey knows Luke's reputation as a **famous hero**, but she is unsure what to expect when she finally meets this mysterious figure.

TERRIFYING TIMES
Luke witnessed the **tragic destruction** of his attempt to **rebuild** the Jedi Order. Afterward, he vanished from the galaxy, and **years** passed. Some say that he left to try and find the **first Jedi temple**.

GROWING STRENGTH
The power of the Force has been **awakening inside Rey** as she travels to Ahch-To. She hopes that Luke, the last Jedi Master in the galaxy, can explain how to **develop** and **use** her new abilities.

247

Q: Who catches cheats and thieves?

A: Visitors to Canto Bight's casinos **expect to be kept safe**, so **vigilant police officers patrol** the resorts and keep an eye out for suspicious activity. It's best not to get on the wrong side of these lawkeepers—they wield **stun rods**, **crowd control rifles**, and **blaster pistols**. Troublemakers beware!

STRANGE ...BUT TRUE
This casino's brightly colored **stained glass windows** are decorated with racing **fathiers**. Bred on Canto Bight, these **elegant, speedy** creatures are forced to compete on the **race tracks**—all for the **entertainment** of wealthy spectators.

PLAYGROUND OF THE RICH

If you want an **exclusive resort** to **gamble** the night away surrounded by the galaxy's **cream of the crop**, head to the **swanky casinos** of Canto Bight. To fit in with this high-rolling crowd, you'll need to own a **fortune in credits**— and be prepared to lose it!

ELITE CLUB
Only the **richest** and most **powerful**—from politicians and celebrities to trade bosses—can **afford** to play in these **luxurious casinos**. The **gilded halls** and **ornate furniture** make them an **opulent** sight.

THE BATTLE CONTINUES...

TOP 4
GAMBLING HOTSPOTS

1. **The Outlander Club, Coruscant**—this popular hangout is famous both as a nightclub, and a venue for gambling on sporting events such as podracing.
2. **Maz Kanata's castle, Takodana**—bounty hunters, criminals, and travelers play at Maz's gambling tables.
3. **Canto Bight, Cantonica**—a golden, glittering city of casinos and resorts.
4. **Cloud City, Bespin**—this floating city is renowned for its chic casinos.

HOT PURSUIT
Canto Bight officers chase runaway criminals on their **Cantonica Zephyr GB-134 speeders**. Armed with laser cannons, these pursuit craft are **nimble** and **lightweight**, which makes zooming through large crowds a **piece of cake**.

LUXURY LIVING: THE CANTO BIGHT WAY!
- Choose a headturning outfit to stand out from the crowds.
- Pick up a good tip and place a winning bet on a fathier race.
- Gamble your earnings in casino games for the biggest thrill of all.

249

Fast Facts

NAME: Praetorian Guards
AFFILIATION: The First Order
TASKED WITH: Personally protecting Supreme Leader Snoke from any threat
SPECIES: Human
SKILLS: Specialists in melee combat
PERSONALITIES: Merciless, persistent

BEARING A GRUDGE...
Kylo Ren may have lost his first lightsaber duel with Rey—but that **doesn't mean** he's given up! Determined Kylo wants to **prove himself** to his mentor, Snoke, and **seeks revenge** on those who defeated him on Starkiller Base.

REALLY?! Among Snoke's many frightening powers are **TELEPATHY** and Force **CHOKES** and **THROWS!**

PRESENT FOR THE BOSS
The Resistance sends **personal messages** to Snoke, but they're **not exactly fan mail**—they're written on **bombs** that Resistance pilots drop onto their First Order targets!

ARMED TO THE TEETH
The Praetorian Guards boast an arsenal of **weapons**, such as **flailing whip-staffs**, and heavy double-bladed **polearms** that can also be separated into single-bladed weapons. The **precise, sweeping movements** of their **martial arts** fighting style strikes fear into the hearts of foes.

RELENTLESS EVIL

Snoke

The Resistance has wiped out the First Order's superweapon, Starkiller Base, but the battle for ultimate control of the galaxy **rages on**. Flanked by his **blood-red Praetorian Guards**, Snoke **rallies** his mighty troops to counterattack. Faces **old** and **new** will enter the fray...

THE BATTLE CONTINUES...

Fast Facts

NAME: Rose Tico
AFFILIATION: Resistance
OCCUPATION: Ground crew technician
PERSONALITY: Independent, focused, some say "crankypants"

GOING UNDERCOVER! Rose and Finn team up on a secret Resistance mission to **infiltrate** the First Order. They **disguise** themselves as First Order **officers** and must hope to **blend in** with the **enemy**.

Rose has **hated** the First Order since her **childhood**!

In numbers

9 plates of armor
Protect each Praetorian Guard's arm and shoulder

8 Praetorians
Make up Supreme Leader Snoke's personal security team

1 flying headquarters
Held in Snoke's enormous *Mega*-class Star Destroyer

1 throne
For Snoke to rule his minions from and look very scary

INDEX

Page numbers in **bold** indicate main entries. Characters are listed according to their most commonly used name, for example Han Solo is under "H" and Asajj Ventress is under "V."

A
A4-D 94
Ackbar, Admiral Gial 66, 150, 151, 215
acklay 170, 171
Adi Gallia 8
Admiral Motti 100
Admiral Kassius Konstantine 66
Admiral Wullf Yularen 100, 105
aerial combat **230-39**
Ahch-To 244, **246-47**
Ahsoka Tano **14-15**
　　and Anakin Skywalker 10, 15, 17, 207
　　and Asajj Ventress 96
　　and Captain Rex 22, 23
　　and Darth Vader 14, 15, 88
　　and the Inquisitors 108, 109
　　lightsaber 14, 240
　　and Saw Gerrera 40
aiwhas 183, 200
Ak-rev 157
Aldar Beedo 158
Alderaan 57, 67, 101, 234, 242
Amanaman 145
Amani 204
Anakin Skywalker **10-11**, 33
　　and Ahsoka Tano 207
　　Boonta Eve Classic 158, 159
　　and Count Dooku 11, 87
　　and Hondo Ohnaka 133, 169
　　lightsaber 240
　　and Obi-Wan Kenobi 10, 11, 12, 13, 15
　　and Padmé Amidala 10, 89, 197
　　and Princess Leia 10
　　and Qui-Gon Jinn 10
　　and Yoda 16, 17
　　see also Darth Vader
anoobas 168
AP-5 36, 38, 39
Arakyd Industries 49
ARC-170 starfighter 230
arena beasts **170-71**, 202
Arihnda Pryce 216

Arleil Schous 152
Arok the Hutt 128, 129
astromech droids 132, 162, 208, 218, 234, 237
　　see also BB-8; Chopper; R2-D2
Atollon, Battle of 66
Attark the Hoover 169
Aurra Sing 122, 133
Azmorigan 134

B
bacta 57, 72
Bail Organa 13, 66
Bala-Tik 134
Balnab castaways 169
banshees 182
banthas 161, 176, 178, 194
Barada 144
battle beasts **172-73**
battle droids 48, 93, 142, 163, 202
Baze Malbus 50, 52, **54-55**
Bazine Netal 154
BB-8 **76-77**, 118, 162
　　and Finn 73, 234
　　and Luke Skywalker 74, 76
　　and Poe Dameron 74, 76, 77
　　and Princess Leia 61
　　and Rey 70, 71, 77, 222, 234
beasts of burden **176-77**
Ben Quadinaros 159
Ben Solo 59, 61, 119
　　see also Kylo Ren
Bendu 30, 31, 103
Beru Lars 56, 57
Bespin **212-13**
Bib Fortuna 144, 169
Bith 156, 157
Black Sun Guard 34, 135
blarths 169
Blizzard Force 208
bloggins 223
Boba Fett 59, **122-23**, 145
Bobbajo 195, 223
Bodhi Rook **50-51**, 106
bogwings 183

Boles Roor 158
Bom Vimdin 153
bonzami 188, 189
Boonta Eve Classic 158-59
Bor Gullet 51
Boss Nass 147
Bossk 145
bounty hunters **120-25**, 194, 199, 200
　　see also individual bounty hunters
Brace Marko 34
Braconnor Bakiska 152
brain worms 185
brezaks 182, 183
Bubo 168, 169
buzz droids 231

C
C-3PO **64**, 76, 207, 219
　　and Chewbacca 63, 64, 145
　　and the Ewoks 59, 64, 141
　　and Jabba the Hutt 144, 188
　　and the Jawas 148, 149
　　and Luke Skywalker 57
　　and Princess Leia 11
Cad Bane **124-25**, 207
can-cells 182, 183
Canto Bight 245, **248-49**
Captain Gregor 23
Captain Tarpals 173
carrier butterflies 182
Cassian Andor 15, **46-47**, 48, 49, 218
Castas 166
Catacombs of Cadera 221
Cham Syndulla 29, 104
Cherff Maota 155
Chewbacca 59, **62**, **63**, 246, 247
　　and C-3PO 64
　　and Han Solo 62, 63
　　and Jabba the Hutt 60, 61, 129
　　Millennium Falcon 234
Chief Chirpa 140, 141
Chirrut Îmwe 50, **52-53**, 54, 55
Chopper **38-39**, 187, 232
　　and Agent Kallus 105
　　and Ezra Bridger 35, 38, 195
　　and R2-D2 38
　　and Zeb Orrelios 35, 38
Cikatro Vizago 135
the Citadel 218, 219
Cliegg Lars 160
clone troopers and commanders **18-25**, 112, 169, 189, 200, 201
Clone Wars 22, 23, 83, 146, 150
Cloud City **212-13**, 249
colo claw fish 175
Colonel Datoo 117

Commandant Aresko 109, 111
Commander Cody 13, 20, 21
Commander Fox 21
Commander Gree 20
conduit worms 185
convorees 168, 182
Coruscant **198-99**
Count Dooku **86-87**, 89
　　and Anakin Skywalker 11, 87
　　and Asajj Ventress 96, 97
　　and Darth Sidious 86
　　on Geonosis 203
　　lightsaber 241
　　and Padmé Amidala 93
　　and Qui-Gon Jinn 11
　　Separatists 93
　　and Yoda 86, 87
the Crèche 75
creepy-crawlies **184-85**

D
dactillions 182, 183
Dagobah **210-11**, 247
darksabers 130, **240-41**
Darth Maul **84-85**, 247
　　and Darth Sidious 82, 85
　　and Ezra Bridger 32, 85
　　and Kanan Jarrus 30, 32, 33
　　lightsaber 84, 85, 241
　　and Obi-Wan Kenobi 12, 85, 97, 195
　　and Qui-Gon Jinn 84
Darth Plagueis 82
Darth Sidious **82-83**
　　and Cad Bane 124, 125, 207
　　and Count Dooku 86
　　and Darth Maul 85
　　and Darth Vader 89, 108
　　lightsaber 82, 241
　　Mustafar 206, 207
　　and Yoda 17
　　see also Palpatine
Darth Tyranus *see* Count Dooku
Darth Vader **88-89**
　　and Ahsoka Tano 14, 15, 17, 88
　　and Darth Sidious 89, 108
　　Darth Vader's castle 207
　　and Emperor Palpatine 82
　　and Han Solo 59, 123
　　and the Inquisitors 109
　　and Kylo Ren 118, 119
　　lightsaber 88, 241
　　and Luke Skywalker 56, 82, 89, 213
　　and Obi-Wan Kenobi 12, 13, 109, 207
　　and Princess Leia 61
　　see also Anakin Skywalker
Dathomir 85

INDEX

Death Stars 107, 214, **242-43**
   construction 143, 203, 242, 243
   and Galen Erso 106
   and Grand Moff Tarkin 100, 101, 218
   Jedha 220, 221
   and Jyn Erso 45, 48, 66
   and Luke Skywalker 56, 57
   and Princess Leia 61, 64, 234
death troopers 110, 112
Death Watch **130-31**
Dengar 145
Depa Billaba 31
dewbacks 176, 177, 194
dianoga squid 243
Dr. Evazan 134, 152
dokma 187
droid starfighters 230, 231
droids 94, **162-63**, 208, 218, 230
Droopy McCool 156, 157
duracrete slugs 184
Duros 152

E

Eadu Energy Conversion Laboratory 107
Ebe E. Endocott 158
Echo Base 208, 209
Eighth Brother 109
Elan Mak 158
Embo 168
the Empire **98-113**, 216-17, 218, 219
Empire Day 33
Endor **214-15**
   Battle of Endor 61, 140, 141
eopies 176, 177, 194
Ephant Mon 144
Ephraim Bridger 33
Even Piell 8
Ewoks **140-41**, **214-15**
   and C-3PO 59, 64, 141
   and Chewbacca 62
executioner trooper 113
exogorths 180
Ezra Bridger **32-33**, 66
   and Agent Kallus 105
   and Ahsoka Tano 15
   and Chopper 38
   and Darth Maul 32, 85
   Ghost 232
   and Hera Syndulla 28, 207
   and Hondo Ohnaka 133
   and Kanan Jarrus 31, 33
   lightsaber 240
   and Obi-Wan Kenobi 33
   and Sabine 34, 35
   and Yoda 16, 17, 32

F

Falleen 135
falumpasets **172-73**
fambaas **172-73**
Farns Monsbee 34
fathiers 248, 249
Fenn Rau 34, 51
Figrin D'an 156
Finn (FN-2187) 51, **72-73**, 116, 251
   Millennium Falcon 234, 235
   and Poe Dameron 73, 74, 75
   and Rey 62, 70, 73
   Starkiller Base 224, 225
First Order 74, 114-19, 198, 250, 251
   Finn (FN-2187) 51, 72, 73
   Starkiller Base 224-25
   stormtroopers 110, 112-13
Fives 21, 23
flametroopers 113
Fodesinbeed 159
the Force 10, 17, 220, 246, 247
   Force spirits 13, 16
   Force vision 17, 70
Fort Anaxes asteroid 181
frog-dogs 168
Fulcrum, Agent 105, 232
fyrnocks 180, 181

G

Galactic Senate Building 199
Galen Erso 50, 106, 198, 219
Gall Trayvis 35
Gamorreans 144
Gannis Ducain 58
Gardulla the Hutt 10, 11, 129
Garven Dreis 236
Gasgano 158
Gauron Nas Tal 145
General Cassio Tagge 100
General Crix Madine 67
General Grievous **94-95**, 167
General Jan Dodonna 217
Geonosis **142-43**, **202-203**, 242
   Battle of Geonosis 20, 87, 132, 202
Ghost 103, 187, 228, **232-33**
ginnthos 205
Gooti 32
Gor, the roggwart 166, 167
Gorga Desilijic Aarrpo 128
Grand Inquisitor 108, 241
Great Grass Plains 172
Greedo 153
Grummgar 154
Guardians of the Whills 53, 54, 221
Guavian Death Gang 134, 135
gundarks 12, 166, 167
Gungans **146-47**, **196-97**
   battle beasts **172-73**
   bogwings 183
   creepy-crawlies 184
   Gungan Grand Army 146, 147, 172, 173
   pets 169
gutkurrs 166
Gwarm 132
Gwellis Bagnoro 169

H

Han Solo **58-59**, 135
   and Chewbacca 62, 63
   and Darth Vader 59, 123
   and the Death Star 57, 58, 59
   and Finn 73
   is frozen in carbonite 59, 123, 207, 212
   and Greedo 153
   and Jabba the Hutt 59, 123, 129
   and Kylo Ren 118
   Millennium Falcon 234, 235
   and Princess Leia 59, 61, 119
   and Rey 70
   Starkiller Base 224, 225
happabores 176
Has Obitt 41
Hem Dazon 153
Hera Syndulla **28-29**, 31, 134
   and Agent Kallus 105
   and Chopper 38, 39
   Ghost 232, 233
   Mustafar 207
   and Zeb Orrelios 37
Hesten monkeys 169
holocrons 30
holoprojectors 41, 117
Hondo Ohnaka 87, **132-33**, 169
Honor Guards of Lasan 36
horaxes of Nelvaan 178
Hosnian Prime 198
Hoth **208-209**
   Battle of Hoth 61, 209
Hoth Asteroid Belt 181, 209, 235
Hurst Romodi 100
Hutt family 124, 128-29, 135, 194
Hutt Grand Council 128, 129
Hux, Commandant Brendol 110
Hux, General Armitage 116, 117, 118
   Starkiller Base 224, 225

I

ice beasts **178-79**
ID9 seeker droids 109
IG-RM droids 217
ikopi 186, 187
Imperial Academy 111
Imperial military officers **100-101**, 108
Imperial Navy **238-39**
Imperial Security Bureau (ISB) **104-105**
Inquisitors 31, **108-109**, 205, 217
intelligent beings **138-63**
Izby 169

J

Jabba the Hutt **128-29**, 144-45
   and Chewbacca 129
   and Han Solo 59, 123, 129, 179
   musicians 157, 215
   pets 169, 189
   and Princess Leia 60, 61
   rancor beast 57, 167, 194
Jakku 101, **222-23**
Jango Fett **122-23**, 124, 171, 200
   and Asajj Ventress 97
   and Hondo Ohnaka 133
Janyor 35
Jar Jar Binks **146-47**, 174, 197
Jawas **148-49**, 177
Jedha 152, **220-21**
Jedi Archives 125, 200, 218
Jedi High Council **8-9**
Jedi Order **6-17**, 57, 87, 247
   Jedi hunters **108-109**
Jedi Temple 9, 17, 32, 57, 130, 199, 217
   and Ahsoka Tano 15, 21, 23
Jek Porkins 236
Jiro 132
Joh Yowza 215
joopas 188
Jun Sato 66
Jyn Erso **44-45**, 67, 218
   and Baze Malbus 54
   and Cassian Andor 46, 47
   and Death Star 66
   and K-2SO 48
   and Saw Gerrera 40, 41

K

K-2SO **48-49**
kaadu **172-73**
Kalani 22
Kaliida Nebula 181
Kallus, Agent 15, 51, **104-105**
Kamino **200-201**
Kanan Jarrus **30-31**
   and Agent Kallus 105
   and Darth Maul 30, 32, 33
   and Ezra Bridger 31, 33
   and Grand Inquisitor 108, 109
   lightsaber 240
   and Saw Gerrera 41, 45
   and Yoda 17, 31
   and Zeb Orrelios 37
Kanjiklub 135
Kanjiklubber 154

253

Kashyyyk 20
Kel Dor 8
Kes Dameron 74
Ketsu Onyo 34, 51
Ki-Adi-Mundi 9
Kiros birds 168, 169
Kit Fisto 94
Kitwarr 63
Klik-Klak 41, 143
Knights of Ren 70, 118
kouhun 184, 185
Krell, General Pong 21
Krennic, Orson 100, 106, **107**
krykna 166, 167
Kullbee Sperado 41
kyber crystals 44, 118, 217, 218, 221
    Death Star 243
    Inquisitors' crystals 14, 108
    lightsabers 241
    Project Celestial Power 198
    theft of 132
Kylo Ren 116, 117, **118-19**, 250
    and Darth Vader 118, 119
    lightsaber 72, 241
    and Poe Dameron 74
    and Rey 70, 71
    TIE silencer 119

L

land beasts **186-87**, 194
Lando Calrissian 39, 51, 134, 212, 235
lava fleas 206, 207
Leia Organa, Princess **60-61**, 67, 150
    and Anakin Skywalker 10
    Battle of Scarif 67
    and Chewbacca 63
    and Death Star 61, 234
    and Han Solo 59, 61, 119
    and Jabba the Hutt 60, 61, 144
    and Luke Skywalker 57, 60
    and Obi-Wan Kenobi 13
    and Poe Dameron 74
    and R2-D2 61, 64
Lieutenant Mitaka 116, 117, 118
Lieutenant Yogar Lyste 105, 216
lightsabers **240-41**
    see also under individual characters
Lobot 212
Lor San Tekka 74, 75, 116, 118, 222
Lothal **216-17**
luggabeasts 176, 177
Luke Skywalker 33, **56-57**, 148
    and BB-8 74, 76
    and Darth Vader 56, 82, 89, 213
    Death Star 234, 236, 243
    on Hoth 209
    and Jabba the Hutt 144
    lightsaber 11, 155, 240
    and Obi-Wan Kenobi 12, 13, 56, 57, 61
    and Poe Dameron 74
    and Princess Leia 57, 60
    and R2-D2 65
    and Rey 70, 246, 247
    X-wings 236
    and Yoda 56, 210-11
Luminara Unduli 31

M

Mace Windu 8, 9, 31, 203
    lightsaber 123, 240
    and Palpatine 83
Maketh Tua 216
Malakili 167
Mandalore 23, 34, 35, 84, 122, 130-31
Marlo the Hutt 128
Marrok 168
Mart Mattin 104
massiffs 169, 202
mastmots of Toola 178
Max Rebo 157, 215
Maz Kanata 70, **154-55**, 157, 247
ME-8D9 154
medical droids 94
Meebur Gascon 23
merdeths 202
midi-chlorians 10, 11
Millennium Falcon 58, 59, 181, 233, 234-35, 247
milodons 188
Mira Bridger 33
Miraj Scintel, Queen 168, 169
Modal Nodes **156-57**
Momaw Nadon 153
momong 187
Mon Calamari 146, **150-51**
Mon Mothma 28, 35
    and Cassian Andor 47
    and the Rebel Alliance 66, 67
monsters **164-89**
Morad Sumar 216
Moralo Eval 124
Moroff 41
Mos Eisley 195
Mos Eisley Cantina **152-53**, 195
Mos Espa Grand Arena 158
Mother Talzin 96
motts 186, 187
mouse droids 76, 242
Muftak 152
musicians **156-57**
Mustafar **206-207**
mynocks 181

N

Naboo **196-97**
    Battle of Naboo 147
    creatures on 147, 169, 172-73, 184, 187
    Naboo Crisis 83, 92, 125
Naboo Abyss 174-75
Nabrun Leids 152
Nahdar Vebb 151
narglatch 178, 179
neebray mantas 180, 181
Neimoidians **92-93**, 97
Neva Kee 159
New Republic 117
nexu 170
Nightbrothers 84, 97
Nightsisters 85, 96-97
nightwatcher worms 184, 185
Niima Outpost 222
nos 188, 205
nuna 186, 187
Nute Gunray **92-93**, 97, 147

O

O-MR1 65
Obi-Wan Kenobi **12-13**, 104, 247
    and Anakin Skywalker 10, 11, 12, 13, 15
    and Commander Cody 13, 20
    and Darth Maul 8, 12, 85, 97, 195
    and Darth Vader 12, 13, 109, 207
    and Ezra 33
    and General Grievous 95
    and Hondo Ohnaka 133, 169
    lightsaber 13, 240
    and Luke Skywalker 12, 13, 56, 57, 61
    and Princess Leia 13
    and Yoda 16
Ody Mandrell 159
Oked 97
Old Jho 216
Oola 144
opee sea killers 175
Orn Free Taa, Senator 186
Oruba the Hutt 128, 129
Otoh Gunga 197

P

Padmé Amidala, Queen 147
    and Anakin Skywalker 10, 89, 197
    arena beasts 171
    and Bail Organa 66
    and Count Dooku 93
    Naboo 196, 197
    and Rebel Alliance 66
Palpatine 239
    and Cad Bane 125
    and Darth Vader 82
    and Mace Windu 83
    Order 66 13, 20, 23
    and Trade Federation 92
    see also Darth Sidious
Parade Grounds 224
Parsel 132
Pau City 205
Pau'ans 108, 204, 205
Petranaki Arena **170-71**, 202
pets 168-69
Phantom II 232-33
Phasma, Captain 116, 225
Phoenix Squadron 15, 22, 28, 39, 61, 66, 104, 217
picadors 171
Piit 132
pikobi 187
Pilf Mukmuk 169
pilots, podracing **158-59**
planetary systems **192-225**
Plo Koon 8, 15
Pluma Sodi 188
podracing **158-59**, 194, 195
Poe Dameron 73, **74-75**, 76, 77, 224, 236
Poggle the Lesser, Archduke 142, 143, 171, 203
police officers 249
Ponda Baba 134, 152, 194
Pons Limbic 152
porgs 187, 246
Praetorian Guards **250-51**
Pre Vizsla 130, 131
Prince Lee-Char 150, 151
Profundity 151
protocol droids 39, 93, 154, 162, 163, 208, 218
    see also C-3PO
Pyke Syndicate 134, 135
PZ-4CO 76

Q

Quarren 150
Quarrie 150, 151
Que-Mars Redath-Gom 132
Qui-Gon Jinn 15, 197
    and Anakin Skywalker 10
    and Count Dooku 11, 86
    and Darth Maul 84
    and Jar Jar Binks 147
    lightsaber 240

R

R2-D2 **65**, 77, 125, 148, 247
    and Chopper 38
    and Luke Skywalker 65
    and Princess Leia 61, 64
R5-P8 132

INDEX

Raddus, Admiral 50, 67, 151
Rako Hardeen 124
rancors 167, 194
Rappertunie 156
rathtars 167
Ratts Tyerell 159
Rebel Alliance **42-67**, 214
    bases 67, 208
    crest 40
rebels **26-41**
Red Key Raiders 135
Ree-Yees 144, 145
reeks 170
Reeksa 166
the Republic 201
Republic Judiciary Detention Center 124
the Resistance **68-77**, 117, 246, 247, 250, 251
resputi 205
Rex, Captain 13, 21, **22-23**, 201
Rey **70-71**
    and BB-8 77, 222
    and Finn 73
    and Han Solo 62, 70
    and Kylo Ren 70, 71, 118
    and Luke Skywalker 70, 246, 247
    Millennium Falcon 234, 235, 247
    and Yoda 17
Rieekan, Rebel General 61, 208
Ring of Kafrene 46
rishi eels 188
Rishi Maze 200
rock vultures 205
rock warts 184
roggwarts 166, 167
rontos 176, 177, 194
Roodown, "Crusher" 223
Rose Tico 251
Rotta the Hutt 97
rupings 176, 177, 182
Ryder Azadi 169, 216

S

Saak'ak 93
Sabine Wren **34-35**, 51, 233
    and Agent Kallus 105
    and Ezra Bridger 34, 35
    and Pre Vizsla 130
Saelt-Marae 144, 145
Saesee Tiin 9
Salacious B. Crumb 144, 169
sandcrawlers 148, 149
sando aqua monster 174, 175
Sarco Plank 57, 223
Sarlacc 188, 189, 194

Satine Kryze, Duchess 12, 13, 130, 131
Savage Opress 82, **84-85**
Saw Gerrera **40-41**, 106, 111, 220
    and Captain Rex 22
    and Chirrut Îmwe 52, 53
    and Kanan Jarrus 41, 45
scalefish 174, 175
Scarif **218-19**
    Battle of Scarif 28, 61, 67
scout troopers 113
sea creatures **174-75**
Sebulba 158
security droids 48-49
the Senate 198, 199
Senator Meena Tills 151
Sentinal 108
sentry droids 117, 162
the Separatists 86, **92-97**, 150
Seventh Sister 108, 109
shaaks 186, 187
Shag Kava band 157
Shara Bey 74
Shasa Tiel 144
Shield Generator Station 215
Shmi Skywalker 10, 11, 160, 161
shoretroopers 113, 219
Shrikes 59
Sidon Ithano 154
Sifo-Dyas 20, 86
the Sith **80-89**
Sith Temple of Malachor 32
Sixth Brother 108
skalders 186, 187
slug-beetles 184
slugs 184
Snap Wexley 224, 236
Snoke, Supreme Leader 116, 117, 118, **250-51**
snowspeeders 209
snowtroopers 113
space slugs 180, 181
space travel **228-39**
Stalgasin Hive 203, 242
Star Destroyers 228, **238-39**
starfighters 230, 231
Starkiller Base 59, 72, 73, 117, **224-25**, 234, 237, 250
    Poe Dameron's attack on 74, 75, 76
Steela Gerrera 40
steelpeckers 182, 223
stormtroopers 52, **110-11**, 112, 116
    Blizzard Force 208
    command of 105, 108
    on Scarif 218
    and Zeb Orrelios 36, 37
Suralinda Javos 75

swamp slugs 211
Sy Snootles 145, 157

T

Tarkin, General Moff Wilhuff 108
    the Citadel 218
    Death Star 100, 101
    on Lothal 216, 217
    and Orson Krennic 107
    Sovereign 109, 207
Taskmaster Myles Grint 109
Tasu Leech 135
Tatooine **194-95**, 247
tauntauns 176, 177, 178, 179
TC-14 93
Teedos 222
Teemto Pagalies 159
Temple of the Kyber 53, 54, 221
Tessek 145
Teth 25
Thanisson, Petty Officer 117
Theed 196
Thrawn, Grand Admiral **102-103**, 105
tibidees 178
TIE fighters 228, 229, 236, 238, 239
TIE silencer 119
Tion Medon 205
Tipoca City 201
Todo 360 125
tookas 168
Trade Federation **92-93**, 142, 147, 197
tribubble bongo sub 174, 175
tri-fighters 230
Troig 158
troopers **112-13**
Tseebo 104
Turk Falso 132
Tusken Raiders 10, 89, 159, **160-61**, 177, 194
Twi'leks 28-29, 144, 166, 181

U

Ugnaughts 213
Umpass-stay 157
Unamo, Chief Petty Officer 117
the underworld **126-35**, 199
Unkar Plutt 234, 235
Utai 204
Utapau **204-205**

V

vehicles **228-39**
Ventress, Asajj 51, 85, **96-97**, 201, 241
vixus 188, 189
void striders 187

vulture droids 229, 231

W

wampas 178, 179, 208
Watto 10, 11
weapons
    bounty hunters 123
    clone troopers **24**
    Death Star **242-43**
    Ewoks 140
    Honor Guards of Lasan 36
    Rebel Alliance 52, 55
    the Resistance 70
    stormtroopers 110
    Wookiee 62
Wedge Antilles 104, 105, 236
Weequay 132
Wolffe 21, 23
womp rats 185
Wookiees 37, **62-63**, 76, 123, 183
Wooof 144
worms 184, 185
worrts 195, 223
Wuher 152
Wullffwarro 63

X

X-wings **236-37**
Xanadu Blood 125
xandu 182, 183
Xrexus Cartel 135

Y

Yaddle 8
Yarael Poof 8
Yarkora 145
Yarna d'al'Gargan 144
Yavin, Battle of 61
yobshrimp 174
Yoda 9, **16-17**, 203, 247
    and Bail Organa 66
    and Count Dooku 86, 87
    and Ezra Bridger 16, 17, 32
    and General Grievous 95
    and Kanan Jarrus 31
    and Luke Skywalker 56, 210-11
    and Princess Leia 61
Yoda's hut 211
Yuzzum 214, 215

Z

Zare Leonis 217
"Zeb" (Garazeb) Orrelios 36-37, 104, 167
    and Chopper 38
    and Kallus 104, 105
Zillo Beast 166, 167
Ziro the Hutt 125, 129, 145
Ziton Moj 135

Project Editor Ruth Amos
Editor Lauren Nesworthy
Designer Chris Gould
Additional design by Lisa Rogers, Abi Wright
Senior Pre-Production Producer Marc Staples
Senior Producer Zara Markland
Managing Editor Sadie Smith
Managing Art Editor Ron Stobbart
Art Director Lisa Lanzarini
Publisher Julie Ferris
Publishing Director Simon Beecroft

DK would like to thank: Katy Lennon, Cefn Ridout, David Fentiman, and Julia March for additional editorial; Owen Bennett, Karan Chaudhary, Pranika Jain, Simon Murrell, Robert Perry, Anna Pond, Clive Savage, Anne Sharples, and Toby Truphet for additional design; and Vanessa Bird for the index.
Many thanks to Brett Rector, Shahana Alam, Bryce Pinkos, Erik Sanchez, Newell Todd, Tim Mapp, Nicole LaCoursiere, Leland Chee, Pablo Hidalgo, Matt Martin, and Michael Siglain at Lucasfilm.
Special thanks to *Star Wars* fans Luke Harris for the Fan Fact on p17, Joshua Divall for the Fan Fact on p89, and Mark Newbold for the Fan Fact on p129.

In 2014 Lucasfilm reclassified what is considered canon in the *Star Wars* universe. *Star Wars: Absolutely Everything You Need to Know* draws upon a little information from the Expanded Universe that Lucasfilm now considers to be "Legends"–that is, stories beyond the original six films and the TV shows *Star Wars: The Clone Wars* and *Star Wars Rebels*.

First American Edition, 2017
Published in the United States by DK Publishing
345 Hudson Street, New York, New York 10014

Page design copyright © 2017 Dorling Kindersley Limited
DK, a Division of Penguin Random House LLC
17 18 19 20 21 10 9 8 7 6 5 4 3 2 1
001–280842–Oct/2017

© & TM 2017 LUCASFILM LTD.

All rights reserved.
Without limiting the rights under the copyright reserved above, no part of this publication may be reproduced, stored in, or introduced into a retrieval system, or transmitted, in any form, or by any means (electronic, mechanical, photocopying, recording, or otherwise), without the prior written permission of the copyright owner.
Published in Great Britain by Dorling Kindersley Limited.

A catalog record for this book is available from the Library of Congress.

ISBN 978-1-4654-5563-5

DK books are available at special discounts when purchased in bulk for sales promotions, premiums, fund-raising, or educational use. For details, contact: DK Publishing Special Markets, 345 Hudson Street, New York, New York 10014 SpecialSales@dk.com

Printed in China

A WORLD OF IDEAS:
SEE ALL THERE IS TO KNOW

www.dk.com
www.starwars.com